JUST ANOTHER QUIET MORNING...

On October 31, 1999, at 8:56 A.M., Dirk Greineder called the Wellesley Police Department.

In a high-pitched, panic-stricken voice, Greineder told police someone had attacked his wife at Morses Pond. They were walking their dog and his wife hurt her back. He left her to continue walking the dog. When he came back, he found her. She'd been attacked.

Wellesley police officer Paul Fitzpatrick was dispatched to the scene. Greineder flagged Fitzpatrick down. The officer stopped and told Greineder to get in the back of the car. Greineder directed him to drive down to the circle, then turn right onto the path. Fitzpatrick drove as far as he could, then stopped the car, got out, and went around to the front of the vehicle.

Greineder tried to get out of the cruiser but couldn't. He panicked. He screamed and Fitzpatrick finally came around and opened the door. He went down the path and down the rise, like a shot, to May. Of course, she hadn't moved. He tried to take her pulse again. He looked into her eyes, but he couldn't even tell if her pupils were moving. Then he picked up her shirt but couldn't get a heartbeat. She was gone. He knew it. But he didn't believe it.

"What's your name, sir?" Fitzpatrick asked.

"Dirk Greineder. I'm a doctor at Harvard and Brigham and Women's Hospital."

"What happened here?"

The doctor repeated what he said on the phone.

"Is she dead?" Greineder asked Fitzpatrick about thirty minutes later.

"Yes."

"Are you going to arrest me?"

MURDER at MORSES POND

LINDA ROSENCRANCE

PINNACLE BOOKS
Kensington Publishing Corp.
http://www.kensingtonbooks.com

Some names have been changed to protect the privacy of individuals connected to this story.

PINNACLE BOOKS are published by

Kensington Publishing Corp.
850 Third Avenue
New York, NY 10022

All Kensington Titles, Imprints, and Distributed Lines are available at special quantity discounts for bulk purchases for sales promotions, premiums, fund-raising, and educational or institutional use. Special book excerpts or customized printings can also be created to fit specific needs. For details, write or phone the office of the Kensington special sales manager: Kensington Publishing Corp., 850 Third Avenue, New York, NY 10022, attn: Special Sales Department. Phone: 1-800-221-2647.

Pinnacle and the P logo Reg. U.S. Pat. & TM Off.

First Pinnacle Books Printing: November 2004

10 9 8 7 6 5 4 3 2 1

Printed in the United States of America

For my mother, Mary Fanelli, my son, Adam Rosencrance, and his wife, Dawn, and in memory of my father, John Fanelli. And for the other Adam in my life—may we one day find the truth.

ACKNOWLEDGMENTS

I wish to thank several people for helping me get the information necessary to write this book. First, Wellesley Police Chief Terrence Cunningham, who agreed to sit down with me and go over the Greineder case in detail; second, the employees of the Norfolk Superior Court in Dedham, Massachusetts, especially court clerk Michael Hulak, who allowed me unfettered access to the entire court file; and finally court reporters Peggy Morris and Dawna Chapin, who graciously took time from their very busy schedules to print out the voluminous trial transcript for me. I'd also like to thank my agent, Janet Benrey, of the Hartline Literary Agency, and Miles Lott, my editor at Kensington Books, for all their hard work on my behalf.

Linda Rosencrance

AUTHOR'S NOTE

In the beginning of the investigation into the murder of May Greineder, Wellesley police detective Jill McDermott was known as Jill Hogan. However, in order to avoid confusion I have decided to refer to her as Detective McDermott throughout the book.

L.R.

It is a man's own mind, not his enemy or foe, that lures him to evil ways.

—Buddha

Prologue

Wellesley, Massachusetts, is an affluent bedroom community located approximately thirteen miles west of Boston, the state's capital. The town, which covers about ten square miles, is home to CEOs, doctors, lawyers, politicians, media personalities, entertainers, and even famous athletes. It's a town where people like Dirk and Mabel Greineder want to raise their families. The Greineders, who married on July 7, 1967, moved to Wellesley from Maryland in 1975 after Dirk became a research fellow at Boston's Robert B. Brigham Hospital, a precursor of the current Brigham and Women's Hospital, and Harvard Medical School. Their three children, Kirsten, Britt, and Colin, grew up in Wellesley and graduated from Wellesley High School.

Incorporated as a town in 1881, Wellesley offers its residents the best of both worlds: proximity to the sights and sounds of the big city, such as the historic Freedom Trail, world-class museums and hospitals, numerous theaters and sports venues, as well as the Boston Pops and the Boston Symphony Orchestra; and the convenience and safety of a small town.[1]

Named in honor of wealthy businessman and town benefactor Horatio Hollis Hunnewell, whose man-

---

1. Hinchliffe, Beth, "Wellesley Today."

sion was named Wellesley after his wife, whose maiden name was Welles, the town of Wellesley consists of "beautiful, well-established residential neighborhoods laid out along tree-lined, winding roads."[2] Its shopping districts feature specialty shops as well as branches of larger chain stores.

One of Wellesley's best-known buildings is the majestic nineteenth-century Town Hall situated on top of a tree-shaded hill in the center of town. Built entirely of stone, the building is modeled after a French château. Its grounds make up Hunnewell Park, which boasts a collection of beautiful shrubs, trees, and flowers. Next to Town Hall is the Duck Pond, which delights young and old alike throughout the year.[3]

Wellesley is home to three well-known colleges. Wellesley College is a four-year liberal arts college for women, established in 1875. Wellesley, the alma mater of former first lady Hillary Clinton, sits on a five-hundred-acre campus that includes Lake Waban and the nine-hole Nehoiden Golf Course. Babson College is a four-year coeducational college offering undergraduate and graduate degrees in a variety of business-related subjects. Babson, founded in 1919 by Wellesley resident Roger Babson, also includes schools of management and executive education. Massachusetts Bay Community College, which was founded in 1961, sits on a hill where Indians used to camp. Massachusetts Bay is a two-year coeducational school offering associate degrees and certificates in subjects ranging from accounting and computers to child development.[4]

---

2. Ibid.
3. Ibid.
4. Ibid.

Wellesley is also known for its school system, recognized as one of the best in the state, and its low rate of crime. The first armed bank robbery in Wellesley took place in 1969. And until 1999, the last recorded murder in the town occurred on December 13, 1969, when a jilted lover shot and killed his twenty-two-year-old girlfriend at her parents' home on Crown Ridge Road, and then tried to kill himself.

That's why friends, neighbors, and townspeople were shocked and frightened when Mabel Greineder, or May as she liked to be called, was stabbed and bludgeoned to death at Morses Pond on a clear, crisp Halloween morning in 1999. May's murder was the third murder in Norfolk County in less than a year, all of which occurred in public parks in towns that began with *W.*

In December 1998, Irene Kennedy, a seventy-five-year-old Foxborough woman, was choked, stabbed, and sexually mutilated in Bird Park in Walpole. In August 1999, Richard Reyenger, an eighty-two-year-old Westwood man, was beaten to death while fishing at Westwood's Buckmaster Pond. Because police had no suspects in either case at the time May was murdered (as of this writing they have charged convicted killer Martin G. Guy with Kennedy's death), Wellesley residents were concerned that a serial killer was on the loose.

Although Wellesley police and state police detectives assigned to the Norfolk County District Attorney's Office knew right from the beginning May's murder wasn't the work of a crazed serial killer, they also knew they couldn't release that information to the public until they had a suspect in custody—something that wouldn't happen until four months later.

And police knew one other thing for certain—the people of Wellesley, Massachusetts, would be even more shocked when they learned who really stabbed and bludgeoned fifty-eight-year-old May Greineder to death.

Chapter 1

Tuesday, February 3, 1998.

The first time Thomas Young met Elizabeth Porter, she threw him for a loop. At twenty-five, she had a body to die for—hard, tight, curves in all the right places. Not old and soft like his wife's. And that wild red hair. He had really lucked out.

After years of using telephone sex lines and getting off looking at pictures of naked women on the Internet, Young had finally mustered up the courage to solicit a prostitute for sex and called a Boston-area escort service.

Sometime that day, a driver for the Commonwealth Entertainment agency picked Porter up at her home in Quincy, Massachusetts, and approximately thirty minutes later dropped her off at the Crowne Plaza Hotel on Route 9 in Natick. Known as the Crowne Plastique among locals, the hotel on the slick, Vegas-like strip was the perfect place for a clandestine rendezvous.

Young was already in the room when Porter arrived. Hoping to take the edge off their first encounter, he had filled the chamber with champagne, roses, chocolate-covered strawberries, and an assortment of fruit and candy.

But still feeling awkward and somewhat uncomfortable about what he was about to do, the man, known only to Porter as Tom, spent a good deal of their hour together just talking with her.

"I'm a cancer researcher . . . from Baltimore," Young told Porter, trying to break the ice after the initial introductions were over. "I get to Boston a few times a month."

Noticing the gold band on his finger, she said, "I see you're married."

"Oh, I'm separated."

"Well, why are you wearing your wedding ring?"

"Oh, I don't know. Out of habit, I guess. Why? Does it make a difference?"

"Well, if you're separated, why would you want to wear your wedding ring?" she responded, not really answering his question.

"Oh, it really makes a difference?"

"Well, if you were out and you were at a bar or something, a woman would first notice a wedding ring and think you're married," she explained.

"Oh, okay," he said.

Pouring each of them a glass of champagne, Young explained that he was in the process of divorcing his wife because the passion had gone out of their marriage and he just wasn't attracted to her body anymore.

"But you know how that goes," he said, staring at her young, taut breasts straining against her sweater. "Divorce takes a while."

Unable to wait any longer, Young took Porter's hand and led her to the edge of the king-size bed. He pulled her sweater up over her head and flung it to the floor. He reached around and unsnapped her bra. He leaned down and placed his mouth on her swelling right breast, running his tongue around her sensitive nipple. At the same time, he unbuttoned her skirt, letting it fall to her feet. Porter kicked it aside, then stepped out of her shoes.

Knowing there wasn't time for foreplay, Young hurriedly stripped off his own clothes. He pushed Porter down onto the bed, pulled off her panties, and climbed on top of her.

"I'll be back in Boston next Wednesday, and I'd really like to see you again," Young said as they put their clothes back on.

"Okay, but let's do it without letting my boss know, because it will benefit me moneywise," Porter responded. "Here's my pager number."

Young called Porter the very next day.

"I can't wait to see you again," he said.

After arranging to meet on Wednesday at the ritzy Copley Westin Hotel in Boston's Copley Square, they continued to chat for a few minutes. Young agreed to pay Porter $450 for ninety minutes of her time. Then, maybe trying to impress Young, Porter concocted a story about going to nursing school at Boston City Hospital—a far cry from her life as a prostitute.

The first thing Young did when Porter got to the room at the Copley Westin was hold up his left hand to show her the gold band was gone.

"I took your advice and got rid of the wedding ring for you," he said, handing her one of the two beautiful red roses he had purchased especially for this occasion. "This one is for you to take home. The other is to rub up and down your body while I massage you with sweet-smelling oils."

After they had sex, Porter went into the bathroom to

take a shower. Young followed and asked if he could join her. She said no, but allowed him to watch.

As she left, Young told Porter he would call her soon.

Beginning the next day, Young left numerous messages on Porter's pager, but she never returned his page.

"I really want to see you again. Why haven't you called me back?"

Although Porter had lost her pager after her second encounter with Young, she could still retrieve her voice mail messages. The problem was, Young never left his telephone number in any of his verbal messages, choosing instead to punch his number in numerically so Porter would see it on her pager. However, without her pager, Porter couldn't see the number. And Young couldn't even reach Porter through the escort service, because she no longer worked there.

After several weeks, Porter got a new pager and stopped checking the messages left at her old pager number. But even if she had been able to access Young's telephone number, she probably wouldn't have called him back anyway.

"I had a funny feeling, the second time I was with him, that he was kind of strange," she said later.

Chapter 2

Luis Rosado was hard at work installing a new bath-room in the Wellesley, Massachusetts, home of Dirk and May Greineder. As he was about to mount the custom-made shower door, he realized he had a problem—he didn't have the right hinges.

No big deal, he thought. But he couldn't have been more wrong.

He told May about the glitch around 4:00 or 4:30 P.M. and said he would take care of it. But May started to cry, saying Rosado hadn't finished the bathroom and it cost her so much and things weren't going properly.

Again, Rosado told her not to worry and promised May he would take care of everything she needed done.

"Please calm down," he told her.

He thought maybe she was still upset because earlier in the day, as she was working on a paper for school, her computer crashed and her husband, Dirk, had to come up and unfreeze it for her. Then about fifteen or twenty minutes later, he came back up and asked her if she had used his computer. She said no.

* * *

Saturday, October 30, 1999.

It was Saturday, the day before Halloween. Dirk and May Greineder awoke sometime around 6:00 or 6:30 A.M. It was a foggy, misty morning in tony Wellesley, Massachusetts. The kind of damp weather that always caused May's sinuses to act up.

Typically, on the weekends, after their customary breakfast of cut-up fresh fruit and bagels, the pair, accompanied by whichever of their three adult children happened to be home, would take Zephyr, one of their two German shepherds, to Wellesley's Morses Pond for some much-needed exercise. For the past several years, the family had been forced to leave Wolf, their other dog, at home. Despite being on doggy Prozac to curb behavioral problems, Wolfie was still aggressive, particularly around other dogs.

That Saturday, however, Dirk, a world-renowned allergist, decided to take Zephyr to the pond alone. They did their usual walk down to the beach and after about an hour and a half they went home.

It seemed May, who planned to spend most of the day working on some projects for school, was afraid if she went outside she'd end up with a whopper of a sinus headache and have to take to her bed for several hours. If that happened, she'd never finish her paper and slide presentation on asthma on time. She just couldn't afford to take the chance.

A stay-at-home mom while her three children were growing up, May returned to work in 1993 as a triage nurse at what was then the Kenmore Harvard Community Health Plan. She stayed there until 1998, when she left to care for her ailing mother, who passed away on January 23, 1999. In September of 1999, May enrolled in a program at Massachusetts

General Hospital School of Nursing to get her nurse practitioner's degree.

On any given day, numerous joggers and dog walkers use the forty-six acres of parkland and wooded trails surrounding Morses Pond. And the day before Halloween 1999 was no exception. However, in addition to those Morses Pond regulars, Russell Road residents Hugh and Artemis Halsey and several other adults spent the day setting up a scary walk and scavenger hunt for the Halseys' thirteen-year-old son and five of his friends.

For most of the day, they mapped out the route the kids would travel that evening. They set up about six or seven stations in the woods, making sure to steer clear of the path that led to the parking area and the access road to Morses Pond.

When the event began around 7:00 P.M., the adults split the six boys into two groups, gave each group a map, and sent the teens on their way along a predetermined path to the various stations manned by adults dressed in scary costumes. At each point, the boys had to stop and endure whatever "torture" the adults put them through. Artemis was in a hut in the pine tree forest—along the ridge of the sand pit—that was made out of branches that had fallen off the trees.

As the boys made their way from one location to another, they also had to locate certain items, such as small Santa Claus dolls, E.T. figures, and packets of stars or labels the adults had hidden in the woods, and place them in a canvas tote bag donated by a Boston-area insurance company. At the end of the night, the boys had a chance to display the items they had collected.

Parents arrived at Morses Pond around 10:00 P.M. to pick up their children at a place the Halseys called Hecate's Fire, an actual bonfire in the center of a sand pit.

When Dirk got home from walking Zephyr, he worked in the backyard of the Greineders' split-level home, getting it ready for fall. The next day, he and May were going to put out the bird feeders and he wanted to make sure everything was in tip-top shape. So he cleaned up the dog droppings—something he did every week—picked up around the yard, and put the hoses away. He swept out the doghouse in preparation for insulating the floor with foam, which he did each winter.

When he finished his chores, Dirk loaded up his Chrysler Town and Country van with yard waste and other trash, which had been piling up for several weeks, and headed for the town dump on Great Plain Avenue. As he drove out of the dump after unloading the rubbish, Dirk realized that he was directly across the street from the Wellesley Sports Club. Although he had just joined the club that summer, he was thinking of canceling his membership because he really wasn't working out regularly. And he certainly didn't want to continue paying for something he wasn't using.

He had just received two new research grants at work and he had one still running, and with the holidays coming up, he knew he wouldn't be going to the gym. Although the membership was moderately expensive, he was reluctant to suspend it because he thought he'd have to pay a penalty, but he decided to go in and discuss it with the club's management anyway.

As it turned out, the process was pretty painless. For

a small fee, Dirk was able to freeze his membership for three months.

Before heading home, he stopped at Roche Brothers supermarket to pick up a few things, since May was occupied with her schoolwork and didn't have time to go shopping.

In addition to working on her projects for school, May was also busy planning her oldest daughter's wedding. Just two weeks earlier, on October 16, Kirsten, twenty-eight, became engaged to her long-time boyfriend, Aleks Engel, a native of Denmark. Kirsten, who lived in Ann Arbor, Michigan, where she was a resident in emergency medicine at the University of Michigan, told her family the news the very next day. The couple planned to marry in June 2000.

"I was doing very little, she was doing a lot," Kirsten later testified. "She had called about fifty places where we could have the wedding and she was beginning to contact florists and photographers."

When Dirk arrived home from running his errands, May was upstairs working on her paper. She had turned her daughter Britt's old room into a mini office, where she typed her papers on an older model desktop computer. But May Greineder was far from computer savvy. She refused to get online. In fact, she didn't even have a printer in her office. Dirk had to print her papers out for her from his computer and leave them on the kitchen table for her to read.

That Saturday evening, in addition to doing his own work, Dirk helped May with her studies.

"I know I printed out her paper for her so she could proofread it," he said later. "I would have to put it on a three-and-a-half-inch floppy disk and take it to my computer to print it out."

He also typed her bibliography on his computer to

save her some time and then got out some of his slides on asthma—his area of expertise—to help with her presentation. He got the slide carousel out and May went through the slides, selecting a small number to use.

"I started helping her around eleven P.M. and probably worked until a little after midnight. I actually may have spent some time on the Internet as well," Dirk recalled later.

The pair turned all their clocks back an hour—it was the end of daylight savings time—and retired a little after 12:30 A.M. May got ready to go to bed, but Dirk was still saving the files and printing them out. He went to bed as soon as he was finished.

Sunday, October 31, 1999.

Halloween. A picture-perfect fall day in Wellesley, Massachusetts. The fog and mist of the day before had burned off. Although it was a clear, crisp morning, the temperature was expected to reach the low seventies by midafternoon.

Dirk and May Greineder got up around 6:00 A.M.—the time they usually awoke on the weekends. Dirk went upstairs to the kitchen—because the house was a tri-level the master bedroom was on the bottom level—to prepare their breakfast of cut-up fruit and muffins.

While Dirk was slicing the apples, oranges, and pears, May stayed downstairs and did a few small chores, which included stripping the sheets off their bed and putting them in the washing machine, then went up to join her husband for breakfast.

As they were eating, they decided they would go to

the pond to walk Zephyr later that morning. It was a beautiful day, and it looked like May's paper was in good shape. And even though she was still feeling a bit of pressure about it, she decided she could afford to go for a walk. She'd been cooped up for a number of days and really wanted to get out. So while Dirk cleared the kitchen table, washed the dishes, and cleaned out the sink, May picked up a bit downstairs.

When they were finished, the couple got dressed and gathered up the dog's toys and other things they were going to take with them. May donned a dark blue velour pullover top, blue pants with white stripes, white sneakers, and a bright red jacket.

Dirk put on black pants, a black-and-red pullover jersey, white sneakers, and an old yellow-and-white windbreaker-type New England Barracudas Swim Team jacket which belonged to one of his daughters. The three Greineder children, Kirsten, Britt, twenty-six, and Colin, twenty-four, were all avid and accomplished swimmers, as was their father. Growing up, they had all been on competitive swim teams. In fact, Dirk and May went to all their children's swim meets. They even got certified in stroke techniques and became starters so they could participate along with their children.

When he finished dressing, Dirk got his small red backpack, which usually held Zephyr's leash, some balls for her to play with, and a variety of other items like an extra pair of gloves, or maybe some small plastic bags if May planned on picking berries to put in the bird feeder. May liked to add berries to the regular birdseed that she put out because she knew that some birds were fruit eaters. She was so concerned about those birds that she planted a mountain ash tree, which produced little red berries, for them in the front yard.

After they were ready, they struggled to get Zephyr into the garage and into the van. Apparently, Zephyr was distracted by Wolfie, who was in the house and trying to get into the garage with the rest of the family. Wolf, it seemed, was not at all happy about being left home alone all the time. While Dirk was getting Zephyr into the garage, May was standing by the passenger side of the van, in between the van and their other car, a Toyota Avalon. When Dirk finally got Zephyr around to the passenger side of the van, May had a nosebleed. She had been having nosebleeds about once every month for at least six months. They were so severe that Kirsten had encouraged her mother to see a physician and have some blood tests done to rule out any serious problems.

Dirk opened the door to his car, the Avalon, and pulled out the towel he always kept for emergencies. He passed it to May, who had been using a tissue which was now saturated with her blood.

"I had acquired this particular towel from the Ritz-Carlton Hotel in Atlanta in the summer of '98," Dirk said later. "Soon after I brought it home, it ended up in my car. It was perfect to put on my lap if I was having coffee while I was driving or if I was eating a sandwich or something like that so I wouldn't spill anything on myself. If I had eaten something, I would use it to wipe my face or hands. It was an all-purpose 'clean towel,' to keep in the car for that kind of purpose, [not] the more dirty terry cloth rags I used to wipe up the floor if anything spilled on the floor or something like that."

May's nosebleed lasted for about two or three minutes.

At this point, Zephyr, who was becoming increasingly confused and frustrated because the family didn't seem to be going anywhere, made a beeline for the Toyota's open door. Seeing this, Dirk grabbed hold of her, put her steel collar around her neck, yanked her out of the Avalon, and tried to get her into the van.

"As she was jumping in and out of the van, her head banged my nose—not real hard, but hard enough to give me a nosebleed," Dirk testified later. "My wife noticed it—now I was having a nosebleed and she handed me the towel while she continued to pinch her nose with her hand. I used the towel to stop the bleeding and to wipe my hand. I remember handing it to her at one point. I don't know if she actually used it again, but then I finally closed the door on Zephyr. She handed me the towel and I threw it in my car mainly because I was concerned that Zephyr would be sniffing all over the towel and that the damp towel would be getting us dirty. So I just threw it in [the Toyota], thinking I would deal with it later. I wasn't that concerned about [future nosebleeds] because I knew that I also had stashed some other towels in the van on the other side."

The nosebleeds over, the Greineders left for Morses Pond, arriving sometime between 8:00 and 8:30 A.M. Dirk parked in front of the locked gate on Turner Road, the front of the van facing out. The couple let Zephyr out, walked around the gate, crossed the aqueduct, and took a right into the pine tree forest.

When May Greineder entered the pine tree forest at Morses Pond on that Halloween morning in 1999, she had no way of knowing she would never come out alive.

Chapter 3

Thomas Young was a very busy man in the week leading up to October 31, 1999. On October 23, 1999, while registered at the Sheraton Crossroads Hotel in Mahwah, New Jersey—he was there to attend a meeting of the Immunology Research Institute of New England—he surfed the Internet, looking for an escort service in the area. At 1:41 A.M., 1:42 A.M., 1:43 A.M., and 1:44 A.M., he made four successive cash withdrawals of $100 each; then at 2:46 A.M., he called the Marilyn Escort Service in Brooklyn. The service sent a prostitute named Nora Lopez to Young's hotel room. Young paid her $400 in cash for sex. Then at 3:46 A.M., after Lopez had left, Young ordered a pornographic movie from the hotel's movie service. At 5:50 A.M., he ordered some food, then got back online. Even though Young was scheduled to give a lecture to the group later that day, he didn't take any kind of medication to keep him awake.

After he returned home on October 24, Young entered, browsed, and then joined People2People, an online singles dating service, part of the Phoenix Media Group in Boston. He used the screen name casual_guy2000, with an e-mail address of *casual_guy2000@yahoo.com*. That night, he logged on to the site at 10:00 P.M. and then again at 11:13

P.M., entered the "Men Seeking Women" section and filled out a profile and interest page.

Young said he was forty-nine, Caucasian, five feet ten inches tall, with an average body, light brown hair, and brown eyes. He didn't smoke and drank only occasionally. Young said he had a doctorate and worked full-time. He was looking for a Caucasian woman, thirty-five to sixty years old, who was slim to slightly overweight, and who lived about thirty miles outside Boston and had at least a high school diploma.

The same day, Young signed up at the Ultimate Live Web site—a portal for adult materials, including streaming videos of female models based in Amsterdam with whom visitors could chat via the Internet. He canceled that subscription on November 10, 1999. While at this site, Young chatted with female models and asked them to pose for him.

Young entered the People2People Web site again, on Monday morning, October 25, and between 5:42 and 5:51 sent messages to three fellow members with the screen names macp143sum, mistressrk, and bckallykat.

Harry Page and his wife, Amy, also known as macp143sum, often used the People2People service to meet others for group sex. Young saw their profile—a white couple in their early thirties looking for average to chunky white men for sexual times.

According to their profile, the Pages enjoyed peep booths, adult theaters, rest areas, dark bars, and public places. The couple liked to party, but they didn't drink and the husband didn't smoke. They weren't willing to meet anyone at their home since they had children. However, they might make an exception if they really liked someone. The wife said she was five feet four inches tall, 145 pounds, with a 38D bust, a toned behind and legs—but "a bit of a tummy from having kids"— long brown hair, and brown eyes. Although the couple claimed to have a happy marriage, the husband was into seeing his wife in group situations—and she enjoyed them as well.

The couple was looking for a man aged twenty-nine to fifty, Caucasian, average weight or a few pounds overweight, five feet six inches to six feet two inches, who lived within one hundred miles of their home in East Bridgewater, Massachusetts.

On October 25 at 5:42 A.M. Young e-mailed the Pages with information about himself. He said he was white, forty-nine, clean, drug and disease free, and a few pounds overweight. He told the couple he was a college graduate and was a "managerial type." He said he was married, but his wife didn't "play," so he was looking for a very discreet couple with whom to play. He explained that he loved to give and receive oral sex, loved big breasts to suck on, and loved group activities. He said he was basically straight but could adapt in group situations. He said he wanted to exchange e-mails to see if they would get along. He told the Pages that he couldn't host them at his home but would be willing to arrange for hotel accommodations if they got along. He asked the Pages to respond in an e-mail.

Amy Page responded to Young saying he could e-mail her at *peepbooth@aol.com* and she would send him some pictures. She said she was normally shy, but her husband really liked to see her with another man. "He enjoys seeing me with two cocks in me." She then asked Young if they could meet in a hotel and if he had any special interests.

Young tried to reach the couple at the e-mail address Amy provided, but his messages kept bouncing back. So he used the People2People site to ask them for another e-mail address. Amy then sent him a corrected address and they began to communicate using the free e-mail service available at Yahoo.com rather than the paid message service offered by People2People.

At 8:15 P.M., Young e-mailed the Pages saying he was pleased that they were interested and hoped they would be able to meet. He thought a good way to break the ice was to exchange pictures—he said he had taken some of himself with and without clothes.

He asked the couple if they could meet in a discreet public place to talk and exchange ideas. "I would love to meet for a drink after a few more e-mails or phone calls with the option to stay and play together right after if we are compatible," he said, adding he would be impatient if they couldn't get together the first time they met.

Responding to the Pages' questions about his special interests, he said he loved to please his partners in any way possible. He again said he was very oral and loved dual penetration activities, whether "oral, vaginal, or double anything." Young said he had dabbled in most everything, although his preferences were "pretty vanilla, if you call threesomes vanilla."

The Pages then sent Young five sexually explicit photos of Amy via e-mail.

Young responded to the Pages at 12:13 A.M. on Tuesday, October 26, telling them he loved their pictures and said he would love to play with them. He said since they had sent him provocative photographs, he would e-mail them a nude photograph of himself. He asked the Pages to call him to talk, but he told them there were times when he might not be able to take their calls and would have to call them back.

"I am excited by your cooperation and candor! Look forward to hearing from you by phone or e-mail, Tom." With his message, Young attached a photo of himself showing full-frontal nudity.

At 5:25 A.M., Tom sent the Pages another e-mail, including his telephone number, which he forgot to send with his previous messages.

At 8:55 A.M., Harry Page got another message from casual_guy2000, saying he would like to know a few more things but they could be discussed in person.

"I'm a bit worried about the sig (signature), which suggests you may use rest areas. How careful are you about who, how, you interact?" Young asked the Pages.

He asked if they could meet that Thursday. Young said he couldn't stay the night, but he could meet them after 6:00 P.M. and stay until 10:00 or 11:00 P.M. If that didn't work, he suggested they could get together in a couple of weeks.

The Pages never responded to his message. Young e-mailed them again on October 27 at 10:16 A.M., apologizing if he offended them in any way because he asked about their behavior.

"Forgive me if that's it and let's communicate some more anyways. I really am not offensive. If it's merely that you have been busy, well that's OK. Thanks for listening, Tom."

The Pages and Young never got a chance to meet.

On October 25, 1999, at 5:43 A.M., Young also responded to an ad placed on the People2People Web site by mistressrk, saying he was mature, forty-nine, a few pounds overweight, athletic, with a doctorate degree. He said he was looking for a discreet relationship and was interested in what she had to offer, but he would reject anything that left permanent marks. "Please e-mail if you are still available."

There was no response.

At 5:51 A.M., Young read a profile of bckallykat, whose name was Katherine Irwin, and then sent her a message.

In her profile, Irwin said she was single, forty-five, five feet four inches tall, Caucasian, a smoker, an occasional drinker, with an average body. She said she was classy, intelligent—she had taken some college courses—warm, compassionate, sexy, sensuous, playful, down-to-earth, with a wild and crazy sense of humor. She said she loved to dance and to make romance with the right man.

"I am a very adventurous lover, wonderfully uninhibited and wickedly open to most anything. (So what do you have in mind?)," she wrote.

She explained that she was extremely liberal in most areas of life, including politics. She said her kids were grown and on their own.

"So let's do it, let's do it. What have you got to lose? Meow, prrrrrrrr."

She said she was only interested in men looking for a mutually satisfying, lifelong relationship. She was looking for a Caucasian, Hispanic, or "other" man, forty-nine to sixty years old, five feet nine inches to six feet, athletic, average or a few pounds overweight, single or divorced. She wanted a man who didn't smoke and only drank on occasion, and who lived within one hundred miles of Pelham, New Hampshire.

Young responded to her saying he was forty-nine, white, clean, healthy, and fit, and he was looking for mutual petting and more. "I'm very open-minded. I do live in the Greater Boston area. Where are you? Let's e-mail!!"

She responded at 7:41 A.M., "Hi, I live in So. NH—if you're still interested email to: *Spidrwb121@aol.com—Kapokey@aol.com.*"

The two never hooked up.

Then on October 26 at approximately 8:59 P.M., Young read a profile from Joanne Nichols, daisymae828, who was "a woman seeking a man for a friend or a relationship."

In her profile, Nichols said she was a forty-six-year-old Caucasian female, five feet two inches tall, with an average body type. She said she smoked occasionally but didn't drink. She said she had children. She was seeking a Caucasian male, forty-one to forty-nine, five feet eight inches to six feet three inches tall, average body type, who only drank occasionally and lived thirty miles from Boston, Massachusetts.

After reading her profile, Young e-mailed her and said he was interested in an uncomplicated, intimate relationship. "I'm very clean, educated, good-looking, athletic, drug and disease free, sincere but not ready for long-term relationship. E-mail for more."

But Nichols never responded.

At 4:55 P.M. on October 31, Thomas Young tried to contact a prostitute named Deborah Doolio. Unable to reach her, he left a message on her cell phone.

Chapter 4

Dirk Greineder was born on October 19, 1940, in Berlin, Germany, to Kurt Greineder and Renee Chaoun, Greineder the younger of two boys. His wife, Mabel, was born just about a year later, on August 31, 1941, in Colombia, South America, to Angel and Martina Chegwin. May, as Mabel liked to be called, was the youngest of four children—two boys and two girls.

When Dirk was five, his family moved to Beirut, Lebanon, and he lived there until 1958, when he graduated from the American Community School, a local high school. He spoke four languages: German, English, French, and Arabic. After graduation, Dirk moved to the United States to attend Yale University, majoring in biochemistry. He graduated from Yale in 1962. At that time, he decided to move to Cleveland, Ohio, to pursue a combined M.D./Ph.D. degree in pharmacology and medicine at Case Western Reserve University. He finished his studies in September 1970.

In 1964, while in Cleveland, Dirk met his future wife, May Chegwin, who was pursuing a master's in medical surgical nursing, an advanced nursing degree. He was twenty-four; she was twenty-three. May had moved to Cleveland from New York, where her family settled when she was a year old. She had graduated from New

York's Hunter College with a bachelor's degree in collegiate nursing and a minor in zoology.

The pair dated for a short time, then drifted apart, meeting up again in 1966 and marrying in 1968. While her husband was completing his studies, May graduated from the master's program and joined the faculty at Case Western Reserve Nursing School, rising to the level of assistant professor. When Dirk graduated, the couple moved to Manhattan, where he did his internship and one year of residency at Cornell University's Medical School and New York Hospital. May joined the faculty at Cornell Nursing School as an assistant professor and worked there for one year. She soon became pregnant with Kirsten, who was born on April 22, 1971.

In 1972, the young family moved to Bethesda, Maryland, where Dirk entered a three-year program at the National Institutes of Health in the National Institute of Allergy and Infectious Disease. After spending three years in Maryland, Dirk, May, and their three children—by now Britt and Colin had also been born—moved to Cleveland Road in Wellesley in 1975, because Dirk had secured a position at the then-Robert B. Brigham Hospital in Boston, a precursor of the current Brigham and Women's Hospital. Although he spent most of his time doing research in immunology, he worked with patients approximately one day a week. He remained at Brigham until 1980. During that time, he also moonlighted at the emergency room in a Brockton hospital to make ends meet—something he did until 1986.

But in 1980, Dirk, who by now was a fully trained allergist, decided he wanted to spend more time working with patients. So he signed on at the then-

Harvard Community Health Plan, an HMO with only two health centers and a small membership, where he became the predominant allergist. Because the HMO couldn't afford a full-time allergist, Dirk moved from the Brockton hospital to the Morton Hospital in Taunton and increased his emergency room work to somewhere around twenty-five hours a week. By 1986, when he left the Morton Hospital, he was working in the emergency room only twelve hours a week.

While their children were growing up in the 1980s, the Greineders' family life revolved around swimming, traveling to various swim meets—Kirsten, Britt, and Colin all swam competitively—and studies. May helped them with liberal arts, and Dirk with science and math. After Colin graduated from high school, May went back to work as a triage nurse at what was then the Kenmore Harvard Community Health Plan, which became Harvard Pilgrim Health Care and then Harvard Vanguard. She worked there until her mother suffered a stroke the day after Thanksgiving 1998. After her mother became ill, May spent every week caring for her mother at her home in Queens, New York, then traveling back to Wellesley on the weekends. She did this faithfully until her mother passed away on January 23, 1999.

In the mid to late 1990s, Dirk was head of the allergy department at Harvard Pilgrim Health Care, which had grown into the largest HMO in New England. He also worked in the allergy department at Beth Israel Hospital in Boston. In fact, in the early 1990s, he and his colleagues at Beth Israel had landed a $5 million grant from the National Institutes of Health to study pediatric asthma. Most of Dirk's time was taken up with that project. He worked twelve-hour days, five days a week, from 7:00 A.M. to 7:00 P.M. He usually worked late one night a week in the clinic, often seeing patients until 9:00 P.M. or 10:00 P.M. In addition, he was writing grants and doing a lot of paperwork, much of which he did at home.

In 1997, the family traveled to Europe, spending three days in Heidelberg, Germany, where Kirsten was working on a Fulbright Scholarship, then continued on to Spain, where the entire family stayed for ten days. Then in June 1998, when Kirsten moved to Ann Arbor, Michigan, to do her medical residency, her parents helped her move to her new apartment. They loaded up two cars with Kirsten's belongings and drove out to Ann Arbor. Dirk and May spent five days in Michigan making sure everything was perfect for their eldest child.

"My mom was sad to have me leave New England, and I was sad to leave my parents," Kirsten said later. Kirsten was concerned about what would happen to her parents now that all the kids had moved out of the house. "I was very reassured by the fact that they had gotten Huntington tickets. They were going to the Huntington Theater. They were going to the symphony and they were enjoying activities together, on top of the typical movies and other activities."

It appeared Kirsten was right.

May appeared to be adjusting well to life without her children. She had lost weight, gotten a face-lift, and was dressing more stylishly. In September 1999, she even started school at Massachusetts General Hospital School of Nursing to obtain her nurse practitioner's degree. And she had taken over virtually all the planning for Kirsten's upcoming wedding.

She seemed to be having the time of her life.

Chapter 5

On October 31, 1999, at 8:56 A.M., Dirk Greineder called the business line of the Wellesley Police Department.

In a high-pitched, panic-stricken voice, Greineder told police someone had attacked his wife at Morses Pond. They were walking their dog and she hurt her back. He left her to continue walking the dog. When he came back, he found her. She'd been attacked. He thought she was dead.

What exactly happened that Halloween morning is unclear, but many months later her husband explained it this way:

After the Greineders got out of the car, they started walking down the path through the pine tree forest, continuously throwing the ball for Zephyr on the leafy stretch of open space overlooking the aqueduct. The couple threw the ball down the embankment once or twice to make her run down and back up again, which was good exercise for the dog. The pair then continued walking on the path through the trees, ending up at a flat, raised section of ground in the sand pit area. The sand pit area is approximately thirty or forty feet below the level of the pine tree forest.

As they were going down the gravelly path, May slipped and moaned slightly.

Dirk turned around and saw her frozen in an awkward stance—immobile right where she stood. May had always been prone to back problems. In recent years, she'd get a very sharp, electric pain in her back—almost as if someone gave her a jolt or a stab—that would shoot down her leg. Although she was supposed to wear a back brace, she wasn't wearing one that day.

Dirk asked his wife how she was and she told him she had a pain, but she'd be fine in a minute or two. After resting a bit, May took one or two small, careful steps. Dirk took her hand to make sure she didn't slip. After several minutes, May told Dirk to keep walking with Zephyr down to the beach and she'd meet him at the rock in the parking lot where they used to sit sometimes. Initially, Dirk didn't want to let his wife go on alone, but she finally persuaded him to go ahead without her.

Dirk walked on, taking the same route they normally took, leaving his wife to slowly make her way to their meeting place. He walked down the path, out to the circle area—the cul-de-sac at the end of the path—toward the gate by the beach, which is kept locked. All the while, he threw the ball for Zephyr.

As they walked, Zephyr, who had been distracted all morning, didn't seem all that interested in chasing the ball. Instead, she was doing a lot of smelling near the beach. Usually, Zephyr would run right into the water, but this morning, for some reason, she just wasn't behaving normally.

Rather than going to the beach, Dirk decided to head back and look for May. He walked a little faster than usual, but was still throwing the ball for Zephyr. He didn't see anyone at the edge of the circle. But when he got to the rock, where he was supposed to meet May, she wasn't there. Thinking she might be at another rock on the other side of the parking lot, Dirk drifted out into the circle area to see if he could see her. It had been about ten minutes since the couple had separated. He called out her name in a normal tone of voice. At that point, Zephyr turned and headed back onto the path. Dirk followed the dog but lost track of her as she went down the embankment. It was then he saw May lying at the edge of the path at the bottom of the embankment. By now, Zephyr was nuzzling May, and Dirk was waiting for his wife to look at him. When she didn't, he ran down the rise and over to her. He pushed Zephyr out of the way to stop her from bothering May. He asked May if she was okay, but May didn't answer him or even open her eyes. He noticed a cut on his wife's forehead. Not overly concerned, Dirk tried to rouse her, then tried to take her pulse on the left side of her neck. It was then he saw the blood. He quickly went to the right side of her neck to try to get a pulse that way; he couldn't.

Dirk had no idea what had happened, but he knew his wife was really hurt. Frightened, he shook May, trying to get her to wake up. He leaned in to her, putting his head next to her face, trying to feel her breath on his cheek. But he couldn't feel anything there either. Then he saw the massive wound on the left side of his wife's neck.

Dirk knelt by his wife's right side and tried to pick her up, figuring if he could just get her out of there and get some help, she'd be okay. But he couldn't really get a good grip and wasn't able to lift her. Greineder squatted down and tried again to pick May up, but her head just flopped back and she started slipping out of his grasp. He was afraid he would do her more harm than good. So he tried to lay her back down on the ground. She was so crooked; he had to straighten her out a little.

Unable to scoop her up and get her out of there, Greineder decided to leave his wounded wife and get some help. He walked around, but all he could see was Zephyr; he realized if he did leave May and anybody came on the scene and tried to assist her, the dog might get in the way, or worse, keep them from helping her. So he grabbed Zephyr's leash, which was half around May's waist—she always tied it loosely around her waist—and half on the ground underneath her. Putting it on the dog, he went back with her to the circle, hoping to find a Department of Public Works employee at the pumping station, but he realized the orange DPW truck wasn't there. He looked around and thought he saw movement at the edge of the circle, where the paved path that goes to the edge of the beach begins.

Thinking maybe he saw a runner, he followed the movement a short distance down the path, but he didn't see anyone. So he turned around, planning to run up the access road to get help, and almost immediately bumped into William Kear, a Wellesley resident walking his small dog. Greineder, who had forgotten his own cell phone, asked Kear if he had one. He didn't. Greineder wanted to go back for May, but he knew he had to get help. So he went up the access road as fast as he could.

Greineder ran about halfway up the access road when he saw Rick Magnan, another Wellesley resident, on another path walking toward him. He waved and yelled, trying to flag Magnan down. Greineder asked Magnan if he had a cell phone. When Magnan said no, Greineder kept going, running as fast as he could, down the access road, angry that he couldn't run any faster.

When he got to the car, Greineder immediately opened the passenger door and put Zephyr inside to get her out of the way. Then he went around to the driver's side, opened that door, which was unlocked, and flung himself inside. As he started to dial his car phone, he realized he was calling his home, quickly hung up, then called the business line of the Wellesley Police Department. When he reached the police, he told them he needed help. He was at the gate to Morses Pond. His wife had hurt her back. Then she had been attacked.

The police dispatcher told him to wait and guide the police or ambulance to his wife. But he didn't want to do that; he wanted to get back to May. When he finished the call, he didn't know what to do. He wanted to go back to his wife, but he was terrified that if the police came and he wasn't there, they would never find his injured wife in the woods. Greineder then asked Magnan, who had followed him to his car, to go back to where May was because the police wanted him to stay at the van and wait until they arrived.

But Magnan told Greineder to go back to his wife while he waited for the police. Greineder agreed and started running as fast as he could down the access road. Almost immediately he heard a car behind him. It was Wellesley police officer Paul Fitzpatrick, who had been dispatched to the scene. Greineder flagged Fitzpatrick down. The officer stopped and told Greineder to get in the back of the car. Greineder directed him to drive down to the circle, then turn right onto the path. Fitzpatrick drove as far as he could, then stopped the car, got out, and went around to the front of the vehicle.

Greineder tried to get out of the cruiser but couldn't. He panicked. He screamed and Fitzpatrick finally came around and opened the door. Dirk went down the path and down the rise, like a shot, to May. Of course, she hadn't moved. He tried to take her pulse again. He looked into her eyes, but he couldn't even tell if her pupils were moving. Then he picked up her shirt but couldn't get a heartbeat. She was gone. He knew it. But he didn't believe it.

Greineder looked down at his wife's body and realized her belly was exposed. Not wanting a stranger to see her that way, he knelt down and tried, unsuccessfully, to pull up her pants.

By now, two or three firemen had arrived and they formed a circle around May's body. Officer Fitzpatrick, who had followed Greineder to his wife's body, tapped him on the shoulder and asked him to back away so the paramedics could do their jobs. Still on his knees, Greineder leaned back and looked up at the emergency personnel surrounding his wife. One of the firefighters looked down at him and all of a sudden everything began to make more sense.

When Greineder moved away from his wife's body, Fitzpatrick noticed a large puddle of blood in the middle of the pathway and drag marks that began at the center of the path and ended at May's left foot. Not wanting anyone to contaminate the crime scene, Fitzpatrick told the emergency personnel not to step in that area. He then radioed Sergeant Peter Nahass of the Wellesley Police Department, notified him of May's murder, and asked him to come to Morses Pond.

When he arrived ten minutes later, Nahass told

Fitzpatrick to go back to the circle area to wait with Greineder, who was already there standing under a tree talking with a firefighter. The first thing that caught Fitzpatrick's attention was the bloodstain along the left arm of Greineder's yellow-and-white windbreaker. Fitzpatrick also noted that Greineder's hands were clean.

"What's your name, sir?" Fitzpatrick asked.

"Dirk Greineder. I'm a doctor at Harvard and Brigham and Women's Hospital. Here's my driver's license."

"What happened here?"

"I was out walking with my wife and she tripped on a pebble and threw her back out, which is not unusual. She told me to go on ahead of her and she'd meet me at the rock," Greineder said, pointing to the flat rock near the entrance of the parking area. "So I went ahead to the fenced-in area by the beach with my dog and the dog started acting funny and then ran back to where I had left my wife. That's when I found her in the pathway. I checked her and she felt warm. I checked her carotid pulse and it was weak. So I ran back to the van and called the police."

"Is she dead?" Greineder asked Fitzpatrick about thirty minutes later.

"Yes."

"Are you going to arrest me?"

Just before 9:00 A.M. on Halloween, an emergency medical call came into Wellesley Fire Department headquarters. About a minute and a half later, Lieutenant William DeLorie, a firefighter as well as an emergency medical technician, firefighter Ken De-Merchant, and firefighter Ron Wilson arrived at

Morses Pond. Two paramedics, who worked for a private ambulance company, American Medical Response, had also been dispatched from another Wellesley fire station to Morses Pond on the report of a back injury.

After parking their truck behind Officer Fitzpatrick's cruiser, the firefighters grabbed their gear and made their way down the path to May's body.

"Take her pulse," DeLorie shouted to DeMerchant, noticing May's ashen gray color.

DeMerchant crouched down by the left side of May's body. He attempted to get a radial pulse and checked for signs of life, but he was unable to do so. So he bent down to check her pulse on her neck. As he moved her sweater out of the way, he and DeLorie saw that her throat had been slashed. Seeing the horrific wound, DeLorie immediately radioed the paramedics to determine their location. The paramedics responded that they were within seconds of the scene.

As he waited, DeLorie saw Greineder, who was still in the area, drop to his knees and cry out, "This is my wife. Who could have done this to my wife?"

"Did you lose sight of your wife?" DeLorie asked.

"Yes, we were walking with the dog, throwing a ball out in front of us for her to retrieve," Greineder explained. "May threw the ball to her side and twisted her back, so I went ahead of her to get the dog to stop her from going into the water and I lost sight of my wife."

When the paramedics arrived, they knew right away the woman lying on the ground had not injured her back. Noting the large wound on the victim's neck, the fact that she wasn't breathing, as well as the pool of blood in the path, they quickly determined they were quite possibly in the middle of a crime scene.

"She doesn't have a pulse," DeMerchant told them. Realizing there was nothing they could do, the paramedics backed away, trying not to disturb anything, and they headed back to the circle area, where they saw Greineder, who had left the pathway before them, talking with Officer Fitzpatrick.

Shift supervisor Sergeant Peter Nahass was at the Wellesley police station when he heard the dispatcher say send an ambulance and the fire department to Morses Pond because a woman had hurt her back. He didn't think much of it until several seconds later when the dispatcher said she didn't know if the woman was breathing. As Nahass began to get his gear together, he received a radio call from Officer Fitzpatrick telling him to report to Morses Pond immediately because a crime had been committed. Within three minutes Nahass was at the scene. Because the gate at the end of Turner Road was open, he drove down the Morses Pond access road to the circle, parked his car, and got out. He immediately went down a path to his right and had walked about forty or fifty yards when he saw the firefighters, paramedics, Fitzpatrick, and May's body. When Nahass saw the wound on the right side of May's head and the large gaping cut on the left side of her neck, he knew she was dead. The paramedics confirmed his observation.

When Nahass learned that May's husband was in the area, he told Fitzpatrick to go stand with him. Nahass then asked the firefighters and paramedics to leave the area the same way they entered the path and to take whatever they brought with them. Nahass knew he had to protect the crime scene.

Looking around, Nahass saw a plastic Baggie that had blood on it lying in the pathway near May's body. He also saw a tennis ball covered with dirt. He noticed a heel mark and drag marks in the path that led to May's body, as well as a blue fleece glove on the ground like the one May still had on her left hand. He observed that May's pants were undone and her left pant leg was pushed up to just below her knee. He saw that her shirt was hiked up a little bit over her stomach and the gold chain she was wearing was embedded in the wound on her neck.

Nahass asked Officer Lamar Hughes, who had also arrived at the scene, to take the names of everyone in the area and to note the type of shoes they were wearing. He instructed another officer to take pictures of the shoes and to match the names to the shoes. After he and another officer roped off the area with yellow crime scene tape, Nahass went out to the circle area to talk to Greineder.

As Nahass walked over to Greineder, who was standing with Fitzpatrick, he noted that the man was in constant motion—he couldn't seem to stand still. He also observed reddish bloodstains on the yellow-and-white windbreaker-type jacket the man was wearing. Although the bloodstains went from his shoulders all the way down to the man's wrists, there was no blood on his hands. The sergeant observed dirt on one knee of Greineder's black pants and a reddish brown spot on his white running shoes.

"What happened?" Nahass asked Greineder when he got close to him.

"We took a walk down around the pond, like we usually do, and at some point she was throwing the ball to the dog and she hurt her back," Greineder explained. "I told her to stay there while I continued walking the dog and I'd meet her at the rock where we meet if we split up during our walk. But when I went to the pond area, the gate was locked, so I turned around to come back. Zephyr took off, almost like she heard someone calling her. I followed her back to the path, where I found May on the ground. Zephyr was on top of her, licking her face. I'm a doctor and I tried to take her pulse twice at her carotid artery but couldn't. So I took the leash from around May's waist, leashed Zephyr, and went to the car to call the police. After I made the call, I started to go back to May, and Officer Fitzpatrick picked me up."

Around 11:00 A.M., Greineder and some of the other officers went back to the Wellesley police station, but Nahass remained at the pond for the rest of the day, searching for evidence.

Detective Jill McDermott was sitting at her desk in the Wellesley police station when she heard officers being dispatched to Morses Pond because a woman had hurt her back. Shortly after, however, she heard the dispatcher say the woman might not be breathing.

Knowing she'd probably have to respond to the scene, she started gathering up her belongings. As she was doing this, her telephone rang.

"You should probably start heading to Morses Pond," the dispatcher told her.

When she arrived at the pond some five or ten minutes later, the gate to the access road was open, so she drove down to the circle area. She parked her cruiser in the lot just before the circle, got out, and approached Sergeant Nahass, her superior, who was standing with other officers, firefighters, and paramedics. Looking around, she saw a number of civilians, including a man with a small dog, an Asian man, and a man wearing a white T-shirt and shorts. She also saw a man wearing a yellow windbreaker standing with Officer Fitzpatrick.

As she watched, the man in the yellow jacket began pacing back and forth. At one point, he lay down on his stomach with his elbows on the cement and his chin resting in his hands, then got up again.

While McDermott was talking with Nahass, the man in the yellow windbreaker and Fitzpatrick started walking toward her, so she began walking in their direction. As she got closer, she saw large red smudges, which appeared to be blood, on the front, shoulder, arms, and cuffs of his yellow-and-white windbreaker. She also observed small red droplets on his white sneakers and a reddish smudge on the left lens of his eyeglasses, which he was wearing.

"Hello, I'm Detective McDermott," she said.

After telling Greineder that she was going to pat-frisk him, she put his hands behind his back and had him lock his fingers together. The she patted the outside of his clothing, up and down, front and back. When she was finished, she asked him to empty his pockets and show her the contents, which consisted of some loose change and keys.

"What happened at the pond today?" she asked him, writing the information he gave in a small notebook.

"My wife and I drove to the pond and parked where we usually park every weekend, and we walked our dog Zephyr."

"Where did you walk the dog?"

"We walked through the pine tree forest throwing a ball in front of us so Zephyr could retrieve it. May threw the ball ahead to the dog and she hurt her back in the sand pit area. She told me to go ahead with the dog and she would meet me at the rock," Greineder explained, motioning to the path where his wife's body was found and the rock at the end of the access road.

"I went toward the beach with Zephyr, but we didn't get close to the water because the dog kept running back in the direction we had just come from," Greineder said. "I thought maybe May was calling Zephyr, but I didn't hear anything. So I followed Zephyr back to the rock, but when I got there, I didn't see May. Zephyr ran into the path area, and I followed her, and that's when I found May. Zephyr was on top of her, licking her face, and I thought maybe they were just playing because May usually lies down when she hurts her back. But as I got closer to her, I realized something was wrong. Her pants were open and she had some blood on her neck. I checked her carotid artery for her pulse but couldn't get one. She was still warm and I tried to wake her up, but I couldn't, so I took Zephyr and ran back out to the street and across the path looking for a runner because I needed to get help. That's when I saw the guy with the little dog and asked him if he had a cell phone."

As Greineder was talking to McDermott, Sergeant Martin Foley, a state police trooper assigned to the Norfolk County District Attorney's Office, joined them.

That morning, Foley had been at the medical examiner's office in Boston. Sometime after 9:00 A.M., the trooper got a call from headquarters to call Sergeant Peter Nahass of the Wellesley Police

Department. Nahass told Foley about the murder and asked him to report to Morses Pond.

Foley and other state police officers from the DA's office responded to and investigated all unattended deaths in Norfolk County and acted as the designated investigative representative of the Norfolk district attorney. They also worked hand in hand with local police detectives on all homicides as well as many other types of cases.

Foley finished up his work at the ME's office, hopped in his car, and drove to Morses Pond, getting there at approximately 10:05 A.M. When Foley arrived, he saw Greineder standing beyond the circle area, close to the water.

After speaking with Nahass, Lieutenant Wayne Cunningham, and McDermott of the Wellesley Police Department, Foley followed them down the dirt path to view May Greineder's body. The first things he noticed were the open wound on the left side of her neck and the wound on her forehead. He also noted that her blue-and-white striped pants were open in the front and a blue sweatshirt was pulled up, exposing her stomach.

Looking around, Foley observed a clear plastic bag lying in the path a few feet away from the victim and a bloodstain on the ground in the middle of the pathway. A short distance away in the dirt, he saw a blue fleece glove, similar to a glove on one of the victim's hands. Foley then left the area with McDermott, who introduced him to Greineder.

"Hi, I'm Sergeant Foley with the state police," Foley said. "I'm sorry for your loss."

As he spoke with Greineder, Foley noted that he was wearing a yellow nylon jacket that had reddish brown stains on the front of it, as well as on the tops of the sleeves and both elbows. Foley also noticed that there was a large reddish brown stain on the jacket's left cuff—a stain that ended abruptly in an elliptical shape—but his hands were clean. The trooper spotted a reddish brown swipe on the left lens of Greineder's glasses, which were now hanging down from his sweatshirt, as well as three scrape marks, or scratches, on his neck.

Foley, who already had an understanding of the doctor's version of the day's events from McDermott, asked the doctor what he did the previous night.

"I was home with my wife working on a slide presentation for her school project," Greineder answered. "I awoke at six A.M., prepared breakfast of fresh fruit and muffins, and woke my wife up an hour later."

"Do you and your wife sleep in the same bedroom?" Foley asked.

"Yes, we sleep in a bedroom that was newly remodeled," Greineder responded. "We offered the bedroom to one of our daughters, but she didn't want it and I don't really understand why."

Greineder went on to explain that their house was a mess because May had been preoccupied with her schoolwork and because part of the house was being renovated. Foley thought it odd that Greineder offered so much information in response to his simple question.

"Did you have sexual intercourse with your wife this morning?" Foley asked.

"No, I didn't."

In the event that May Greineder had been sexually assaulted, and police recovered DNA from semen on her body, they would need to know if the couple had had sex in order to rule out Dirk Greineder as a suspect.

"Did you have sex with your wife last night? Did you have sex with your wife last week?"

"No, my wife and I weren't sexually active and haven't been for a few years," Greineder responded.

Greineder then recounted for Foley what happened at the pond that morning and the events that ultimately led him to his wife's bludgeoned body.

He said when he first went back to look for his wife, he found her several hundred feet from where he originally left her, lying on her back to the left of the pathway. He said that he walked closer to her and was able to see a wound on her forehead.

"Did you touch your wife?" Foley asked.

Greineder responded that he first checked her carotid artery on the right side. He said that she was still warm, but he couldn't feel a pulse. He said that when he returned with the police, he went to check her carotid pulse from the left side, where he did a better job of it and that's when he discovered the neck wound. He said he checked her heartbeat but couldn't find any. He also stated he had yanked up his wife's pants because they had been pulled down around her hips and he didn't want anyone to see her in that condition.

Foley had been talking to Greineder for about five minutes when the doctor expressed concern for his dogs—Wolfie at home and Zephyr in the van.

"I really need to get home to take care of the dogs," Greineder said.

Greineder also repeatedly asked police to let him use a cell phone to call his daughter, Britt, but he was not allowed to do so.

After listening to the doctor's story, Foley asked him if he would accompany himself and McDermott to the Wellesley police station, which he did.

Chapter 6

Around 11:00 A.M., Foley and McDermott drove the doctor to the Wellesley police station. On the way, Foley asked him if he had his estate in order. Greineder responded that he and his wife had recently signed some life insurance papers, but added, "It doesn't matter now."

Once at the station, McDermott and Foley took Greineder to the second-floor detectives' office, where he asked if he could telephone his youngest daughter, Britt, who lived in Brookline. When he reached her at approximately 11:20 A.M., he told her something bad had happened to her mother and to please come to the Wellesley police station right away.

"Did you wash your hands since you checked your wife's carotid artery?" Foley asked Greineder when he got off the phone.

"No."

"Then why are your hands clean?" Foley asked. "Why isn't there any blood on them?"

"I don't know," Greineder answered, shaking his head.

"Well, we're going to have to take your clothes and sneakers. Maybe you should ask your daughter to bring you a change of clothes when she comes," Foley said.

"That won't work because I changed the keys and

alarm system to the house so she won't be able to get in," Greineder said. Then he added, "A friend of mine, Terry, he's a lawyer and I think I should call him."

After Greineder finished his telephone call to attorney Terry Segal, he approached McDermott, who was sitting outside the detectives' office.

"He told me not to talk to you anymore," Greineder said. "I've told you everything. I'm not trying to hide anything. I've given you everything I know. You say you want my clothes and it suddenly scares me. This isn't real; this is a movie. I don't know what happened and I was right there."

Segal arrived at the station around 11:50 A.M. and met with Greineder in a second-floor detectives' office. When he had finished talking with his friend, Segal told McDermott he wanted to talk to the district attorney. While Segal was trying to contact the DA, McDermott sat in the office with Greineder.

"I'm thinking of these crazy things. . . . Like this morning, May gave me a back rub, so you'll find my skin underneath her nails," the doctor told the young detective.

"Did you give your wife a back rub?" McDermott asked.

"No."

Just then, Greineder's daughter arrived and went into the office with Segal. Britt was very upset and screaming at her father.

"Britt came in and she was yelling and screaming. I wanted her to come to be with me before I told her what happened. I knew she'd be upset and frightened. I thought I should be with her. I wanted her with me. I needed her," Greineder testified later.

"What the hell is going on? What happened? Is she

really dead? Did someone kill her?" she asked, hugging her father. "What happened between you and Mom today? Did something happen?"

"No, we were walking and she hurt her back. I went down to the water with Zephy and Zephy heard something and she found [Mom]," Greineder said.

"She's hurt her back before. She usually lies down and she's fine," Britt said before going into a separate office to talk privately with her father.

"Why do these fucked-up things always happen to our family?" Britt yelled out as they exited the office. "Why do these psychotic, unexplained things happen to our family?"

"They're going to think it's me," Greineder said. "I've seen it on TV."

Later, Britt explained that the "psychotic things" she was referring to were the multiple murders and suicide committed by Fred Chegwin, her mother's older brother. That crime had shocked another upscale community thirty-one years earlier.

According to newspaper reports of the crime, at 8:00 A.M. on August 7, 1968, Chegwin drove his turquoise Ford Mustang to his father-in-law's home in Hollywood Hills, California, forced his way into the house, and fired "burst after burst" from a .32-caliber pistol, killing his twenty-four-year-old wife, Myra, her nineteen-year-old sister, Debbie Weinstein, and their parents. Chegwin then killed himself.

Those murders ended a nasty love triangle involving Chegwin, his wife, and her sister, according to reports in the *Los Angeles Times*. At the time, investigators said Philip Weinstein had fired Chegwin from his job the day before the murders, because Weinstein had heard that Chegwin had fallen in love with

Debbie and the affair was ruining his marriage to Myra.

While at the station, police photographed Greineder with and without his clothing. They also wanted him to turn his clothes over to them.

"They want you to sign a release to give them your clothes and to let them search your car and your house," Segal said to Greineder after talking with police. "Let's just do that and get out of here."

Ultimately, Greineder agreed to give police his clothing and sneakers voluntarily, as well as his fingernail clippings. Terry Segal's wife, who lived in Wellesley, drove to the police station with some of her husband's clothes for Greineder to wear home. However, Greineder refused to give police his eyeglasses because it was the only pair he had and he needed them to drive. While Greineder was at the station, Foley looked closer at his glasses and noticed that there were two reddish brown swipe marks on the bottom half of the left lens and some dots on the upper portion of the same lens. Foley instinctively knew those eyeglasses were important evidence. Nearly four years later, Wellesley police chief Terrence Cunningham said the only mistake his officers made that day was not taking Greineder's glasses.

After they left police headquarters, Britt took the keys to her father's van and went to Morses Pond to get Zephyr and take her home. Wellesley police planned to tow the Greineders' van to the station to search it. Greineder went home in Segal's car, followed closely by police in squad cars.

When they arrived at the home on Cleveland Road, Greineder went in first. He took Wolfie, who was at the front door, up a few stairs through the kitchen and put him in the backyard.

Then Greineder, Segal, McDermott, state police trooper Julia Mosely, and Foley walked through each room of the tri-level house, starting in the back area where the kitchen, dining room, and Greineder's office were located. Next the group went downstairs to the living room, and from there to the back bedroom, which was the master bedroom, on the lower level of the house. Once in the master bedroom, Foley noticed the bed had been stripped clean.

"Where are your bedsheets?" Foley asked Greineder.

"They're in the laundry room."

Police then followed Greineder to the laundry room. Martin Foley opened the washer, pulled the sheets out, and examined them. He didn't find any suspicious substances on them.

On the way back upstairs to the third level to walk through the other bedrooms and the bathrooms, Foley noticed some reddish brown stains on a Fisher-Price baby gate placed at the bottom of the stairs that led to the third-floor bedrooms. After their three children left home, the Greineders put the gate up so the dogs wouldn't go up the stairs to the bedrooms.

"Are those bloodstains?" Foley asked.

"No, they're stains from when I painted the deck."

Foley, who initially wanted to take the gate to the Wellesley police station, instead took it outside and had it photographed.

Once the walk-through was completed—it took about half an hour—Foley asked Greineder if police could photograph his eyeglasses. Greineder agreed. Foley again asked Greineder if police could take the glasses with them, but Segal answered, saying Greineder needed them for driving.

As they left, police opened the door to the garage and noticed a car inside. It was about 2:30 in the afternoon.

At this point, Foley drove Mosely to meet up with the state police helicopter—Mosely was going to take aerial photographs of Morses Pond—in the parking lot of a church on the eastbound side of Worcester Road in Wellesley, about a mile from Greineder's home. After dropping Mosely off, Foley went back to Morses Pond. By the time he arrived, the state police dive team and the K-9 unit were already there. When he got there, Foley joined Nahass, another state trooper, and an employee of the Wellesley Department of Public Works in a search of the area.

The group walked down the paved pathway where Greineder went when he came out of the woods after finding his wife's body. They saw a catch basin with an iron grate that was covered with leaves, branches, and other debris. Earlier the K-9 dog had alerted his handler that he was drawn to that storm drain. The DPW worker pulled the grate off the storm drain. Foley looked down into it and saw the head of a hammer, the brass end of a knife, and a brown glove on top of the knife. After police removed the items from the storm drain, Foley determined the hammer was a two-pound Estwing drilling hammer with a short handle, almost like a mini sledgehammer with a head that is identical on both sides. The knife, a Schrade, which was closed when police found it, had a four-inch folding blade. The brass end of the handle had the name Old Timer inscribed on its side. The right-hand glove was made of brown cotton. The palm area, the baby finger, the first finger, and the thumb were all covered with a plastic-type material that had dots on it. All three items appeared to have blood on them. There were also dog hairs on the glove.

Later that afternoon, Foley went back to the Wellesley police station to draft an application for a warrant to search Greineder's home.

Chapter 7

After working the night shift at a hospital emergency room in Ann Arbor, Michigan, on October 30, 1999, Kirsten Greineder drove to her fiancé's house in Dearborn, where she spent the night. The next morning, the couple had a leisurely breakfast and were watching television when the telephone rang. Kirsten's fiancé, Aleks Engel, got up from the couch to answer it.

"What?" he said, then put the phone down and looked Kirsten. He was as white as a ghost.

"Kirsten, something terrible has happened. We have to go to Boston right away."

"Oh my God. Oh my God," she screamed.

The first thing that flashed into Kristen's head was that her parents had had an accident and both of them were hurt. She had tried to call her parents that morning but was unable to reach them. She really hadn't been worried because she knew they always walked Zephyr on Sunday mornings.

"You have to tell me what happened," she demanded. "I can't go to Boston and be two hours in a plane without knowing what happened."

Aleks didn't know what to say, so he called the telephone number Britt had given him when she called.

When she answered, he handed the receiver to Kirsten.

"Kirsten, Mom's dead. She's been murdered." Britt sobbed uncontrollably.

After talking with her sister, Kirsten and Aleks quickly packed some clothes, booked a flight, and got to the Greineders' Wellesley home around 4:00 P.M.

When they pulled up in front of the Cleveland Road home, Terry Segal and Nancy Gans, a neighbor, were standing on the sidewalk talking. Britt was also outside and Dirk was at the front door. Kirsten and Aleks gave everybody a hug and went inside.

"My dad looked distraught, exhausted, devastated," Kirsten later testified. "He looked like I'd never, ever seen him look before. He looked so horrible, physically, that I was worried about him from a physical standpoint."

"Are you all right?" Kirsten asked her dad.

Almost immediately Greineder began to tell his daughter what had happened that morning at Morses Pond.

"Your mother and I went on a walk and she twisted her back, throwing the ball to Zephyr," he explained. "We discussed what we should do and she said Zephyr needed exercise, so she said I should continue walking her. I continued on and she said she'd walk slowly and meet me at the flat rock in the circle. So we split up in the sand pit area. When I got back, I didn't see her where we were supposed to meet. Zephyr tore off ahead of me and I followed her. That's when I saw your mother lying on the ground. My first thought was that she hurt her back. Zephyr was licking her face. I went up to her and I knew something was terribly wrong. I was shaking so much I couldn't even tell if she had a pulse. I remember I couldn't get her pulse. I never got her pulse. She was a little warm. I tried to pick her up so I could do something. I knew I needed to help her. So I got the cell phone in the car and called police. Then I went back to her. A police officer brought me part of the way back, but I had trouble getting out of his car. I was afraid because I thought I wouldn't be able to get back to your mother. But finally I did."

Colin Greineder, a medical student at Yale University in New Haven, Connecticut, slept in a little later than usual on Sunday, October 31, 1999. He had been out late the night before attending Halloween parties. After dressing, he went to play soccer with friends. In between games, he headed back to his apartment to check his messages. The first message he heard was from his sister Britt, saying he had to call her, and leaving him the number. The second message was from the Segals, who, like Britt, told him to call them immediately.

Colin knew something was wrong, so he called Britt, who tried to cushion the news of their mother's murder by making small talk. But Colin pressed her to tell him what had happened.

"Mom was murdered at the pond," Britt told her younger brother.

Colin heard the words but couldn't quite comprehend the gravity of the situation.

"Did they take her to the hospital? Are they trying to revive her? Where is she in the hospital?" he asked again and again.

When Britt explained that their mother hadn't been taken to the hospital, Colin was furious.

"How can they not take her to the hospital?" he screamed into the receiver.

Colin just couldn't understand that his mother couldn't have been saved even if she had been taken to the hospital.

Finally Britt just said, "Come home, and don't drive."

So Colin went next door and asked his friends to drive him to Wellesley.

But even when he arrived home, he kept insisting to his father that his mother should have been taken to the hospital.

Trying to help his son come to grips with his mother's death, Greineder told Colin everything that had happened at the pond.

"They couldn't have done anything for her at the hospital," Greineder said.

After spending most of the evening going over the day's events with their father, the Greineder children and Aleks turned in around midnight and were awakened about an hour later by the sound of voices.

At 1:00 A.M. on November 1, 1999, a total of ten officers from the Massachusetts State Police and the Wellesley Police Department arrived at the house to execute a search warrant. Based on the events of the previous day, Sergeant Martin Foley, who applied for the warrant, believed police would find evidence of May's murder at the Greineder home.

When the bell rang, Greineder, who hadn't yet gone to bed, opened the door to see Foley standing inside the storm door. Greineder grabbed the door trying to keep the dogs, which were not happy about having company at that hour, inside.

"Let us in," Foley said. "We have a search warrant and we're coming in right now."

"You'd better not, unless you want to kill these dogs."

"Secure the dogs, we're coming in," Foley said.

"Fine."

Greineder went upstairs, through the kitchen, let the dogs out the back door, then slammed it shut. After doing that, he went to the upstairs bedrooms to wake his three children, then back to the front door.

In the meantime, Foley had pulled the storm door open again and was already standing in the doorway. As soon as the doctor approached him, Foley handed him the search warrant. Greineder took the paper but didn't read it immediately.

As Greineder turned to walk back up the four stairs that led to the lit foyer landing, he felt a mass of bodies behind him, with Foley next to him, propelling him up the stairs. They all moved together to the landing.

"We need to talk," Foley said. "Let's go into the living room and sit down." Greineder tried to switch on the living-room light, but Foley told him to leave it off.

"Just go sit down, we have to talk," Foley said.

Greineder went in and sat down on the sofa. Foley sat right next to him. Some of the officers were in the foyer, others in the living room.

"I need your help," Foley said in a calm, pleasant voice. "We found a hammer, a knife, and a right-hand glove, and I want your help in telling me where the left-hand glove is."

"I don't know what you're talking about."

"If you tell us where the left-hand glove is, it will be a lot better for your family," Foley told Greineder.

"We found the hammer, knife, and right-hand glove in a storm drain right off the path that you went in, and I've got the timeline all figured out and I know what you did. If you tell us what happened and help us find the glove, it will be a lot easier for your family."

Greineder still didn't understand what Foley was saying.

"We've got DNA," Foley said.

That statement hit Greineder like a ten-ton truck. Although he wasn't an expert on DNA, Greineder knew a fair amount about the subject and figured there was no way the police could have DNA in such a short period of time. But he was still scared. During this conversation, another police officer was reading Greineder his Miranda rights because he was officially considered a suspect in his wife's death.

Greineder was getting nervous and decided he'd better get some help, so he first called Terry Segal and then telephoned his neighbor, Nancy Gans.

About this time, Kirsten got up, put on a robe, and walked downstairs. She saw her dad sitting in the living room, surrounded by numerous police officers. She continued walking outside and went next door to the Gans home.

About fifteen or twenty minutes later, Dirk, Britt, Colin, and Aleks joined Kirsten at the Ganses' home so the police could search their house. While at the Ganses', Dirk Greineder read the search warrant, which he had taken with him. According to the warrant, the police were looking for a work glove with a textured palm, a package for an Old Timer knife, as well as a package for a two-pound Estwing hammer, store receipts, and bloody clothing. Although Greineder knew he had purchased that type of work glove in the past, he had no idea where the gloves were now.

Dirk, Kirsten, and Colin, who had all studied molecular biology at one time or another, also talked about how quickly material gathered from a crime scene could be processed in order to generate DNA evidence. During the prolonged discussion, the participants, who also included Nancy and her husband, Jerome, questioned whether police could have obtained DNA evidence in six hours. The group also discussed what material DNA could be extracted from, as well as the potential for its misinterpretation.

"There was a misunderstanding regarding Father and Mother being intimate and whether DNA from one could be on the other," Kirsten testified later.

Around 3:00 A.M., the Greineder family was allowed to go back home. Once inside, they realized the police had searched every room of their house. Too tired to determine what, if anything, the police had taken, they decided to put off an inventory until the next day and went to bed.

The next morning, they surveyed the house to see what police had confiscated and what damage, if any, had been done to the house. When the police left, they had given Terry Segal and Nancy Gans a list of items they had taken from the house which included an American Express card cut in half, a bag containing shredded paper, a Ziploc bag containing latex gloves, a pair of eyeglasses, and credit card statements. Despite the list, Greineder wanted to make sure nothing else was taken.

So he went into the garage to see what police had seized from his work area. When he walked through the door, he noticed that the drawers of the cabinet that held all his gardening and work gloves had been pulled out and the gloves were either on the floor or spread out on the Toyota. Greineder looked around and soon realized he didn't see his newer work gloves, the ones with the textured palms, which he usually kept in the cabinet.

"I wasn't really looking for them," he said later. "But the only reason I noticed they were missing was because textured work gloves were listed on the search warrant."

While driving to her Manhattan home from a swim meet with two of her three children on October 31, 1999, Belinda Markel, May Greineder's niece, received a cell phone call from her other daughter, who was at home.

"Mom, Britt called and left a message for you and she left this number for you to call."

Belinda didn't recognize the telephone number Britt left, so she decided to call her from the car. To her surprise, she reached her uncle Dirk.

"Where are you?" he asked.

Belinda told him she was in the car and he asked her to pull over to the side of the road so he could talk to her.

"May's been killed," he said. "And I'm frightened for you."

In a state of shock, Belinda told her uncle she had to get her children home and she would call him again at that point. When she called back, Dirk told her they had been in the park and May had been killed there.

After spending time with her children, Belinda contacted her mother, Ilse Stark, May's only sister, who was at her house on Long Island. Ilse was in pretty bad shape. Earlier that afternoon, Britt had called her aunt to tell her that her mother had been murdered. Ilse and her husband, Murray, returned to their home in Manhattan and met up with Belinda, who lived in the same building. They decided they would drive to Massachusetts in separate cars the next day, November 1.

Belinda and her children left Manhattan the next morning around 5:45 and arrived in the area around 10:00 A.M. When she got close to the Greineders' Wellesley home, she called her uncle, who told her there was a lot of press camped out around the house so it would be better if she checked into the hotel, the Crowne Plaza in Natick, first, then call again before going over. Belinda and her children finally arrived at the Cleveland Road home sometime between 10:30 and 11:00 A.M. She looked around and only saw one photographer down the street, not the horde of media people her uncle mentioned.

Once in the house, the relatives cried and hugged each other, glad they were all together. After they had all calmed down somewhat, Dirk took Belinda into his study, just off the kitchen. Still obviously upset, the pair sat down.

"May and I had intercourse yesterday morning, but there's nothing wrong with that because we're married," Dirk told his niece.

"Right," Belinda said, trying to hide her shock because she had never before had that kind of conversation with her uncle.

After making that odd statement, Dirk told Belinda what happened to her aunt in the park. She had been hit in the head a number of times and her throat had been cut.

"After I found May, I ran out," he explained. "I thought I saw a jogger and went after him. That's when I met the man with the small dog. I asked him if he had a cell phone and he didn't. So I continued up the road to the van and called the police."

Her conversation with her uncle concluded, Belinda left the Greineder home so she could meet her parents at a coffee shop on Route 9 and guide them back to her uncle's house. Her father always got lost trying to find Cleveland Road.

At 10:37 A.M., Thomas Young again tried to call the prostitute Deborah Doolio. Again, he was unable to reach her and left a message.

When Ilse and her husband arrived with Belinda, they were greeted warmly by Greineder, their nieces and nephew, and their grandchildren. Terry Segal and Nancy Gans were also there.

As soon as things settled down again, Greineder took Ilse aside and related to her the events surrounding her sister's death.

"Was my sister sexually assaulted?" a distressed Ilse asked her brother-in-law.

"I don't think so."

"Was she robbed?"

"I don't believe so," he answered. "I think she died instantly," he added.

That afternoon, Belinda took her uncle to Britt's room so he could rest because he was extremely tired. While there, Greineder said some things to Belinda that again caught her off guard.

"The police were here last night and they searched the house looking for a glove, a hammer, and a knife. I'm worried the pants I was wearing that the police kept might have fibers of gloves on them. I may have had work gloves like those at some point and the fibers would be on my hands," he told her, although police had never mentioned to him what type of glove they were looking for.

Belinda didn't quite know what to make of her uncle's statements.

"That's ridiculous, because May would have washed those pants a million times between the time you had the gloves on and the time police took your pants," she said. "So don't worry about it."

Later that day, when he and Belinda were in the living room, Greineder began telling Belinda about the nosebleeds he and May had had just before they left for Morses Pond. He told her about the pair sharing a tissue and a towel to stop the bleeding.

"We shared a tissue, so my blood and mucus would be on the tissue that May was holding and it would able to be transferred if she were to touch the killer," he said.

Greineder also told Belinda he was worried that some red marks on his neck he got from shaving, a scratch on his chest, and some black-and-blue marks on his upper arm would show up in the photographs police took while he was at the station. He was particularly concerned about the three or four small, round black-and-blue marks, the size of fingertips, on the inside of his left bicep. He said he didn't know how he got the scratch on his chest or the bruises on his arm.

At this point, Belinda had no idea why her uncle

was telling her these things or how self-serving his statements really were.

During this conversation, Greineder asked his niece to call her husband, a lawyer, and see if he would help him hire an attorney. Belinda's husband flew into Logan International Airport the next day, Tuesday, and met Greineder and Terry Segal in downtown Boston to begin interviewing attorneys. Greineder ultimately hired Martin F. Murphy, a renowned defense attorney with the Boston-based law firm Bingham, Dana, and Gould. Martin graduated from Harvard Law School cum laude in 1983, the same year he began practicing law. A native of Framingham, Massachusetts, Murphy earned his undergraduate degree, summa cum laude, from Princeton University.

The same day, Greineder asked Belinda if she would go the medical examiner's office to identify her aunt's body and fill out any necessary paperwork. Ilse was outraged. After all, May was her sister and she needed to see her. Greineder, however, was adamantly opposed to Ilse going, and he didn't want his children to go either. Kirsten, however, later testified her father never told her not to go to see her mother's body.

Ilse was just as adamant that she should be the one to identify her sister. Finally Greineder relented and Ilse, her husband, Murray, and Belinda all went to the medical examiner's office.

When they returned to the house, Ilse informed her brother-in-law that May had not been robbed. Whatever happened at the pond, Ilse knew that May's death was not the result of a robbery that had turned horribly wrong because May was still wearing her earrings.

"Whoever would do this to her wouldn't stop and

think, you know. They would just rip the earrings out," she said. "She wasn't robbed."

When Ilse finished talking, she, Murray, Greineder, Belinda, and Terry Segal went to the living room. Greineder sat on the hassock surrounded by the others. He told them that police had found a glove, a hammer, and a knife. He also talked about the simultaneous nosebleeds he and May had before going to the pond and about the fact that they used the same tissue and the same towel. He said when they got to the pond, they were both throwing the same spongy ball for Zephyr.

"I don't understand what this is all about," Ilse said.

"Well, if May had defended herself, it's very possible that there is DNA from the dog and myself that could be on the killer's glove because if May had defended herself, she would put her hand up and there could have been a transference of DNA in that fashion from her glove onto the killer's glove," he explained.

Like her daughter, Ilse had no idea what her brother-in-law was talking about. But only one day after his wife was murdered, and months before he would be indicted for her death, Greineder was already setting the stage for his defense. He was already trying to explain why his DNA would be on the glove worn by the person who savagely murdered his wife. At that point in the investigation, however, no one even knew if, in fact, Greineder's DNA was on the killer's glove.

The family held an hour-long memorial service, attended by nearly eight hundred friends and colleagues, for May Greineder at the Newton Presbyterian Church on Wednesday, November 3, 1999. At the service, her friends remembered the Wellesley woman as devoted to her family and happy with her life.

"I had a long conversation with her two weeks ago and . . . she was happy about the upcoming marriage next summer of her daughter, Kirsten. She was happy with her marriage and it's comforting to know that lasting memory of her will be that she had that happiness in her life," said her friend Carol Ottesen, according to a report in the November 4, 1999, edition of the *Boston Herald*.

Ottesen described her friend as someone who loved children and animals—especially dogs—and how she returned to work as a nurse at Harvard Vanguard Medical so Kirsten wouldn't have to worry about paying off tuition after graduating from Harvard Medical School, according to the *Herald*.

"When Kirsten asked what she wanted in return, May told her that she just wanted her to be happy and that would be payment enough," Ottesen said.

"I'm as numb, as you are numbed by this senseless violence," Reverend Marc Sherrod said in his sermon, according to the *Boston Globe*.

And according to the *Globe*, Dirk Greineder told the gathering, through Ottesen, that "the thread woven through May was her tremendous sense of responsibility to everyone. She needed to know that she made a difference to some person or some animal."

Shortly after the family returned home following May's memorial service, Greineder asked to speak privately with Ilse and the pair went to the family room downstairs.

Once there, a nervous and agitated Greineder asked Ilse if he could borrow some money from her—about $500,000 for such things as attorneys, investigators, experts, and bail.

"The police are bastards. They have it in for me," he explained. "The reason they're after me was because they didn't go after anybody else and they have to come up with somebody to solve this crime, even though there've been other similar crimes in the area."

"Well, I would be pounding their doors down to find out what they were doing to look for somebody else," she said, and went upstairs to be with her family, not responding directly to his plea for money.

That morning before May's memorial service, Greineder had called his niece at her hotel to tell her that he had been going through May's things and had come across her dilator. Because of that, he decided to have a second autopsy done on his wife and he was going to call Murphy to see if he could arrange it. Since he was going to have another autopsy done, May's funeral would be held up. Belinda didn't understand what finding her aunt's dilator had to do with the need to have a second autopsy, but she didn't ask any questions.

That afternoon, Ilse and her husband, and Belinda and her family, went back to Manhattan. On Saturday, Dirk called Belinda to tell her that the second autopsy had been completed and May's funeral would be held the following Monday. So Belinda and Ilse and their families returned to Wellesley on Sunday.

After the ceremony, Ilse asked Dirk if he wanted to put May's ashes in the Chegwin family niche in Queens, New York, until he was able to purchase his own niche. He refused.

Chapter 8

It was about 9:00 A.M. on Sunday, October 31, and Terrence Cunningham, Wellesley's deputy police chief, was just stepping out of the shower in a hotel room in North Carolina when he heard his pager go off. Cunningham, who was set to assume the chief's position on November 15, and the current chief, Ernest Gagnon, who was retiring, had just finished attending the International Police Chiefs Conference and were getting ready to head back to Wellesley.

Cunningham, an eighteen-year veteran of the force, grabbed his pager and saw two messages: one to call the Wellesley police station and the other to call his brother, Lieutenant Wayne Cunningham, who was in charge while Terry and Gagnon were out of town.

Immediately Terry called Wayne at home.

"Terry, I just got a call from Sergeant [Peter] Nahass and he said they had a body at Morses Pond and it appears to be a homicide involving a couple from town," Wayne said.

"What's the name?" Terry asked, thinking he might know the family.

"Greineder," Wayne responded.

Although Terry grew up in Wellesley, a town of

about 27,000 people, and knew a lot of people, the name Greineder didn't mean anything to him.

"Apparently, the husband said he left his wife, and when he came back, he found that she had been killed," Wayne continued. "I'm headed down to Morses Pond; the entire shift is down there."

That meant five officers on patrol, Sergeant Nahass, as well as Detective Jill McDermott, were at the scene of May Greineder's brutal murder. Wayne had also called for mutual aid from the neighboring town of Natick. Police from that town handled routine calls for service while the Wellesley officers were at Morses Pond. Natick police also positioned themselves at various points around the perimeter of the town, so in the event a suspect was located they could secure the borders so he couldn't escape.

Cunningham and Gagnon raced to the airport to catch the next plane back to Boston, but they had a tough time getting a flight and didn't get back to Wellesley until about 7:00 P.M.

Throughout the day, Terry was in constant communication with his brother, Wayne, and Nahass, making sure they handled the crime scene properly.

"One of the critical turning points in the case was the fact that they preserved the physical evidence from the scene—not even so much to prove who killed May, but to prove that only one person could have done it because there wasn't anybody else there at the time," Cunningham said later. "My officers preserved the footwear impressions, they preserved the blood spatter—they did an outstanding job. After an underwater crime scene, an outdoor crime scene is the most difficult to preserve. But they locked the whole thing down. And they did a great job of keeping people away from the scene."

Cunningham recalled that the Wellesley Police Department called in off-duty officers and special police—volunteer police, but with police powers—to help set up the perimeter around Morses Pond. Wellesley police also notified the Norfolk County District Attorney's Office, which took control of unattended death scenes, and the Massachusetts State Police assigned to the DA's office. Cunningham assigned a new detective, Jill McDermott, to work with Sergeant Martin Foley. Wellesley police got support from the state police helicopter, the Air Wing. They wanted to look around from the air to make sure there wasn't a raving lunatic running around in the woods. And because the murder weapons were not readily apparent, and since the frog pond area and big pond were not too far from where she had been killed, police called for a dive team to search the water because it was the likely place to throw murder weapons. Police also asked for help from the state police K-9 unit.

The storm drain where the murder weapons were ultimately found—on the paved path that Greineder went down looking for a shadow or a runner—was hidden from view by leaves and other debris. A person could go by it a hundred times and never see it. The police dog, however, immediately focused on the storm drain. At first, his handler pulled him away from it because initially police were looking for a person, not objects. When they went back and searched the area around the storm drain for a second time, the animal again focused on the storm drain. He was picking up the human scent from the knife and the blood and the glove. This time, police cleaned the area around the storm drain, looked down into it, and discovered the right-hand glove and the murder weapons.

After word of the murder got out, people in Wellesley became concerned that a murderer was running around loose in their town. Although police canvassed the area searching for a suspect or suspects, collected evidence, interviewed neighbors and witnesses, they believed they already knew who May's killer was—her husband, Dirk. In fact, police were looking at him from the beginning because of the circumstances of the crime, his demeanor after his wife was murdered, his inconsistent statements to police, and his clean hands.

"The officers on the scene said Greineder would go from being completely calm and cool to crying and falling on his hands and knees, saying how could this happen, how could this happen, when he saw people watching him," Cunningham said later. "The officers said his actions were inappropriate for this situation— although none of us know how we're going to react in those situations—he was calm most of the time. And his story from Fitzpatrick to McDermott to Foley kept changing. Once, he said something like 'he went down there,' and pointed down the paved path. But before that, he had said, 'I thought I saw a shadow; then it went from 'I thought I saw a shadow' to 'I saw a guy jogging.' The story just kept changing. Statistics say most homicides are done by someone close to you, but here's a doctor from Wellesley walking with his wife. It just doesn't strike you that he committed the homicide, but the red flags went off when his story kept changing, and he's got blood up and down his jacket, but none on his hands."

But police couldn't make any of that information public because they didn't want to tip off Greineder.

"That first night, people were calling—it was Halloween and they were saying is it safe for my kid to be out there," Cunningham recalled.

Although it was early in the process, police believed they had probable cause to get a search warrant and go back to Greineder's house. The police thought they were going in the right direction, but it was difficult because they didn't want to tip their hand and tell people what they were doing. They didn't want to tip Greineder off either, but they did want local residents to feel safe. So they put two extra patrol cars on roads in the area of Morses Pond, in the woodlands area outside the pond, and in the area in the back of it, to make sure people up there felt safe.

The next day, Monday, November 1, police found the second glove in a storm drain, about fifteen feet from the spot where Greineder had parked his van. They had done line searches up and down the road where Greineder had gone and this drain was absolutely the last place they searched. In fact, police were getting ready to reopen the park when one of the officers looked in the storm drain and saw the second glove.

Police called the water and sewer department to open the cover and they also called for Crime Scene Services to come down and recover the glove. They pulled it out of the drain and put it on a paper evidence bag on the hood of a police car, and the blood, which had mixed with water in the storm drain, started running off the glove.

Over the next couple of weeks, police searched Greineder's home, car, garage, and offices. They even turned up with a search warrant and took blood and hair samples from his two German shepherds, Wolfie and Zephyr.

During the first few months of the investigation, the elected officials in town were worried because of Wellesley's proximity to Walpole and Westwood, the scenes of two other unsolved homicides. Wellesley officials didn't want to end up in the same situation, but police didn't believe May's murder was related to those other homicides. In fact, they found evidence on Greineder's computer—evidence that was not allowed in at trial—that he may have staged May's death to resemble the 1998 death of seventy-five-year-old Irene Kennedy of Foxborough and the 1999 murder of Richard Reyenger of Westwood. Irene Kennedy was choked, stabbed, and sexually mutilated in Bird Park in Walpole, while Reyenger, an eighty-two-year-old Westwood man, was beaten to death while fishing at Westwood's Buckmaster Pond. When police searched Greineder's computer, they discovered he had downloaded and saved newspaper articles on those murders.

As time went on, the townspeople were shocked to realize Dirk Greineder was the prime suspect in his wife's brutal murder. The majority just didn't want to believe Dr. Greineder had committed such a horrific crime. After all, he was their neighbor, their doctor. They knew him because he went to his kids' swim meets. People just didn't want to even consider that he could have killed his wife. They grew frustrated—even the elected officials were getting frustrated—waiting for the police to make an arrest. But the police didn't want to make an arrest early on and jeopardize their case.

"On November fifteenth, I was elected chief and there was an article in the *Boston Globe* talking about the new young chief—was he going to be able to weather this storm with the pressure from the town, and the enormity of the investigation," Chief Terrence Cunningham recalled. "For the most part, the elected officials were very good, but they were nervous. They didn't know exactly what was going to happen, the town hadn't seen a homicide in twenty-five years and they weren't even sure of the process. They didn't understand the jurisdiction—the state police, the medical examiner's office, how the whole system worked. They wanted to know why—if we had probable cause that this was the person—we didn't just make an arrest instead of putting the evidence in through the grand jury?"

The police knew what they were doing. The benefit of a grand jury investigation was that it gave investigators access to a lot more records, and the grand jury was able to subpoena more information than police would have been able to access. In addition, using a grand jury meant that a jury of Greineder's peers would be making the decision to indict him. They would, in effect, be saying, "We think there is probable cause to issue an indictment." That meant it wouldn't just be the word of the police. People couldn't be saying that police were railroading this poor doctor.

"So it's a grand jury that voted on it and said it's more likely than not that he committed the crime," Chief Cunningham said. "It was cumbersome because all the information that we'd collected had to go to the district attorney, who had to decipher it all so he could present it to the grand jury in a way they would understand."

Another reason the police didn't rush out to arrest Greineder immediately was because they didn't think he was a danger to the community.

"At some point in this case, we said this wasn't a

crime of opportunity, where he just picked some person and killed her," Cunningham said. "This was his wife—he had his motivations for killing her. We didn't see him as an individual who was going to be out there targeting someone on the street. That's another reason not to make the arrest and put it into the grand jury. But we did have reason to be concerned he was going to be a flight risk, because he knew where we were going. People had called him saying we had interviewed them. I think he felt the noose was tightening and it was inevitable that he was going to be indicted.

"When he hit his wife on the head with that hammer and she didn't die with the first blow, like he planned, and she was still alive, and then he had to cut her throat and whatever his motivation was—whether it was out of hatred or he wanted to get out of the marriage—this was still the person he lived with for the last thirty years," Chief Cunningham said later. "He really thought he could get away with it."

The police theorized that Greineder believed he'd be able to kill her with one hammer blow to the head. But that didn't happen, and Greineder was forced to improvise.

This is how police believed the murder went down: Greineder hit his wife on the head the first time and she screamed; she was probably still alive following this blow. A witness heard the scream. He hit her a second time. She grabbed onto him, leaving a bloody handprint on the front of his jacket. She most likely fell to the ground and he cut her throat there. At some point, she was still alive and she saw him and she looked him in the eye. Greineder stabbed his wife ten times, twice in the face.

Chapter 9

About ten days after May's murder, Norfolk County prosecutors convened a grand jury to hear evidence that Greineder murdered his wife.

State and Wellesley police searched the Greineder house again on November 12. During that search, they confiscated a number of items, including a pair of brown cloth gloves with textured palms and fingers; computer equipment, including computer files; two hand-drawn sketches of the Morses Pond area; financial records; loaf pans; swabs from the passenger seat of Greineder's Toyota Avalon and the car's gear shift that tested positive for blood; a plastic bag containing latex gloves; rubber gloves; receipts from a variety of stores, including Diehl's hardware store; packaging for E-Z foil pans measuring 9"x5"x3" and a plastic rim liner for the pans and a Roche Brothers receipt for the pans dated November 8, 1999.

In addition, police took a box marked "miscellaneous hardware" found in the garage that contained a twelve-pack of Trojan condoms (there were only eleven in the box), one prescription bottle from CVS that contained three 50 mg tablets of Viagra, which Greineder prescribed for himself on April 30, 1998 (the prescription was written for ten pills); another Viagra prescription bottle containing 8.5 pills, which he had prescribed for himself on June 2, 1999 (the original prescription was written for twelve, 100 mg pills); one plastic bag marked Eaton Apothecary; two AA batteries; six sterile cotton tip applicators; one nylon rope with knots tied in it; one piece of Velcro; one marble; one small round brush; a $1.89 price sticker from F. Diehl & Son hardware store; several screws; one tube of toothpaste and a toothbrush.

When police later searched Greineder's computer and financial records, they discovered he was not the upstanding physician and family man he appeared to be in public. They soon learned that this world-renowned asthma and allergy doctor had a secret life—one filled with pornography and prostitutes. They uncovered evidence that Greineder downloaded pornography from the Internet as well as arranged meetings with prostitutes.

"We also found pornographic stories on his computer that he had written," Chief Cunningham said later. "When you read through the stories, you could see that it was all about his life. They were works in progress. Some of the stuff was bizarre, like using rope to tie women up."

A character in one of Greineder's stories was named Thomas Young, the name of one of his college roommates. Police discovered that Greineder used Young's name as a screen name in various chat rooms to meet other people for sex. They also learned that Greineder had an American Express corporate card in Young's name that he used to pay for hotel rooms for his trysts with prostitutes, as well as to sign up for Internet porn sites.

And police doing the computer forensics came across correspondence with a woman with whom Greineder seemed to be having some kind of relationship. After

May's murder, he sent this individual an e-mail saying he wasn't going to be able to talk with her for a while because something had come up in his life. Greineder used the woman's name for a character in one of the sexually explicit stories he had written.

"It wasn't clear that this was a sexual relationship, but it seemed to be," Cunningham said. "We think she was someone he met at a medical conference and she lived in Portugal, but we were never able to find her."

On November 18, Greineder's attorney, Martin Murphy, asked Norfolk County District Court judge Gerald Alch to have the state return computers and research files taken during the November 12 search.

"The search was illegal and the property should be returned. He's not a defendant. He's the husband of the victim," Murphy told the judge. "They have taken all the tools he uses for a living."

Murphy also said that according to the warrant, police were not allowed to conduct the November 12 search past 10:00 P.M., but they continued until 12:30 A.M. on November 13.

Prosecutor Richard Grundy told the *Metrowest Daily News* in Framingham, Massachusetts, that returning the items would jeopardize the state's investigation. And Grundy said police had a warrant that enabled them to continue their search until 6:00 A.M. on November 13.

Alch postponed his decision on the matter until later that month and ordered Grundy to provide him with a list of items the state would be willing to return to Greineder. Then, on November 23, Alch ruled that Norfolk County prosecutors didn't have to return the items police confiscated during their two searches of Greineder's home.

In a statement, Murphy said the judge didn't rule on whether the searches were legal or illegal. "He simply said he was not going to address the issue at this time," Murphy asserted in the statement. "We are disappointed he decided not to address the issues we raised."

At one point during the grand jury investigation, police thought Greineder was going to make a run for it, so they put a bird dog on his car to track him wherever he went. But he never tried to flee.

"He didn't leave for the same reason that I think he thought he could kill her and get away with it," Chief Cunningham said later. "I think he thought he was smarter than everybody else. That he had this sense that he was better than everyone else. He still thought he could get away with it. It was sheer arrogance."

Over the Christmas holidays, Greineder and his family went to Denmark to visit Kirsten's fiancé's family. While they were there, Wellesley police contacted the Danish authorities so they could keep an eye on Greineder.

"We wanted to make sure he got off and on the plane and to make sure he was where he said he was going to be," Cunningham recalled.

Finally the grand jury handed down an indictment. On February 29, 2000, after an exhaustive, four-month investigation, police arrested Dr. Dirk Greineder at his Brookline office and held him overnight at the Wellesley police station until his arraignment on one count of first-degree murder the next day in Norfolk Superior Court in Dedham.

Greineder pleaded not guilty to the charges.

The day Greineder was arrested, District Attorney William Keating held a press conference to talk about the case and calm the fears of Wellesley residents.

"Last Halloween morning, October thirty-first, at Morses Pond area in Wellesley, Mabel 'May' Greineder was brutally assaulted and murdered. Today, after investigating this since the first week of November, on a weekly basis, [a grand jury] indicted Dirk Greineder, also known as Thomas Young, for the murder of his wife."

In a move that Greineder's attorney, Martin Murphy, later said, "clearly violated the rules forbidding a prosecutor from making prejudicial out-of-court statements," Keating gave reporters a detailed presentation, summarizing the results of his officers' four-month investigation.

In fact, Murphy said the DA took the media through a pretrial tour of the prosecution's "evidence," provided dramatic details of the doctor's "secret life," and even went so far as to offer conclusions about Greineder's guilt. In Murphy's eyes, the press conference was a calculated attempt by Keating to assassinate his client's character and poison the jury pool.

Keating told reporters that the investigation into May's murder centered around three areas: the analysis of the crime scene, a look into May Greineder's life and her relationship with her husband, and the forensic work done by the Massachusetts State Police Crime Unit and Cellmark Diagnostic in Maryland.

The DA first talked about the crime scene at Morses Pond.

"This is Morses Pond in Wellesley," Keating said, pointing out the access road to the pond on a map. "We have identified three crime scenes within this area."

Keating then described the area where May's body was found, the location of the first storm drain where police discovered the bloody right-hand glove the murderer wore as well as the murder weapons, and then the site of the second storm drain, at the end of Turner Road, where Dirk Greineder parked his van and where police found the matching bloody left-hand glove.

Keating said a review of May Greineder's background led investigators to believe that she had not been targeted by anyone with a grudge against her. Furthermore, after looking at her relationship with her husband, police determined that there were problems in the marriage.

"In reviewing the background with her husband, looking at business documents, looking at credit cards, looking through computer material, we were able to determine that Dirk Greineder had a focus on pornography, he had a focus on, and a frequency in, engaging with prostitutes, and he even adopted the fictitious name Thomas Young, which he used on the credit card and on documents of the like to try and create a second identity that he followed through his secret life," Keating said. "This background information clearly demonstrated that, in terms of the relationship, there were difficulties and there [was] some strain."

Keating then told reporters that because the Wellesley police did a superb job of preserving the crime scene, investigators were able to remove a great deal of trace evidence from the area.

"We were able to determine, because of DNA testing, that indeed May Greineder's—that it was May Greineder's blood that was on the hammer, that it was on the glove, it was on the knife," he said. "Through other DNA testing, we were able to link Dirk Greineder to the handle of the knife and a portion of the glove."

The DA explained that police had considered

Greineder a suspect from the very beginning of the investigation because of the circumstances at the crime scene, including the fact that he had blood on his jacket, on his eyeglasses, on his sneakers, and on his sleeves.

"But interestingly enough, that blood stopped and there was no blood on his hands," Keating said.

In addition to outlining the state's case, Keating predicted a conviction and went so far as to suggest that, in order to throw investigators off the track, Greineder had set up the crime scene to resemble the scenes of the two other unsolved homicides that had taken place in Norfolk County in the year leading up to the murder of May Greineder.

"Many of the things that made the public make the link were there," Keating said. "Do I think that he anticipated that people would make the link, another woman dead by a pond in a suburban town that begins with *W*? Do I think that maybe he staged the scene to look like those killings? The circumstances were such that you have to wonder if he didn't try to point things in that direction."

During Greineder's arraignment, Murphy argued that his client should be released on $100,000 bail and pointed to the doctor's medical credentials and his strong ties to Wellesley, as well as the fact that he returned home after a Christmas visit to Denmark with his family. But prosecutors outlined the evidence against him that Keating spoke of in his press conference and asked the judge to deny the defense's bail request.

The judge ruled that Greineder should be held without bail in the Norfolk County Jail pending further DNA testing.

Documents released by the Dedham District Court

the day after Greineder's arraignment alleged that Dirk and Mabel Greineder took out $500,000 life insurance policies on each other on October 29, two days before her murder. But Murphy said the policies, which never went into effect, were actually second-to-die policies that named the couple's children as beneficiaries after the death of both parents. Police later conceded that fact.

Even after their father was charged with murdering their mother, Greineder's three children steadfastly stood behind him. The children told reporters they absolutely believed their father was innocent.

"I'm feeling outrage and I'm feeling frustration in a system, with a system, that I feel has failed us, a system that we attempted to trust in and it has failed miserably with putting on trial and indicting an innocent man," Kirsten Greineder told television reporters on March 2. Greineder's younger daughter, Britt, said, "I never questioned as to whether my father was responsible for my mother's death. Never."

And their brother, Colin, said, "We will do whatever it takes to bring to light what we know." Colin said their dad had an answer to the questions swirling around his secret life and would provide those answers at some later date.

"I think there's sadness and I think there's definitely anger and outrage," Colin said. "And I think there's also just this very strong will for us to stay together to do whatever it takes for us to bring to light what we know, which is that our father's innocent."

On Wednesday, March 8, 2000, the Board of Registration in Medicine determined Greineder was a threat to public health and safety and suspended his license for six months.

The day before Greineder was to return to court

for a pretrial hearing, Murphy filed an emergency motion, asking a judge to force prosecutors to provide him with important pieces of DNA evidence in the case. At Greineder's arraignment on March 1, Judge R. Malcolm Graham ordered the state to produce a copy of that DNA evidence to the defense "forthwith." But in a March 10 letter to the state, Murphy told prosecutors the evidence had not yet been turned over to him.

At Greineder's arraignment, prosecutor Rick Grundy said two DNA profiles—one male and one female—were generated from evidence at the crime scene. The profiles concluded that Mabel Greineder couldn't be excluded from the female sample and Dirk Greineder couldn't be excluded from the male sample.

"The immediate production of evidence concerning DNA testing is essential to determine what steps the defense should take to address the question of bail," Murphy said in his motion. Murphy also wanted the prosecution to turn over copies of statements Greineder made to police, as well as grand jury minutes, exculpatory evidence, and witness interviews conducted by police. And he asked that the state share other reports, including the autopsy report of May Greineder as well as photographs, sketches, or drawings of the crime scene. Murphy also wanted to know if Wellesley police tested his client's hands for the presence of blood on the day of his wife's murder.

In a motion filed March 20 at the Norfolk Superior Court, Murphy accused Keating of poisoning public opinion against his client by making statements after Greineder's arrest and destroying his chances of getting a fair trial in Norfolk County. Murphy argued that Keating's statements violated ethical rules that forbid a prosecutor from making prejudicial out-of-court statements about a defendant prior to trial.

Because of that, Murphy asked Judge Graham for a "hearing and relief to remedy the Commonwealth's violations of court rules concerning prejudicial pretrial statements and grand jury secrecy." Murphy added that Keating "unlawfully disclosed secret grand jury information to the news media."

In his motion, Murphy said, "When a prosecutor, particularly the district attorney himself, visibly thumbs his nose at fundamental rules established by the state's highest court to ensure the integrity of legal proceedings in the Commonwealth, forceful action is warranted."

If the judge agreed with Murphy that Keating violated the Massachusetts Rules of Professional Conduct, he could dismiss the indictment against Greineder, change the venue or have jurors selected from another county, and find Keating in contempt.

At an April 10 hearing, Norfolk Superior Court judge Charles Barrett blasted Keating for making the prejudicial statements but denied the defense's request to let Greineder out on $100,000 bail.

In a written statement, Barrett said there was "little doubt that the disclosure rules in criminal matters were flagrantly violated" by the district attorney. Barrett told the DA's office not to commit further violations of the disclosure rules. But he stopped short of ordering that the trial be moved to another county, saying that issue would be handled closer to the start of the trial.

Arguing against letting Greineder out on bail, Grundy cited new evidence in the case—that Greineder was one of only 680,000 white males whose DNA matched the DNA taken from one of the bloody gloves found at the scene. Grundy also said there was a dog hair found inside one of the gloves, although he didn't say whether it matched either of Greineder's dogs. Wellesley police chief Terrence Cunningham said later the dog hair was sent to the FBI for DNA analysis, along with the hair from Greineder's two dogs. He said the FBI identified the hair as belonging to a German shepherd, but it could not be matched to either Wolfie or Zephyr, so Grundy was not allowed to enter it as evidence at trial.

In another pretrial hearing on June 20, Murphy asked Norfolk Superior Court judge Regina Quinlan to set a deadline for the prosecution to turn over the information he had previously requested, including copies of investigators' reports, diagrams, sketches, search warrants, and DNA test results that the state had obtained during its investigation. He also wanted the state to hand over copies of the raw data so he could have an independent DNA expert review the information. He needed all the information so he wouldn't be surprised at trial. The prosecution had been ordered to give the materials to the defense by May 10, but had not yet released all of it to Murphy. Grundy said he had not turned over some materials because he was still waiting for the paperwork to be completed.

In a June 28 ruling, Quinlan ordered Greineder to provide investigators with a sample of his blood to compare it to forensic evidence from the crime scene.

"Since the defendant has questioned the reliability of testing from nail clippings, there is a need for the Commonwealth to conduct further testing and, thus, a need for a sample of his blood," she said in her ruling.

In an affidavit to the court written on July 8, 2000,

Greineder explained why he believed certain evidence should not be introduced at trial.

First he told the court that after finding his wife seriously injured at Morses Pond on Sunday morning, October 31, 1999, he went to his car to call police from his car phone. When they arrived minutes later, he led them to his wife. She was pronounced dead at the scene. He said he was devastated. At the scene, police searched him and several questioned him.

"I told the police I needed to notify my children about their mother's death, but they told me that I needed to stay there at the scene," he said.

After more than two hours, Greineder said police took him to the Wellesley police station. On the way, they continued to question him. Again, he told police he needed to contact his children. He also told them that he needed to attend to his dogs—one had been left alone at his house and the other had been left in the car at Morses Pond.

"The police told me that I could take care of my affairs after I spoke to them at the station," he said.

Greineder told the court that the police continued to question him when he was at the station. Finally he said he was able to call his daughter to ask her to come to the Wellesley police station.

"The police told me that I should ask my daughter to bring me a change of clothes because they were going to take my clothes and shoes," he said in the affidavit. "I called a friend who is a lawyer."

Greineder said from the moment he led police to his wife's body at Morses Pond, he did not believe he was free to leave or not to answer questions of the police.

While at the police station, Greineder said Wellesley police took pictures of him—before and after his attorney arrived—and gave him a consent form to sign concerning the search and seizure of his property. He said he signed them because the police told him they were going to take his clothes and shoes anyway.

"I did not believe I was free to prevent the police from taking photographs of me or not to sign the consent form," he said in the affidavit. "The police took my clothes, shoes, and fingernail clippings. At no time at the scene or at the police station did anyone advise me of my Miranda rights."

Greineder said on November 5, 1999, he met privately with his lawyer, Martin F. Murphy, at his home. The purpose of the meeting was to get legal advice from Murphy. During the meeting, Greineder said he made two sketches of Morses Pond for Murphy to illustrate certain points. Greineder said he didn't tell anyone else about the sketches, which he ultimately threw in a trash barrel.

"My intent was to keep my communication with my lawyer, as illustrated in the sketches, private and not to disclose them to anyone else," he said.

However, he said on November 12, 1999, police came to his house for a third time. Colin and Kirsten were also staying at the Cleveland Road home for the weekend. He said the police ordered them to leave the house because they had another warrant to search it. He said the police gave him a copy of the one-page warrant, but it didn't have any attachments.

Greineder said when he realized they were looking for computers, he asked them not to take Colin's laptop because he would need it when he returned to school.

"The police refused to give me my son's laptop," Greineder said in the affidavit. "They also took the keys to my daughter's car and searched her car and also searched my car a second time."

He said except for Colin's laptop and Kirsten's car, everything police took during the November 12 search was there during the first and second searches on October 31 and November 1. Greineder said on February 7, 2000, police obtained a warrant to search his computer, which they had had since November 12, 1999.

"I did not receive a copy of this warrant, nor was I aware of it until months after I was indicted," he said.

Then on July 11, Murphy filed a fifty-page motion asking a judge to throw out crucial pieces of evidence because he claimed police illegally searched Greineder's home, car, and computers.

Murphy also alleged Sergeant Martin Foley seriously misstated his background and experience when he applied for the search warrants. In the affidavit for the search warrants, Foley said he was a fourteen-year veteran of the Norfolk County District Attorney's Office and had investigated many violent crimes. However, according to Murphy, Foley had not even worked for the district attorney for a year and didn't have very much experience with homicide investigations.

"Because Sergeant Foley knowingly misstated his experience when he sought the authority to search the defendant's home, evidence seized during that search must be suppressed," Murphy argued. Murphy said the warrant should have more specifically described the types of computer records investigators could search and seize.

"The police had no basis for believing that [Dirk Greineder's] computers themselves constituted evidence of any crime," he said. "There is no reason why electronic information stored in a computer should be described with any less particularity than physical paper documents stored in a file cabinet."

Murphy also alleged Foley provided "knowing and reckless" false statements in his application for the November 12 search warrant. In the application, Foley said Greineder used a computer-generated check to make certain purchases from a Roche Brothers supermarket. But Murphy said Greineder actually used a regular bank check to pay for those items.

Murphy said that although police questioned Greineder numerous times at the crime scene and the Wellesley police station, they never read him his rights. In addition, he said, though Greineder repeatedly told police he needed to call his daughter and take care of his dogs, police did not allow him to go about his business, making it clear he was not free to leave.

On July 18, 2000, Elizabeth Porter told the grand jury about her encounters with Greineder, whom she knew as Thomas Young. Porter said she was living in Quincy, Massachusetts, and working for an escort service in 1998, when she met with Greineder. She testified that he gave her champagne, candy, and flowers before having sex with her. Porter told the grand jury that after their second meeting she thought that "he was kind of strange."

During a series of pretrial hearings, Murphy and his client appeared in Norfolk Superior Court, where Murphy continued to argue for the suppression of evidence taken during police searches of Greineder's home.

During the hearings, Murphy questioned Foley extensively about his credentials and job experience, as well as three search warrants and conversations Foley had with Greineder at Morses Pond the morning his wife was murdered. For his part, Foley said the search warrants were legal and police did everything by the book when they seized evidence from Greineder's home, car, and computers. He also testified that Greineder was free to go at any time when police were questioning him on October 31, 1999, about the events leading up to his wife's murder.

In addition to Foley, Wellesley police chief Terrence Cunningham, and Wellesley police detectives, including Jill McDermott, and other police officers were also subpoenaed to testify at the hearings before Judge Paul Chernoff about the searches and the events at Morses Pond on October 31, 1999.

During one of the hearings in August 2000, prosecutors played a tape recording of the emergency call Greineder made to police after he found his wife's body.

"Help," a seemingly hysterical Greineder told the police dispatcher. "I'm at the pond. I need some . . . someone attacked my wife. . . . I left her 'cause she hurt her back."

The dispatcher asked Greineder if his wife was alive, and he responded, "I think she's dead, I'm not sure." The dispatcher then told Greineder help was on the way and told him to relax because she couldn't understand him. While the tape was played, Greineder, who showed little emotion during the previous hearings, lowered his head and broke down.

The prosecution claimed that Greineder lied to the dispatcher and the emergency call was made just to cover up the fact that he had murdered his wife. During the hearing, Dennis Mahoney, the first assistant district attorney, told the judge that, in his opinion, Greineder's call was not truthful. Mahoney, however, admitted he had not actually listened to the tape of the call himself but had been told of its contents by other investigators who had heard it. Although Murphy objected to Mahoney's statement, Chernoff let it into the court record.

On October 18, Chernoff denied most of Murphy's motions and ruled that the majority of the evidence police collected against Greineder through search warrants, as well as statements he made to police, would be allowed at trial.

In his ninety-four-page ruling, Chernoff said police did not deliberately violate Greineder's rights. However, he did point out "errors" and "procedural irregularities" that "were sufficiently significant to warrant exclusion of some of the evidence at trial."

Chernoff ruled that prosecutors could not use some of the material they found on Greineder's computer, including the sexually explicit stories he wrote and e-mail. According to Chernoff's ruling, investigators may have overstepped the bounds of that particular search warrant.

"The majority of the information searched and seized [from the computer files] is suppressible because of the lack of particulars in the affidavits and in the warrant," Chernoff said in his ruling.

Although Greineder claimed that police didn't have probable cause to seize some of this belongings, including the work gloves found in the doghouse in his backyard, which were identical to the gloves found in the storm drains at Morses Pond, Chernoff disagreed.

"A plethora of information known to investigators existed to establish probable cause to believe that the defendant's home, including his home computers, contained evidence linking him to his wife's murder," Chernoff wrote.

In addition to suppressing some of the material found on Greineder's computer, Chernoff threw out some of the statements Greineder made to police the day his wife was murdered. Chernoff said that although Greineder wasn't under arrest, the police should have advised him of his Miranda rights. Chernoff also said the two cut-up credit cards police found in Greineder's house could not be introduced as evidence.

It had been nearly one year and seven months since May Greineder was killed and her husband was about to go on trial for her murder.

Chapter 10

After two days of questioning three hundred prospective jurors, a jury of ten men and six women was selected. They included a student in political science at Johns Hopkins University, an employee of the U.S. Postal Service, a computer software salesman, a student at New York University, an English professor, a dentist, a vice president of an investment bank, and a president of a start-up software company. At the end of the trial, twelve jurors would be selected at random to enter into deliberations. The others would serve as alternates.

"Good morning, Mr. Clerk, would you please call the case," said Judge Paul Chernoff.

"This is the matter of Dirk Greineder, number 108588."

"Mr. Clerk, would you read the indictment?" the judge asked.

"At the superior court, begun and holden at Dedham, within and for the County of Norfolk, on the fifth Tuesday of February 2000, the jurors for the Commonwealth of Massachusetts on their oath present that Dirk Greineder of Wellesley, in the County of Norfolk, on or about October 31, 1999, at Wellesley, in the

County of Norfolk, did assault and beat Mabel Greineder with intent to murder her, and by such assault and beating did kill and murder said Mabel Greineder in violation of Massachusetts General Laws, c. 265, section 1.

"To this indictment, the defendant at the bar has pleaded not guilty and for trial places himself upon the county which county you are. You are sworn to try the issues. If he is guilty, you will say so. If he is not guilty, you will say so, and no more. Members of the jury, hearken to the evidence."

So began the murder trial of Dr. Dirk Greineder on Wednesday morning, May 23, 2001, in Norfolk Superior Court in Dedham, Massachusetts.

With the formalities concluded, Chernoff explained to the jurors that before they heard any testimony, they were going to take a fifteen-minute bus ride to Morses Pond to see exactly where May Greineder had been murdered.

"We are going out to take a look around," the judge told them. "We are going out to get an appreciation as to what the scene was like at the time and place in question, because that will help illuminate the testimony of witnesses in court and may even illuminate some physical evidence in the case, so we're not collecting evidence out there. You're taking a look around so it will help you to understand the evidence that will be presented in court."

Chernoff explained that he and the jury would take very passive roles as they toured Morses Pond. They wouldn't ask questions. They wouldn't talk with one another. They would just simply look.

The judge then turned the proceedings over to prosecutor Richard Grundy. Grundy, fifty-two, earned his undergraduate degree from Seton Hall

University in New Jersey and his law degree from the University of Virginia. He had been practicing law since 1987.

Grundy advised the members of the jury that once they arrived at the corner of Turner Road and Halsey Avenue, they would see the access road and the gate that closed it off to cars. The prosecutor asked the jurors to pay close attention to the neighborhood that surrounded Morses Pond.

"We're going to open up the gate and go into Morses Pond and we will go down that access road a little ways. I ask you to notice, both on your left and your right, certain openings of pathways. We are going to stop at one of those pathways and get off the bus shortly after, just a couple hundred yards into that access road," he noted.

The start of the Morses Pond trail is at the intersection of Turner Road and the Crosstown Trail, at the beginning of the access road to the town beach. The trail runs along a paved path to the beach parking lot, goes past the water treatment facility, and turns right toward the edge of the pond. It climbs to the ridge of the sand pit, cuts through the woods, descends the bank to the Cochituate Aqueduct, and ends on the Crosstown Trail. The length of the trail is six-tenths of a mile.

Grundy told the jurors they would be going into a path that goes into a wooded area—a path that would be referred to during the trial as the "pine forest." The jurors would then be asked to walk along the path, paying close attention to the surroundings and imagining how it would look at different times of the year.

"[Pay close attention] to how the area is vegetated, how that may or may not change depending on the seasons of the year, what is underneath your feet, how that may affect your ability to walk and travel in that area, and what is surrounding the distance that you can see," he instructed them. "As we come through the pine forest area, we are going to come to an area where there is a dramatic drop-off, and it is down to an area that you will hear referred to in the coming weeks as the sand pit."

Grundy asked the jury to pay specific attention to the drop down to the sand pit area, as well as the texture of the ground in the area.

"I'm going to ask you to look down at a small wooden area that you will be able to see as you stand atop of that sand pit, as well as the crescent-shaped rib of where it will be in the pine forest as you travel around that sand pit area," he continued. "We will also take the opportunity while we are on top of that to see what other landmarks you might be able to see, whether it is the pond itself, structure of the building, or the water-pumping station. . . . You can see those and how they are located."

The jurors learned they would then leave the pine tree forest, get back on the bus, and travel to the cul-de-sac, or circle, at the end of the access road. Once there, they would get off the bus and walk about 100 to 150 yards down a dirt pathway and then down an incline.

"You will go down that incline and just in front of you, less than fifty yards, will be that small wooded area that I will ask you to look at when we are on top of the pine forest looking down into the sand pit," Grundy explained. "I am going to ask each of you to walk through that pathway. . . . I am going to ask you to pay attention to either side of the woods, the thickness of the woods, and, again, how that vegetation may have been different depending on the time of year. I am going to ask you to look at where certain cones may be placed, orange-type traffic cones."

The jurors would next walk through that pathway to the sand pit area, from which they could look up and see the pine tree forest.

"As the rim of that pine tree forest comes around the sand pit, there will also be some cones following a certain path, and I am going to ask you to look at those and follow those and come back out through the path, back out toward that cul-de-sac," Grundy said. "The water-pumping station is there. I am going to ask you to pay attention to where that is, how it is structured, some fences that are around it, and we will have an opportunity to walk down toward the beach and the pond area. . . . I am going to ask you to go to a particular area that I suggest you will hear referred to as the 'Old Beach' in the next several weeks, and a gated latch there.

"I am also going to ask you to come back to the cul-de-sac at that point and make certain observations from the cul-de-sac to another pathway, a paved pathway, and a storm drain down that pathway," he continued.

At that point, everyone would get back on the bus and travel back to the gated area at the top of the access road. Once there, the jurors would be asked to look at the orange traffic cones placed just beyond the gate and to note their proximity to another storm drain at the intersection of Turner Road and Halsey Avenue.

"Finally, ladies and gentlemen, we will come around the perimeter of Morse [*sic*] Pond and stop just off of [Route] 135, and you will have the opportunity to see areas of train tracks where it would run parallel to the pond," Grundy said.

Grundy told the jurors that it was important for them to familiarize themselves with the area around Morses Pond so that when they heard the evidence and facts at trial, they would be able to apply what they learned, what they saw, and what they felt during the tour to those facts.

Now it was defense attorney Martin Murphy's turn to inform the jurors about what they would see as they toured Morses Pond.

"I, too, ask you to pay careful attention to the surroundings," he began. "You will hear much testimony about these surroundings over the next few weeks. You will also get a chance, as you hear the testimony, to see photographs of the way Morses Pond looked back on October 31, 1999. A few things in particular that I would point your attention to are places that Mr. Grundy didn't mention. I will ask you to walk over a footbridge that connects the area that Mr. Grundy describes as the cul-de-sac to the beach."

Murphy asked the jurors to observe the beach house and the gate that was on the near side of the beach house.

"And I am going to ask you to walk around the outside edge of that beach house so that you can see where the pond is from the far side of the house," he explained.

Murphy told the jurors that the bus would first stop next to the path on the right that Grundy said went through the pine tree forest.

"I am going to ask you to look to your left at another path," he said. "I'm not going to ask you to walk down the path. When we come back on the bus up the hill from the cul-de-sac area toward the top of the gate, I'm going to ask that we get out and ask that you look at a path that leads off that road to the right as we're coming back up the hill."

Murphy said he would also point out other paths within the wooded area to the jurors.

With that, the attorneys, jury, judge, and some court staff members boarded the bus for the fifteen-minute trip from Dedham to Morses Pond in Wellesley. The view was closed to the public and the press, although members of the media were allowed to tour the site after the official site visit was completed.

As the jurors boarded the bus to go back to the courthouse, they were reminded not to go back to Morses Pond on their own.

After the members of the jury went home, juror number seven, David Lazowski, met with opposing counsel, as well as Judge Chernoff, in the judges' lobby.

"Mr. Lazowski, you gave me this note," the judge said. "I think I can read your writing, but I'm not going to count on it. Would you please read your note to us?"

"Judge, in talking with a friend, I believe Jill Mc-Dermott is a witness, as well as Faryl Sandler. I believe I could not be unbiased if these are material witnesses," Lazowski read.

"And what is your relationship to these people?" the judge asked.

"Jill McDermott has been a close family friend for a long time," Lazowski responded. "I know her aunt and uncle very well. I have met her several times and just feel that my relationship with them is just strong—"

"With them or with her?" Chernoff interrupted.

"Both, the whole family," Lazowski replied. "I just feel that if she said something, I couldn't look at it in an, you know, unbiased way. If she said something,

I would kind of lean toward whatever she said as being the way it was."

Chernoff asked Lazowski why he didn't mention this before he was impaneled as a juror.

"Refresh my memory, when we were upstairs going through the individual voir dire, did you mention her name?" Chernoff asked.

"No, I didn't see—I'm not quite sure if her name was actually on there. If it was, I didn't see it at the time," Lazowski said.

"Has she recently married or changed her name?" the judge asked.

"No, but she is married and has a husband."

"And when is the last time you saw Jill McDermott?"

"It has probably been about a year."

"Who is the other individual?"

"The other individual is not a close family friend, but I have daily dealings with some friends of his. We talk in my business constantly, almost on a daily basis. This happens to be their cousin. She is with the medical examiner," Lazowski responded. "I don't really know her per se, but I have been close with her family. That's the other relationship."

"Now, does the first person give you more trouble than the second person?" the judge asked the juror.

"Yes, definitely."

The judge then asked Lazowski to step into the hall while he conferred with Grundy and Murphy.

"Well, I'm certainly sorry we didn't have him disclose this to us during the impanelment process," Chernoff told the attorneys. "I hate losing a person so early in the proceeding. Do either of you have any objection if I were to excuse him?"

Neither attorney objected. In fact, Murphy requested that the judge excuse him.

Chernoff brought Lazowski back into the judges' lobby, thanked him for his candor, excused him from the case, and asked him not to tell anyone, particularly members of the media, that he had been excused from the case, or why he had been excused.

"You will just leave right now," the judge said. "I don't think the press are around here now. I think they're all at the pond. But if somebody were to contact you—and I don't think they will—you know, when the trial is over with and we have a jury verdict one way or the other, you can talk to whomever you please about whatever you please. You can write a book if you want to, but not now."

Lazowski thanked the judge and left the courthouse.

Before opening statements began, Justice Roderick Ireland, a Massachusetts Supreme Court justice, denied the state's request to stop the defense from suggesting that a serial killer could have been responsible for May Greineder's murder.

Norfolk Superior Court judge Paul Chernoff earlier ruled that Greineder's defense attorney could cross-examine police about whether they knew of the two previous murders in neighboring communities. The prosecution then appealed that decision to the state's supreme court.

The murder trial of Dr. Dirk Greineder was being held in a courtroom on the first floor of the courthouse.

Judge Paul Chernoff had hoped to be able to start the trial in the historic Sacco and Vanzetti courtroom on the second floor of the courthouse. However, he told those present—members of the jury had not yet been brought into the room—the move probably wouldn't take place until Tuesday or Wednesday of the next week because it was being used for another trial.

Chernoff told members of the press they were not to take any photographs of the jurors' faces, and they were only to use cameras specifically adapted for courtroom use—cameras that didn't make any noise.

The members of the jury were then brought into the courtroom, seated in the jury box, and the court clerk called the case.

"This is indictment number 108588, the *Commonwealth* versus *Dirk Greineder.* Would counsel please identify themselves for the record?"

After the introductions, Chernoff welcomed the jury and spoke a few words to them.

He first explained that although sixteen jurors had initially been impaneled, there were now only fifteen jurors, because one of the jurors suddenly realized that he and his family were very friendly with one of the people who would be testifying for the state.

He explained to them that at the end of the trial, a lottery would be held to determine the names of the twelve jurors who would be deciding this case. The other three jurors would serve as alternates. He apologized in advance to those who would be selected as alternates and said that in the event one of the jurors had to leave during deliberations, for whatever reason, one of the alternates would take his place.

Chernoff next told the jurors they would be privy to two kinds of evidence in the trial—testimonial evidence, the answers witnesses give to questions posed by the attorneys, and the physical evidence.

"You will be deciding how accurate the witness is

and how credible the witness is," he said. "What you do is compare the testimony and the physical evidence throughout the trial, and it might be that you started with one feeling about a witness and then by the time the trial is over with, your feeling may be a little bit different because you not only decide what to accept and what to reject, you decide how much weight to give it."

The judge asked the jurors to keep an open mind throughout the trial, because they really wouldn't know how much weight to give something until they could compare it to something else.

Judge Chernoff then described the objection process for the members of the jury and followed that with an explanation of physical evidence—evidence that would be in the jury room during deliberations.

Continuing with his remarks, Judge Chernoff broke the trial down into phases for the members of the jury.

"The first thing you will be privy to in this case will be the opening statement by the assistant district attorney, who is responsible for prosecuting the case. Following that, the attorney for the defendant has an opportunity to give his opening statement," he said, noting that the defense attorney could also reserve the right to give his opening statement at a later point in the trial.

He stressed that nothing either attorney said in his opening statement or closing statement was to be considered evidence, but merely a road map for where each attorney thought his case was going.

"After the initial opening stage of the proceedings, you will then be privy to the evidentiary phase where each witness will testify," he continued. "The attorneys will each have an opportunity to examine each and every witness in this case. . . . After the evidentiary phase of this case, which takes the lion's share of the trial, you will then hear from the lawyers again in their closing arguments. . . . After you hear from the attorneys, then you are going to hear from me again in what is known as the judge's charge to the jury."

Judge Chernoff explained that at the end of the trial he would give them all the law they needed to know to reach a verdict.

"You will take the facts as you find them and apply them to the law as I give it to you and, hopefully, you will be able to reach a unanimous verdict as far as the issues that are involved in this case," he said.

Finally, after reminding the jurors not to discuss the case with anyone, read newspaper reports about it, or listen to radio or television news regarding the case, Judge Chernoff thanked the jurors for their willingness to participate and turned the proceedings over to the attorney for the Commonwealth for his opening statement.

"Is she dead? Am I going to be arrested?"

So began the prosecutor's opening statement in the murder trial of Dr. Dirk Greineder.

"Thirty to forty minutes after this defendant called the Wellesley Police Department to say that his wife had been attacked, he stood in that circle area that we visited yesterday, with Officer Paul Fitzpatrick, a uniformed Wellesley police officer, and those were his words, this physician: 'Is she dead? Am I going to be arrested?'"

Rick Grundy told the jury that on October 31, 1999, Dirk Greineder struck his wife, May, a woman he had been married to for thirty-one years, in the back of the head with a two-pound drilling hammer, stabbed her in the head and chest, and then slit her throat with an Old Timer Buck knife from under her ear to her Adam's apple, severing the carotid artery. Later testimony would prove that wasn't exactly the case. While May Greineder's jugular vein had been sliced, her carotid artery was not cut.

"This defendant . . . then tried desperately to get rid of those items and couldn't," Grundy said, pointing to Greineder.

He assured jurors that he would present witness statements, expert testimony, and evidence, including DNA and blood evidence, that would convince them beyond a reasonable doubt that Dirk Greineder did, in fact, murder his wife while they were out walking their dog at Morses Pond that fateful Halloween morning. He stated that experts would tie Greineder to the murder weapons, as well as to other items recovered from the scene, items that included the bloody gloves worn by the murderer.

"Ladies and gentlemen, in that path down that embankment lay the items of an elaborate plan gone awry, too elaborate, too thought-out, a gone-off plan, items left behind, items that will have a link, as you will see, to the defendant," Grundy said. "You will see that the other areas of the pond that this defendant was at that day will find other items [*sic*]. Where this defendant was seen, there will be other items, items used in the murder of May Greineder."

Grundy went on to describe the murdered woman to the jury.

"May Greineder was fifty-seven years old. She was a nurse with a master's degree, but first and foremost she was a mother and a dedicated wife," Grundy stated as Greineder bowed his head and wiped his eyes. "Anyone that you will hear from will tell you how she loved, cared, and nurtured for her children, how they were first and foremost in her life beyond anything, and how important it was to her, the projection of a perfect family. Beautiful, bright, accomplished children, her physician husband, living in Wellesley."

However, he painted a very different picture of her husband.

The jury heard that on the surface Dirk Greineder was a demanding, no-nonsense, straightforward, softspoken, highly regarded individual in his field of medicine and a person whose image meant a great deal to him.

But they also heard that he was a man of secrets, deeply and closely held secrets—secrets that his wife may have uncovered.

"You will hear that, ladies and gentlemen, as we examine just one week, just one week, of those secrets. It will be the week before the death of May Greineder," Grundy said. "You will hear, ladies and gentlemen, that this defendant, a prominent physician, a prominent allergist, straightforward and demanding, had many secrets and . . . in addition to Dirk Greineder, the defendant was Tom Young. Tom Young is this defendant's college roommate who hadn't seem him or heard from him in over twenty years."

Grundy explained to the jurors that as Tom Young, Greineder led a secret life—a life filled with prostitutes and pornography. And Grundy detailed some of the defendant's sexual encounters and activities for the men and women of the jury.

As Grundy talked about Greineder's sex life, his youngest daughter, Britt, though on the verge of tears, looked adoringly at her father. Her brother,

Colin, as well as her father and his attorney, couldn't take their eyes off the prosecutor.

"Ladies and gentlemen, you will also hear that on the date prior to the murder of May Greineder, the defendant called a number and didn't get in contact with a woman he had known as a prostitute," Grundy said. "You will hear that the day after the murder of May Greineder, he called the same number."

He continued, "Ladies and gentlemen, the physical evidence of this case will show you what happened, where it happened, and who did it. The location of the evidence, the testing of the evidence, the actions and words of this defendant, ladies and gentlemen, will leave you with no doubt whatsoever. There will never be a rationale for such a brutal and horrible crime having this person's life taken away, but the facts, I suggest to you, ladies and gentlemen, will be clear. . . . At the close of the evidence, I ask you to do one thing, to return a verdict that speaks the truth. Thank you."

Although Grundy had delivered a rather low-key opening, he seemed to captivate the jury with his approach. Because the jury did have the opportunity to see the murder scene beforehand, they were better able to follow his remarks.

After Grundy finished, Greineder turned to talk to his children. Britt, trying to show support for her father, smiled through her tears, but it was obvious her heart was breaking.

After a brief recess so the jurors could stretch their legs, Greineder's attorney, Martin Murphy, stood to address the jury. During Grundy's opening statement, Greineder, who had lost more than thirty pounds in prison, appeared nervous, continuously fidgeting with his fingers. Now that his attorney was about to speak on his behalf, he seemed to relax.

"I want to begin, if I may, by asking you to think back to Monday of this week, when you and so many others were called here to begin the jury selection process. That day, we had an opportunity to talk to each of you individually," Murphy said. "You had all filled out those questionnaires, and some of you had indicated that you heard something about this case. Some of you said you had even formed some opinions about this case, but all of you said that you could put whatever you heard, whatever you learned, whatever opinions you had, aside because as Judge Chernoff said, a case like this gets decided on what he called the 'real stuff.' It doesn't get decided on pointed fingers. It doesn't get decided on acting-class theatrics. It gets decided on the 'real stuff'—the evidence."

Murphy went on to say that the evidence would show that May Greineder was "horribly, savagely, and brutally" killed at Morses Pond on Halloween morning, 1999. But it would also show that whoever smashed the back of May Greineder's head with a two-pound drilling hammer, whoever cut her throat, and whoever stabbed her twice in the chest and stabbed her five more times in the head, whoever that was, it wasn't his client.

"What the evidence will show, what the 'real stuff' in this case will show, most of all, is that the man who is seated with me at the counsel table, Dirk Greineder, is an innocent man wrongly accused of a terrible, terrible crime that he did not commit," Murphy continued. "What the evidence will show is that the state cannot meet its burden of proving beyond a reasonable doubt that he was May Greineder's killer, and it can't do that for one very simple reason: he's not the man who did it."

Murphy made it clear to the jury that despite the

prosecution's attempts to muddy the waters of the case by harping on his client's fascination with prostitutes and pornography, the case was not about whether Dirk Greineder was guilty of infidelity, adultery, or using the Internet for sexual gratification.

"If Dirk Greineder was charged with infidelity, the evidence would show that he is guilty of infidelity," Murphy stressed. "If the charge here was that Dirk Greineder committed adultery, the evidence will show that he is guilty of that charge. If the charge here was that Dirk Greineder used the Internet for sexual gratification in ways that you might very well find distressing, if that were the charge, the evidence will show that Dirk Greineder is guilty of that charge."

Murphy explained that those issues had nothing to do with the murder of May Greineder and everything to do with the prosecution's desperate attempt to find a motive that would explain why Dirk Greineder would kill his wife.

"The evidence in this case, the 'real stuff' that you will hear from the witness stand, will show that Dirk Greineder had no motive to kill his wife, and that, in fact, he didn't," Murphy said.

He told the jury that the Massachusetts State Police officers assigned to the Norfolk District Attorney's Office jumped to the conclusion that Dirk Greineder was lying and that he was responsible for the savage and brutal death of his wife, even though they knew about two unsolved homicides that had taken place in recreation areas in the twelve months before May Greineder was murdered.

Murphy went on to tell the jury that the evidence would show that, in an effort to pin May's murder on her husband, the police and the prosecutors were still jumping to conclusions, and they were still not getting their facts straight.

The jury also heard that the state's own DNA experts found DNA from an unknown stranger on May Greineder's left-hand blue Polar Tech glove.

"Who is that stranger?" Well, the answer is, members of the jury, we don't know. We don't know because the state, the police, and the prosecutors did not conduct a fair and objective search for the truth," Murphy explained. "They never sought out other suspects."

Murphy also told the jury the defense would address each of the prosecution's contentions with the "real stuff," with evidence from the witness stand.

"I am going to ask you as this case progresses to listen carefully to that evidence, and I suggest to you that what the evidence will show is that Dr. Greineder had no reason to kill his wife, that he didn't kill his wife, and that the state can't prove beyond a reasonable doubt that he did, for one simple reason, he is the wrong man. Thank you."

Chapter 11

After a fifteen-minute recess, the prosecution began its case with testimony from Jason Harris, the first paramedic to reach May Greineder's body. Harris, a nurse in the intensive care unit of Addison Gilbert Hospital in Gloucester, Massachusetts, at the time of the trial, testified that when he was within eight feet of May's body, he saw blood in the path. When he was three or four feet away, he noticed a large gaping wound on her neck that appeared to be fatal, as well as a laceration from May's forehead to the top of her head. Because the neck wound was obviously fatal, Harris said he did not attempt to resuscitate her.

During this part of Harris's testimony, Grundy entered into evidence a graphic photo depicting the horrendous wound on May's neck and passed it around to the members of the jury. That photo would be the first of 473 exhibits, including more photos of the crime scene, the murder weapons, the gloves, Greineder's bloody clothes, his clean hands, as well as charts showing the results of DNA and blood tests, that would be entered into evidence throughout the five-week trial.

As Harris spoke, Greineder took copious notes, showing little emotion. His well-groomed, good-looking children sitting behind him were there to support him. If they believed their father didn't murder their mother, maybe the jury would believe it as well. But members of the jury said later they paid little attention to the children's defense of their father because that's how they expected them to behave. The jury felt no children would ever believe their father killed their mother.

When Harris testified that he saw the defendant at Morses Pond that day, Grundy asked him if he remembered what Greineder was wearing.

"What I remember was a yellow-type either windbreaker of rain-type slicker and wearing tennis shoes," Harris said, adding that he didn't recall seeing anything on the jacket.

"At some point, you indicated you saw him in tennis shoes; is that correct?" Grundy asked.

"That's correct."

"What did you notice there?"

"There appeared to be blood spatter there," Harris replied.

Murphy was up like a shot to object.

The word "spatter" took on a connotation Murphy didn't want the jury to consider—that his client was near his wife's body when she was bludgeoned and stabbed to death.

The judge agreed and sustained the objection, saying, "I think it's a matter for evidence developed by a person with different qualifications."

"You saw some markings on his sneakers; is that correct?" Grundy continued.

"Yes."

"And could you describe them as far as the coloration was concerned?"

"They were red."

"And could you describe specifically the shape and sizes of those?"

"Almost like a splatter effect, if you spilled water," Harris responded.

Again, Murphy was up in a heartbeat, objecting to the word "splatter."

And again the judge sustained the objection.

Next up was Lieutenant Ken DeMerchant, a Wellesley firefighter since August 1994. He was the first firefighter to reach May Greineder's body. De-Merchant, who was also an emergency medical technician, told the jury he went up to May to see if there was something he could do to help her.

The jury heard that DeMerchant knelt down beside the left side of her body to check to see if she was still alive. When he moved her sweater down a little bit so he could take her pulse on her neck, he noticed a large wound. At that point, he decided to check her pulse on her wrists because he wanted to stay away from the neck wound. Unable to get a pulse that way, he was forced to try her neck. But he still couldn't get a pulse or find any signs of life, he told the jury. He also noted that her skin was an ashen gray.

DeMerchant also testified to seeing what looked like a plastic bag with blood on it in the pathway near May's corpse.

When court resumed a little before 2:00 P.M., after an hour break for lunch, Judge Chernoff made an unexpected announcement to the attorneys outside the presence of the jury.

"Counsel, one of the jurors is a sufferer of migraine headaches and he said that he gets them periodically, maybe once a month, and one came on this morning. He is not feeling well. In fact, he is feeling terribly. I had him separated from the other jurors at lunch and given him access to a couch and he is lying on a couch in this courtroom. All he wants to do is go home and he thinks he will be fine to come back tomorrow morning if today's headache is like the other headaches he has had. I am not prepared to release this juror from this case. I don't want to, but I will impose on counsel and everybody affiliated with the case to bear with us and be here at nine o'clock tomorrow morning. I expect he will be here and ready to go. I know that means you might have to take some people out of turn because people might not be available, but we'll just simply have to go with the flow. I thank you all for being so understanding."

With that trial was adjourned until Friday, May 25, 2001, at 9:00 A.M.

When court reconvened the next day, the judge did not have very good news. With the jury present, Judge Chernoff explained that the ill juror had not recovered from his migraine and would not yet be available to continue his work on the jury.

"What I am unaware of is the likely duration of his illness and perhaps, even more importantly, the likelihood of a recurrence of his illness," the judge told the court. "This is all information I should become privy to once we have some medical advice on this case on his situation. What we are going to do is we are going to proceed with the trial today. I am not excusing that juror, at least as of this time. The people in the media have been extremely kind to me and would be willing to put together a tape of the proceedings for today so that, should this juror continue in this case, we would be able to make him privy to absolutely everything that the remaining members of the jury will be privy to today. . . . We are going to continue with fourteen people seated here and one person not seated here."

The unusual solution to the court's dilemma, which both attorneys agreed to, was the judge's way of protecting the integrity of the trial. However, it was odd that no one seemed worried about the possibility that the juror, for whatever reason, might not watch the entire tape and miss a crucial portion of the testimony.

With that piece of business out of the way, the state called William DeLorie, a lieutenant with the Wellesley Fire Department, to the stand. His testimony both helped and hurt the defendant.

DeLorie testified that while emergency personnel were surrounding his wife's brutally murdered body, a visibly upset Greineder, his clothes stained with blood, fell to his hands and knees and cried out, "This is my wife. Who could have done this to my wife?"

In other testimony, DeLorie said that when Greineder was explaining to him what happened, he said his wife hurt her back while throwing a ball for their dog to retrieve. But that explanation contradicted statements Murphy made during his opening remarks, when he told jurors May hurt her back while walking down the incline into the sand pit area, not throwing a ball.

After the usual midmorning recess, the prosecution called Wellesley resident Patricia Andrews, who told the jurors she saw the defendant walking his dog in the pine tree forest at Morses Pond a little after 9:00 A.M. on October 30, the day before May was murdered.

Grundy was laying the groundwork to show that Greineder had the opportunity to hide the items found near May's body, including the lighter fluid, plastic bags, foil loaf pans, and latex gloves—items the prosecution claimed the defendant planned to use to clean up the murder scene and dispose of evidence that could implicate him in his wife's death.

The next two witnesses, Hugh and Artemis Halsey, told the jury that they were at Morses Pond that Saturday morning setting up for a scary walk and scavenger hunt they were holding later that evening for their thirteen-year-old son and five of his friends.

The Halseys said they and some of their friends hid various items such as little dolls and packets of labels and stars for the kids to find during the scavenger hunt. They testified that no one in their group brought lighter fluid, foil loaf pans, or surgical gloves to the pond that day. However, during cross-examination, Hugh Halsey said the site where the scavenger hunt took place was not really all that close to the path where May's body was found. He said it was about thirty yards away from the sand pit area. And Artemis's testimony also helped the defense, because she told the jury that each time she visited the pond she always saw a number of people jogging, walking their dogs, or just walking around. Murphy's point—why would his client choose such a public place to murder his wife?

Later that afternoon, Grundy called Wellesley resident Rick Magnan to the stand. At approximately 8:30 A.M. on October 31, 1999, Magnan left his home on Willow Road to jog to Morses Pond. As he was running around the pond, he heard someone yelling. He said he looked around and saw a man he later learned was Dirk Greineder, with a German shepherd, about thirty feet away from him on the access road.

The man asked Magnan if he had a cell phone. When Magnan responded he didn't, Greineder headed away from the pond toward the parking lot. Not running, not walking, sort of sprinting, Magnan testified. Curious, Magnan followed Greineder to the parking lot, where he saw Bill Kear on the far side of the lot. Kear, who had been walking his small dog at the pond, asked Magnan if he saw anyone. Magnan responded that a man asked him if he had a cell phone.

Magnan said later that Kear told him Greineder's wife was lying on the path and pointed in the direction of the pine tree forest. Figuring the woman was having chest pains, Magnan testified he told Kear he didn't know CPR and would run to the houses at the front of the access road to get some help. When he got to the top of the access road, Magnan saw Greineder sitting in the driver's side of his van with one leg on the ground. Magnan testified that as he got closer to the van, he could hear Greineder on the telephone.

When Greineder finished the call, Magnan said he got out of the van and walked toward him. Magnan told the jury Greineder then asked him to go back to help his wife while he waited for the ambulance to come.

"I said, 'Why don't you go, and I'll stay here and wait for the ambulance,'" Magnan testified. Greineder told Magnan not to let anyone go into the van because the dog was in it, then went back to his wife.

The prosecution scored some points here, showing the jury, through Magnan's testimony, that Greineder couldn't have been too concerned about his wife if he was willing to send a complete stranger back to help her. And the prosecution implied that Greineder didn't want anyone to go into the van because it contained some evidence linking him to his wife's murder.

On cross-examination, Magnan helped the defense a bit by admitting Greineder appeared distraught, emotional, and upset when he was calling for help.

Two things were evident from the day's testimony: If Greineder were guilty of killing his wife, he was either very smart or very stupid to have chosen Morses Pond as the murder site. If he were smart, then selecting a familiar place to do the deed was a good idea because he knew how to get in and out of the area quickly. On the other hand, why would he kill his wife in such a public place where people knew him, as Murphy pointed out? The answer probably lay in those stories about the murders of Irene Kennedy and Richard Reyenger he downloaded and saved on his computer. He wanted to make people think a serial killer was on the loose and his wife was the killer's next victim.

The last witness of the day was Wellesley police sergeant Peter Nahass, who was called to Morses Pond shortly after May's body was discovered. Nahass testified how police handled the crime scene once they realized May was murdered. His testimony was necessary to let the jury know that, although Wellesley police didn't have much experience with homicides, they were organized in their approach to this investigation.

Nahass also told the jury that while talking to Greineder about what happened at the pond that morning, he noticed Greineder's hands were clean, even though his clothes were covered in blood.

"He also had two scratch marks on his neck," Nahass said.

Nahass gave riveting testimony about finding the murder weapons in the storm drain.

"After [DPW worker] Walter Adams came and took the drain cover off that was covered with leaves, I used my flashlight, put it into the area, which was probably four feet deep, and I observed something that had a blue handle, a glove, and what appeared to be a knife, a closed Buck knife . . . and the handle of a hammer over the top of the knife."

The next day, Nahass said, he went back to Morses Pond and around 4:00 or 4:30 P.M. discovered the second glove in a storm drain near the spot where Greineder had parked his van the previous day.

"I put my flashlight on so I could light up the bottom of the drain," he explained. "On the bottom of the drain, there was water and leaves floating around, and amongst the leaves I saw what appeared to be a glove."

"Do you remember the texture to those gloves?" Grundy asked.

"I believe they had little bumps on them."

This was an important moment for the prosecution because the bumps on the gloves would later be linked to patterns on Greineder's glasses and on the jacket he was wearing the morning his wife was murdered.

After Nahass testified about finding the second glove, the judge adjourned the trial until Tuesday, May 29, because Monday the 28th was the Memorial Day holiday.

The Greineder children, who continued to support their father, tried to remain stoic throughout the day. But when the prosecutor projected a picture of the crime scene, showing May's legs sticking out into the path, on a large screen, and also held up the two-pound drilling hammer and the folding knife used to kill their mother, the siblings, obviously distraught, turned away from the gruesome displays, shaking their heads and clutching each other by the arms. Unable to hold in her tears any longer, Britt began crying when, at one point, her cell phone rang twice, interrupting the day's proceedings.

"I'm sorry, I keep shutting it off," she apologized the second time it went off.

Although the day's testimony was focused on piecing together what happened on the morning May Greineder was brutally murdered and what the various witnesses saw, it was as much focused on what they didn't see—another person in the area. Only Dirk Greineder saw that person.

Chapter 12

When court began on Tuesday, Judge Chernoff told the jurors that their colleague who had taken ill was not going to be able to continue with the trial. Some type of infection, the judge said, had fueled his migraine, and it was unlikely that he would be able to concentrate for several days. Fourteen jurors remained, eight men and six women—twelve of them would decide Greineder's fate.

"What that means is that you all have to remain healthy," Judge Chernoff said. "You may have to consider some kind of supplements, but please remain healthy."

The judge's decision to continue the trial without the fifteenth juror was probably for the best. At least now the court wouldn't have to deal with the myriad questions that would likely be raised by letting the ill juror view the trial on tape. The trial system is built around having the jurors in the same room with witnesses so they can see how they act and speak and so they can watch how the defendant reacts to the witness testimony. A juror watching the trial on tape would miss those things. Having the juror view a tape of the trial might also be grounds for a mistrial.

After Sergeant Nahass finished testifying, the prosecution called Terence McNally to the stand. McNally, who had lived in the Morses Pond area for seven and a half years, said he was walking his dog, Theo, near the sand pit on the morning May Greineder was murdered. McNally said he stayed in that area playing fetch with his dog for about ten minutes until about 8:50 or 8:55 A.M. At the beginning of his walk, McNally told the jurors, he heard someone yell—a couple of short, high-pitched yells—from a distance. The screams lasted about ten seconds.

"I really couldn't make out what it was, and I really didn't think much of it at the time," he said. Under questioning from Murphy, McNally said he didn't hear anyone arguing before he heard the screams. McNally also testified that he didn't call police to report what he had heard until he learned about the murder the next day.

The state's premise was that if McNally, who was not too far from the path where May was bludgeoned and stabbed to death, heard screams, then why didn't Greineder hear them? The defense, however, was trying to point out that if McNally didn't think much of the screams, then maybe Greineder didn't hear the screams because they weren't very loud.

After the morning recess, Grundy called Shannon Parillo, the Wellesley police dispatcher who took Greineder's emergency call 8:56 A.M. on October 31, 1999.

While Parillo was on the stand, Grundy played a tape of the call for the jurors. Greineder wiped tears from his eyes as jurors listened to him call for help. His children shook their heads and fought back tears as they heard their father report their mother's murder. Kirsten handed her younger sister, Britt, a tissue and tried to console Colin, who just shook his head and rubbed his cheeks with his hands.

Dispatcher (D): Wellesley Police. This call's recorded.

Greineder (G): Help. I'm at the pond. I need some . . . someone attacked my wife, trying to get (inaudible).

D: Sir, where are you?

G: I'm at, at the pond, at Morses Pond. Walking . . .

D: At Morses Pond?

G: Walking the dog, someone attacked, I left her 'cause she hurt her back.

D: Okay. You just need to relax 'cause I can't understand what you're saying.

G: Please, please, send a car.

D: Okay, you're at Morses Pond.

G: Pond, yeah.

D: Whereabouts at Morses Pond? Whereabouts at Morses Pond?

G: I'm, I'm outside my, my car's outside by the gate.

D: Okay. Hold on one second, okay?

G: Please send someone.

D: Wellesley Control to fourteen zero five.

G: Oh my God.

D: What, what happened?

G: I, I, I, we were walking the dog.

Officer Fitzpatrick: Fourteen zero five.

G: She hurt her back.

D: Is she injured?

G: I think she's dead I'm not sure. I'm a doctor. I went back, I . . .

D: Can you start over to Morses Pond . . .

G: She looks terrible.

D: . . . for an unknown medical at this time.

G: The dog heard something. She went back.

D: Okay, just relax. Is this your, is this your, is this your daughter?

G: My, my wife.

D: You're right at the entrance to Morses Pond?

G: *I'm right at the main entrance where, where it's blocked.*

D: *Negative fourteen zero five. It's right at the main entrance at Morses Pond.*

G: *And, and you got to have someone unlock the door so the cars can get in.*

D: *Okay, what's your name?*

G: *Dirk, Dirk Greineder,* G-R-E-I-N-E-D-E-R.

D: *Okay. Listen. Listen to me.*

G: *Yeah.*

D: *You need to relax. I have people on the way. But I can't understand you. So, you need to just relax.*

G: *All right.*

D: *Okay?*

G: *Yeah, I just ran over here.*

D: *Okay. What's your name?*

G: *Dirk.*

D: *Dirk?*

G: *Yeah.*

D: *And this is your wife?*

G: *Yeah, yes, yes.*

D: *And you were walking your dog and what happened?*

G: *She twisted her back. She's got a bad back.*

D: *She twisted her back?*

G: *I left her.*

D: *Okay, is she conscious and breathing?*

G: *I, I don't think so. I don't think so.*

D: *Okay.*

G: *I went back for her.*

D: *He doesn't think she's conscious.*

G: *The dog . . . someone attacked her. It's definitely an attack.*

D: *Okay. Just hold, are you with her right now?*

G: *No, no, I'm way out. I had to go out to call you.*

D: How, how old is she?

G: Oh God, Please send someone. I don't know.

D: They're on their way. How old is she?

G: Fifty-eight. We live, we lived in Wellesley for twenty-five years, thirty years. I don't even know.

D: Okay.

G: Please.

D: Hold on one second, okay sir? Wellesley Control to fourteen zero five.

Officer Fitzpatrick: Zero five.

G: I found her and I'm . . .

D: Be advised that's a fifty-eight-year . . .

G: I tried to see if there was anything to do.

D: . . . old woman . . .

G: There's nothing I can do.

D: Fell, possibly . . .

G: Please.

D: . . . twisted her back. Unknown if she's conscious and breathing at this time. Sir?

G: Yeah.

D: Are you on a pay phone?

G: No, I'm on, I'm on my cell phone in the car.

D: Okay. Can you take your cell phone and go to her?

G: No, it's in the car. I don't have my portable.

D: You can't . . .

G: Just send someone. I, someone inside with her, there was someone else walking his dog, and I, he went in there. There's a runner here.

D: Do you see the ambulance? We have them on the way.

G: No, I don't see anything yet.

D: Okay. What I'll . . .

G: Do they have a key to this gate? Because they can't get in unless they have the gate.

D: *Yeah. Call the fire department back. Tell them they need the key to the gate lock. Okay, sir, what . . .*

G: *DPW has the key, I think that they're always in there.*

D: *Sir?*

G: *Yeah.*

D: *What I'm gonna do is, I'm gonna hang up the phone with you. I want you to keep an eye out for the ambulance.*

G: *Okay. Okay.*

D: *And the police officer.*

G: *All right, all right.*

D: *When you see them, get them.*

G: *I'm waiting. I'm waiting. I'm waiting.*

D: *Okay.*

G: *Yeah.*

D: *Go back to your wife.*

G: *Yeah.*

D: *See if she's okay.*

G: *All right.*

After they listened to the tape, Grundy handed each juror a transcript of Greineder's 911 call and played the tape for them again while they read along with it. When the jurors heard the tape, they heard a man who was frantic with worry, but why was he frantic—because his wife was dead or because he killed her?

The state now called retired Wellesley patrolman Paul Fitzpatrick, the first officer to respond to the scene after Greineder's emergency call, to the stand. Like most of the law enforcement officials, Fitzpatrick chose to stand during his testimony. Fitzpatrick, a soft-spoken man, had been a Wellesley police officer from 1971 until his retirement in 2000.

Fitzpatrick took the jurors back to the morning of

October 31, 1999, and told them exactly what happened when he arrived at the pond. He testified that when he asked Greineder what happened to his wife, the doctor said they were out for a walk and she tripped on a pebble or something and threw her back out. Again, this was a different story than he told DeLorie. Greineder told the paramedic that his wife threw her back out throwing a ball for Zephyr.

Fitzpatrick said Greineder told him that he checked his wife's carotid pulse and it was weak—Greineder never said this to anyone else; he told other people that he couldn't get a pulse—and that's when he went to the van to call police. At this point, Greineder hadn't told anyone at the pond he picked his wife up, then dropped her again because she was too heavy to move.

Fitzpatrick said after he was with Greineder for about twenty or thirty minutes, the doctor asked him, "Is she dead?"

"I told him she was dead," Fitzpatrick said. "Then he asked me if I was going to arrest him."

Grundy's reason for pointing to this conversation was obvious—why would a man whose wife had just been murdered be worried about being arrested if he were innocent?

Under questioning from Murphy, Fitzpatrick told jurors when he arrived at Morses Pond, he saw a car parked in front of the Greineders' van near the entrance to Turner Road, but didn't notice its license plate or any other identifying information.

Next, Grundy called Wellesley resident William Kear to the stand. Kear's testimony was particularly damaging to the defense.

Kear, who was walking his Australian silky terrier the morning of the murder, testified he saw Greineder, with Zephyr on a leash, come out of the path where May's body was found and walk quickly across the circle at the end of the access road to the paved path. The murder weapons and the murderer's right-handed glove were later discovered in a storm drain on that paved pathway.

Kear, who continued walking down the access road, said he didn't hear the doctor say anything. About forty-five seconds to a minute, or a minute and a half later, Kear said Greineder exited the path and asked him if he had a cell phone.

"I said no, I didn't have a cellular phone. The defendant asked me if I would call—go make a call," Kear testified. "I just said, you know, no, and I asked what happened. He said his wife had been attacked."

Kear asked Greineder where the attack happened, and Greineder pointed back in the woods to the path. After Greineder said he was going to his car to make a call from his car phone, Kear went to see if he could help May. When he got near the spot where May's body was, Kear said he could see some legs sticking out in the path.

"At that point, I had a question, you know, relative to my safety. How safe would I be in going to where this woman had been attacked? I hadn't seen anybody else, so my thoughts were whether—if there was anybody in the woods," Kear explained. "At that point, I turned around and came out of that pathway and headed up the walkway toward the exit of Morses Pond."

After running into Magnan, the jogger, Kear decided to go back to see if he could help May. But when he got within twenty feet of her body, he saw that her torso was exposed and noticed that she wasn't breathing, so he turned around and went back to the access road. While there, he saw Greineder standing outside a police car. At one point, Kear said, Greineder threw himself on the grass and said, "I'm a doctor. Why can't I help my family?" Kear said Greineder also told him he saw shadows.

On cross-examination, Murphy got Kear to admit that when he talked to police the day of the murder, he told them Greineder had only spent twenty or thirty seconds down the paved pathway. Murphy's point was that twenty or thirty seconds didn't give his client much time to dispose of the murder weapons.

Murphy then questioned Kear about what, if anything, he saw Greineder holding in his hands when he crossed the circle and went down the paved path.

"And I take it, sir, that when you saw Dr. Greineder walk across the back of the circle with his red backpack on his shoulders and the dog leash taut in his right hand, you didn't see him with a two-pound drilling hammer in his left hand, did you, sir?" Murphy asked, holding the hammer in his hand, slightly swinging it up and down.

"No."

Murphy asked Kear if the doctor was carrying or wearing a left-handed glove when he emerged from the paved path and asked if he had a cell phone.

"I never saw any gloves."

Murphy then asked Kear whether he ever told police that Greineder said he saw the "shadow of a person," not just a shadow, go down the paved path. Kear said he may have said that, but he really couldn't remember after a year and a half. Murphy's contention was that his client followed his wife's murderer down the paved path. Grundy, however, claimed that Greineder just made up the story to explain why he went down the path where the murder weapons were later found.

Before court recessed for the day, Wellesley police detective Jill McDermott took the stand. McDermott testified that Greineder had blood on the front, shoulders, arms, and cuffs of his yellow-and-white windbreaker. She also said he had small red drops of blood on his sneakers and on the left lens of his glasses. However, she said he didn't have any blood on his hands. The prosecution maintained that his hands were clean because he was wearing gloves when he killed his wife.

The jurors heard Greineder's version of the events of October 31, 1999, from McDermott. She said before she spoke with Greineder, she patted him down and asked him to empty out his pockets. Greineder told her his wife hurt her back throwing a ball to Zephyr while they were walking through the pine tree forest. He said they then separated—he to continue walking the dog and she to walk back and meet him at the rock in the parking lot. But, he said, when he went to find her, she wasn't there, so he followed Zephyr back to the pathway, where he found May's body. Greineder told McDermott that as he got closer to his wife, he saw that her pants were open and there was some blood on her neck. He told her he checked her carotid artery, but he didn't feel a pulse, so he left to get help. She also testified that Greineder said he went down the paved path looking for a "runner," for help, not a shadow, as he told Kear.

At 4:00 P.M., Judge Chernoff adjourned the day's proceedings and admonished the jurors to steer clear of media coverage of the trial.

"I thank you so much for your courtesy thus far, and please stay well," he said. "See you tomorrow morning."

Before McDermott was recalled to the stand the

next day, Wednesday, May 30, the attorneys and the judge held a sidebar to talk about how to treat a statement Britt Greineder made to her father at the Wellesley police station when she went to see him there after her mother's murder.

"I'm concerned that the Commonwealth may seek to elicit from this witness a statement that the defendant's daughter made to him at the police station and I would ask for a ruling in advance, excluding any such statements," Murphy told the judge.

Chernoff then asked Grundy for his response.

"Your Honor, what the Commmonwealth would be offering is the initial statement: 'What happened between you and Mom today? Did something happen?' To the extent that this, then, prompts Dr. Greineder to make the statement 'No, we were walking and she hurt her back. She's hurt her back before. She usually lays down and she's fine.' This again occurs at the police station but does not involve the police in any way, and I would not go into that," Grundy said.

"Your Honor, I'm not asking that the court exclude the defendant's statement. I'm asking the court to [exclude] the defendant's daughter Britt's statement, 'What happened between you and Mom today? Did something happen?' You know, I do not think that it is necessary to explain the context of the response that follows. I think it could be elicited simply by asking the detective, as you would with any out-of-court statement by a witness: 'Did the defendant's daughter say something to him? Yes. And what did the defendant say in response?' It is very prejudicial, Your Honor. It is an out-of-court statement by a witness that is hearsay. You know, what she says is not relevant; it's what the defendant says. So there is a hearsay objection and a relevance objection there. Your Honor, plus I think that it is substantially more prejudicial than probative."

But Chernoff disagreed with Murphy's argument.

"I would allow you to use the first part of the statement, 'What happened between you and Mom? Did something happen?' Then, the defendant's answer to that, I would exclude 'She's hurt her back before. She usually lays down and she's fine.' I would exclude that if the defendant wants that out."

Chernoff told the attorneys that Britt's statements were more than "res gestae" kind of statements. Res gestae is a peculiar rule, used mostly in criminal cases, which allows hearsay if the statement is made during the excitement of the event that is being litigated.

"It seems to me that this is also—there is real spontaneity to her statements. She arrives at the police station. Her mother is dead. Her father is there. . . . So there is spontaneity to it," he said.

Murphy, however, was concerned that if the jury heard Britt's statements, they would get the idea that there were some prior acts of violence between Dirk and May.

"The context of the statement makes it sound like the daughter is making a comment that, you know, they're fighting all the time and that some kind of physical violence is common. Number one—there is no evidence of that," he told the judge.

But Grundy's reason for wanting to include Britt's statement to her father was that his response that May hurt her back was not really what happened to her.

"Does the Commonwealth offer this as a spontaneous utterance?" Chernoff asked.

"Yes, Your Honor."

But Murphy wasn't ready to give up.

"Again, Your Honor, there is a hearsay objection, but there is also a relevance. The content of the statement, you know, brings us into an area where it is just not, I would suggest, appropriate for the jury to hear at this juncture. We're not putting character evidence in. The daughter has not been called to ask about the nature of the relationship, so it's an out-of-court statement about the nature of the relationship between the husband and wife that is just incredibly prejudicial, more prejudicial than probative, given all that it is being used for is to elicit a response.

"'What happened' would be fine, but 'What happened between you and Mom today? Did something happen?' It's the 'between' that really makes this incredibly prejudicial, Your Honor. I would really ask the court to reconsider."

But Grundy wasn't buying Murphy's explanation.

"Your Honor, as many times as Mr. Murphy says that, that doesn't make it inappropriate evidence for this court to allow, and it doesn't even open a door for it to change what the evidence is. The Commonwealth is willing to cut back and not offer what obviously has a prejudicial effect with respect to 'Why do these f'd-up things keep happening to our family, psychotic, unexplained things?' Obviously, there is some prejudice to this, but this is—"

"Your Honor—" Murphy interrupted, but Grundy continued.

"This is a spontaneous statement that elicits a response that the Commonwealth indicates and will argue is not a truthful response," Grundy said.

But Murphy said the prosecution was really not giving anything up by not including those statements because Britt told the grand jury that when she said, "Why do these f'd-up things always happen to our family," she was referring to the murder/suicide May's brother was involved in a number of years ago in California, which had nothing to do with the case at hand.

"Additionally, she indicated to the police that there were problems in their parents' marriage several years ago that she refused to speak about that day, and I'm not offering that as well," Grundy said.

Finally Judge Chernoff said he would allow the prosecution to ask McDermott about Britt's statement to her father.

After the sidebar, Grundy continued questioning McDermott from where he left off the previous day.

McDermott testified again that Greineder told her that after he found his wife, he ran down the paved pathway, looking for a runner to get help. When he turned around, he saw the man with the little dog and went back toward the roadway. McDermott said Greineder then asked the man if he had a cell phone, and when he said no, Greineder said, he went to his van to make the call.

McDermott told the jury Greineder said that after he made the call, he went back to his wife a second time with Officer Fitzpatrick and that's when he saw the wound on her neck. Greineder told McDermott that he touched his wife, but didn't say how he touched her. During their conversation, McDermott said Greineder told her that he needed to get home to take care of his other dog, Wolfie.

After speaking to Greineder for about five or ten minutes, McDermott left him with Officer Fitzpatrick and went to view May's body. She returned to the circle area, where she spoke with Sergeant Foley. She testified that they both then went to talk to Greineder. But, she said, when Greineder explained to Foley how his wife injured her back, he said they were walking in the sand pit area and May stumbled and injured her back. When he told McDermott the story, he said she hurt her back throwing a ball to Zephyr while they were walking in the pine tree forest.

McDermott told the members of the jury that once they got to the Wellesley police station, Greineder was brought to a small conference room, where he was left alone to make some telephone calls, while she sat on a chair outside the room. She said several times Greineder came out to talk to her and told the jurors about the statements he made to her at that time, including "I've told you everything. I'm not hiding anything. You asked me for my clothes and it suddenly scares me." She said Greineder also told her May had given him a back rub the previous evening—later during cross-examination, she realized he had actually said the back rub occurred that morning—and she would probably have his skin underneath her fingernails. But he told McDermott he had not given his wife a back rub.

The jury also heard about Britt Greineder's statements to her father when she first arrived at the police station. McDermott told the jury that Britt said, "What happened between you and Mom? Did something happen?" And Greineder told his daughter that her mother hurt her back while they were walking and that he left her for a moment, and when he went back, Zephyr found her.

McDermott also talked about the walk-through at Greineder's home that afternoon and the search in the early-morning hours of November 1. During the search, McDermott said, she saw a small white hand towel, made out of a rough knobby material, in Greineder's Toyota Avalon. But she didn't see the bloody towel Greineder claimed he threw in the car after he and May used it on their bloody noses.

She said the towel she saw, which she held up and looked at on November 1, was stained with coffee or dirt. But she didn't take it out of the car. About five or six months later, she said, she saw another white towel, which Greineder's attorney had turned over to the state per order of the court, but it was not the towel she saw on November 1, 1999. The towel that Murphy turned over was twice as large as the towel McDermott observed in the Toyota and had a blue Ritz-Carlton emblem on it. It was also a different texture, she said.

McDermott testified that during the November 12 search, she seized wrapping for foil loaf pans, like the one discovered near May's body, in a garbage can in Greineder's garage. She said she also found a receipt for foil loaf pans bought at Roche Brothers supermarket in Wellesley on November 8, 1999. And she said she found foil loaf pans in the attic and the kitchen of Greineder's house. She testified that she also found two hand-drawn sketches of Morses Pond in a wastebasket in a room on the bottom level of the home. One picture included a stick figure depicting the area where May's body was found.

During cross-examination, Murphy pointed out McDermott's inexperience by asking her how long she had been a detective and whether this was her first homicide. She responded she had been a detective since January 1999 and said this was the first murder that she had ever investigated.

Murphy zeroed in on the fact that the only person McDermott frisked that morning was his client, indicating that he was considered a suspect in his wife's death almost immediately, and because of that, police never even looked for anyone else. He also questioned her about why she shredded the notes she took when she was talking to Greineder at Morses

Pond. McDermott said it was because she had typed up her handwritten notes and didn't need them anymore. But Murphy's point was that maybe there was something in her notes that she left out when she transcribed them.

Murphy also asked McDermott whether police had tested his client's hands at the police station for the presence of blood. She had said that there was no blood visible to the naked eye.

"I believe we could not get a chemist to the station—none of us were chemists—so at that time, no testing was done," she said.

"Okay. You understand that there is a test that can be performed to determine whether there is blood on someone's hands; is that right?"

"Yes."

"And did you know then the name of that test?"

"No, but I have since learned it."

"Okay. But you knew back then that there was a test?" Murphy was referring to the orthotoludine test.

"Yes. I knew that there was a test that could test to see if there was blood on someone's hands you visibly cannot see."

Murphy questioned McDermott about the towel she saw in Greineder's Toyota on November 1.

"Did you tell any of the other officers, report back to any of the other officers present, that you had seen a towel that appeared to be bloodstained in that Toyota?"

"No, I did not, and I could say that it did not appear to be bloodstained at that time. That's probably why I didn't say that to anybody."

"All right. But you certainly didn't report that. You didn't report seeing a bloodstained towel to anyone; is that correct?"

"No, because what I observed I did not believe to be a bloodstained towel; I believed to have seen a dirty towel. Obviously, to me, I didn't think there was any significance. Therefore, I didn't seize it and also, therefore, I didn't tell anybody about it."

"All right. Now, was that the only towel that you saw in that car?"

"In that car, I believe so, yes."

"Is there some uncertainty on your part about that?"

"No, but there were more towels in the van. But in the Toyota Avalon, on that search that I did, there was that one towel."

McDermott testified that although photographs had been taken on the subsequent searches of Greineder's house, car, and offices, none were taken of the Toyota Avalon during the November 1 search. Nor did she take notes or write a report of the findings of that search.

"So, you're simply relying on your memory; is that right?" Murphy asked.

"Yes."

During his cross-examination of McDermott, Murphy pointed out inconsistencies between her testimony at trial and her testimony at a pretrial hearing the previous summer.

In her direct testimony, McDermott, testifying from memory, said Greineder had told her May had given him a back rub the previous night, but after Murphy showed her a transcript of her testimony from the hearing, she admitted her mistake.

"And as far as the towel is concerned, the towel that Mr. Grundy showed you that you have testified was not in the car in the early morning of November first, there were no notes about that, correct?"

"Correct."

"No report about that?"

"No, there isn't."

"And you're relying on your memory and your memory alone; isn't that right?"

"Yes."

"And you never communicated to any other police officer that you discovered a bloodstained towel in Dr. Greineder's car in the early-morning hours of November first?"

"No, because I did not believe I observed a bloodstained towel. I thought I observed—I did observe—what appeared to be a dirty towel and I found no significance to pass it on to anybody."

On redirect, McDermott testified that she may have told people about the towel, but she never characterized it as bloodstained.

Grundy also asked her if she ever saw an umbrella in the backseat of the Toyota Avalon during the November 1 search.

"No."

"If you had, would you have taken that into evidence?"

"Yes."

"Do you recall seeing any bloodstaining on any of the seats of that Toyota Avalon on November first?"

"No."

Later that afternoon, Grundy called state police sergeant Deborah Rebeiro to the stand. Rebeiro, whose testimony continued the next day, examined footprint impressions at the crime scene, and she told the jury she found a heel mark that matched one of Greineder's sneakers touching the edge of the pool of May Greineder's blood. The heel mark was facing her body, right next to marks indicating she was dragged off the pathway after she was killed.

"The heel area of foot mark seven was located with the curved surface of the heel toward the victim," Rebeiro told the jury.

Rebeiro testified that she didn't find any footprints that were completely unidentifiable, putting a small dent in the defense's theory that May was killed by an unknown attacker. She told the jury of the thirty-eight footwear impressions found in the area around May's body; thirty were matched to police or firefighters. An analysis of the remaining eight prints showed that seven of them belonged to Greineder; while, she said, the last print could have been made by either Greineder or his wife.

On cross-examination, Rebeiro admitted that she didn't find footprints belonging to some of the public safety officials at the scene that morning. The jury also heard that Rebeiro found only one paw print in the puddle of blood on the ground.

"Now, there was only one paw print that you located at location; is that correct?" Murphy asked.

"On the trail, there were two."

"But at that location?"

"That's correct."

"All right, so all you saw there was one paw?"

"That's correct."

"And, Sergeant, you would agree that there aren't too many one-pawed dogs?"

"That's correct."

"So, is it fair to say that the surface that was available didn't capture the impression of three other paws at that location?"

"That's correct."

"Or perhaps there were marks on that surface

made after the other three paws of the dog left their marks; is that correct?"

"That's correct."

Murphy scored some points with Rebeiro. Maybe the person who murdered May Greineder didn't leave any prints because of the consistency of the surface, or maybe someone else walked over them.

Chapter 13

Later that day, the prosecution called Gwen Pino to the stand. Pino, who worked in the state police crime lab, tested May and Dirk Greineder's bloodstained clothing.

Pino testified that she found human blood on Dirk's yellow windbreaker, black jeans, and white sneakers, as well as on the outside of the red backpack he was wearing the morning his wife was murdered. She also found blood on the handle and edges of Zephyr's leash—Greineder said the leash was wrapped around his wife's waist when he found her body in the pathway and he removed it to put it on the dog when he went looking for help. But she didn't find blood on the items inside the backpack, which included three tennis balls, three dog leashes, and a pair of dishwashing gloves, size small.

That testimony didn't fit with the prosecution's theory. William Kear said he didn't see anything in Greineder's hands when he saw him go down the paved pathway. But since the knife, hammer, and one glove were found in a storm drain on that path, the prosecution believed that Greineder carried the bloody murder weapons and the two bloody gloves in the backpack when he went to dispose of them in the storm drain. Yet, Pino testified that there was no blood inside the backpack. Grundy had to wonder how much this hurt his case.

Greineder and his three children were visibly upset when Pino showed the jurors May's blood-soaked clothes. Pino told the jury there were cuts on her pants, sweatshirt, and T-shirt, as well as her bra and underwear.

Pino, whose testimony continued on Monday, June 4, said she did not find blood on Greineder's cell phone, the steering wheel of his van, or the door handle in Fitzpatrick's police car. She also testified she was never asked to test Greineder's hands for the presence of blood, although she did test his fingernail clippings. She said a screening test indicted his fingernails tested positive for the presence of blood, but added they would also test positive if they came in contact with any oxidizing agent, including vegetable material.

On Monday, June 4, the trial of Dr. Dirk Greineder moved to the historic main courtroom, more commonly known as the Sacco and Vanzetti courtroom, on the second floor of the courthouse. Although one of the largest and most historic in Massachusetts, the courtroom had two drawbacks—there was no air-conditioning and the acoustics were not all that great.

The courtroom was the site of the infamous trial of Italian anarchists Nicola Sacco and Bartolomeo Vanzetti, who were arrested outside Boston in 1920 and charged with robbing and killing a shoe factory paymaster and his guard.

This is their story.

On April 15, 1920, at 3:00 P.M., paymaster Frederick Parmenter and his guard were carrying a shoe factory payroll of nearly $16,000 through the main street of

South Braintree, Massachusetts, when they were murdered and robbed by two men, who then jumped into a waiting car that fled the scene. Witnesses at the scene described the men as Italian-looking.

The crime was similar to an attempted robbery that had occurred on December 24, 1919, in the town of Bridgewater, which was not all that far from Braintree. Therefore, the Bridgewater police chief, whose investigation led him to suspect Italian anarchists were involved in the robbery in his town, believed the two crimes were linked and set a trap to snare the perpetrators.

On May 5, 1920, Nicola Sacco and Bartolomeo Vanzetti, poor Italian immigrants and anarchists, fell into the chief's trap and were arrested. Although they were not originally considered suspects, the two men were ultimately indicted for the South Braintree murders and robbery, because they had been carrying guns when they were arrested, and because they lied repeatedly when authorities questioned them.

In addition, Vanzetti was indicted for the Bridgewater robbery attempt and ultimately found guilty, even though he had an alibi that was corroborated by several witnesses. Judge Webster Thayer sentenced him to twelve to fifteen years in prison, a sentence that was harsher than usual, signaling to the two men and their supporters that there was a political bias against them.

Two months later, Sacco and Vanzetti were indicted for the South Braintree murders. The trial began in May 1921. Even though his bias against anarchists was evident, Judge Thayer asked for, and was given, the case. Fred Moore, a well-known labor lawyer from the West, came to Dedham to defend Sacco and Vanzetti.

Moore decided early on that he couldn't just defend the pair against the murder and robbery charges. Moore felt he had to acknowledge the defendants' anarchist leanings in court and then try to convince the jury that they had been arrested and implicated in the crimes not because they were truly guilty, but because of their political activities. But his strategy didn't work. After a six-week trial, and only five hours of deliberations, the jury found both men guilty.

The ghosts of Sacco and Vanzetti were surely taking an interest in Dirk Greineder's case because the two trials were eerily similar.

For one thing, both cases were primarily built around circumstantial evidence. And in both cases, it appeared the defendants were being tried for something other than murder. Although the prosecutor trying Sacco and Vanzetti assured the pair they would be tried for murder and "nothing else," their radical politics were still a focus of their trial. And it seemed Greineder was on trial as much for his sexual behavior as he was for murdering his wife.

The next witness for the prosecution was Wellesley police chief Terrence Cunningham.

Cunningham testified about finding the murder weapons and gloves worn by the murderer during searches at Morses Pond, as well as the evidence seized during searches of Greineder's home and cars. He told the jury that plastic bags, latex surgical gloves, and foil loaf pans found in Greineder's house were similar to the plastic Ziploc bags, latex gloves, and loaf pans found near May's body.

Like McDermott, Cunningham testified that the bloody towel Greineder said he and his wife shared to stop their nosebleeds, which had been turned over by the defense months after May's murder, was not the towel that was in Greineder's Toyota Avalon on November 1.

But the most damning testimony came when Cunningham said he found a pair of work gloves, identical to the ones found at Morses Pond, hidden in the doghouse in the backyard of Greineder's home. Cunningham said that while he was standing at the corner of the wooden doghouse, Kirsten Greineder told him that if he lifted up the lid of the doghouse, he could see inside it. He said when he lifted the lid, he saw something on a two-by-four board in the upper left-hand corner.

"It was dark at the time. I could see something and I used my flashlight to illuminate the object in the corner," Cunningham told the jury.

"And when you put your flashlight onto those objects, could you tell me what they were, sir?" Grundy asked.

"Yes, sir. They were a pair of brown cloth work gloves, with a textured palm and fingers."

Court was adjourned at 3:00 P.M. and reconvened at 9:00 A.M. on June 5.

While the jurors were being brought into the courtroom the next morning, the judge held a bench conference with the attorneys. The subject was two cash register receipts from F. Diehl & Son hardware store in Wellesley. The first, found in Greineder's garage, indicating that someone in the Greineder household had purchased nails at 8:58 A.M. on September 3, 1999. The other receipt, produced by Diehl's, indicated that two and a half minutes after the purchase of the nails, someone purchased and paid cash for a two-pound Estwing drilling hammer at the same cash register.

Murphy told the judge he had only learned that the receipts were going to be introduced as evidence the previous night and asked the judge to exclude the receipts, which he said were "damaging" to his client, because they were produced late. However, Murphy said if the court were not willing to do that, he asked for more time to go over other records and receipts from Diehl's. The judge decided rather than exclude the receipts, he would give Murphy more time to examine them.

After Cunningham concluded his testimony, Grundy called state police detective sergeant Martin Foley as his next witness.

Foley testified that after he viewed May Greineder's body, he went back to the circle area, where he saw Dirk Greineder. Foley said when he first saw the defendant, he observed that there were bloodstains on his jacket, white sneakers, and eyeglasses. However, he said Greineder's hands were clean, despite the fact that the defendant told him he twice checked his wife's carotid artery—once on the right side when he first found the body and once on the left side when he returned with police—to see if she had a pulse and also tried to pick her up once. Greineder's own testimony would contradict Foley's. Later, Greineder testified that he first tried to take his wife's pulse on the left side and saw blood, so then he tried to take it on the right side. He also said that he tried to pick his wife up three times—but he never said that to police at the scene.

Foley said he asked Greineder if he had washed his hands at anytime after discovering his wife's body and he said he hadn't. On cross-examination, Foley admitted that Greineder never said he touched his wife's neck, only that he went to check her pulse. He also said that police never tested Greineder's hands to check for the presence of blood.

Foley also told the jury Greineder's version of the events of that morning and described his conversation with the defendant. Foley testified that Greineder told him he didn't see the gaping wound on his wife's neck—he said he did notice a wound on her forehead—until he tried to check her carotid artery on the left side when he returned to the scene with police. Foley, though, said he was able to see the wound from fifty feet away. And during his direct-examination, Greineder would say that he saw his wife's neck wound when he first discovered her body.

Because May Greineder's pants were open from the waist and her shirt was pulled up around her chest, Foley felt she might have been the victim of a sexual assault. So he decided to ask Greineder whether he had sex with his wife that morning, the previous night, or anytime in the past week, in order to rule him out in the event police found semen samples on the victim.

"He said that he and his wife weren't sexually active for a few years. He said she had a bad back," Foley testified under direct examination. But during a search of Greineder's home on November 12, Foley said he found a cardboard box in the defendant's garage that contained the anti-impotence drug Viagra and a package of twelve condoms. Foley said Greineder had prescribed twelve Viagra pills for himself on June 12, 1999, but when he seized the evidence on November 12, several pills were missing. Although Grundy talked about Greineder's interest in prostitutes and pornography in his opening statement, this was first evidence of his secret sex life the jurors heard.

As Foley testified about their father's sexual dalliances, his children sort of slumped down in their seats, not wanting to hear this information about the dad they thought they knew.

During direct-examination, Foley also testified that after talking with Greineder for about five minutes, Greineder told him that he needed to get home to take care of his dog and that he was concerned about Zephyr, who was in the van.

Grundy was about to ask Foley about what happened when he took Greineder to the Wellesley police station, when the prosecutor asked for a sidebar. He wanted to talk to the judge about how much information Foley could give the jurors about Terry Segal, Greineder's neighbor and an attorney, whom Greineder called to meet him at the police station.

While Grundy wanted to be allowed to identify Segal as an attorney, not just a friend and neighbor, Murphy argued that, although a person has a right to an attorney, telling the jury he exercised that right was prejudicial. If the jury heard that Greineder immediately called an attorney, they might infer that he was guilty and felt he needed one.

Chernoff wasn't sure how prejudicial it would be to let the jury know that Segal was there as an attorney, as well as a neighbor, especially since Greineder actually hired Murphy several days later, before he was even charged with his wife's murder.

"I just wonder how much prejudice, if any, and maybe it just serves to really explain if it came out that an attorney/neighbor/friend came down, and part of what he did was give him a ride home and to be in his house," Chernoff said.

"Well, you know, I think that it all depends on the context from which it is coming. We object to any reference to him as an attorney in the context of this case," Murphy responded.

For his part, Grundy said the Commonwealth was going to elicit testimony that Greineder made several calls, one of which was to Terry Segal, who identified himself as a friend and an attorney.

"Your Honor, I object to any reference to Mr. Segal as an attorney," Murphy said again.

"But this is not an issue of the defendant invoking a right, a formal right, to counsel. In fact, one of the issues was whether or not he was ever advised of his Miranda rights, and he was not. So, this is not the defendant responding to the police saying okay, you can have a lawyer, or you cannot have a lawyer. It just seems to me this is just a happening. The defendant was given an opportunity to make some telephone calls. A friend/neighbor who was an attorney showed up, and his daughter showed up. The friend/neighbor/attorney gave him a ride home and was there when the police were there and was with him at the time he signed the consent form," Chernoff explained.

"What he is doing is exercising his right," Murphy responded. "Now the court has said that he should have been advised of his Miranda rights, so he is exercising a right that is clear that he had, even though he was not afforded it, which was a right to consult with an attorney. That right is now—I think the case law is clear that if the price of exercising your right is revealing that, you know, that you have exercised it, that is not much of a right at all."

Ultimately, Judge Chernoff decided to exclude, at that point at least, the fact that Segal was an attorney. He also decided to exclude the fact that Segal was Greineder's friend.

After the bench conference, Grundy continued questioning Foley about what happened once Greineder was brought to the police station.

Foley said that Greineder called Terry Segal, and when Segal arrived, he and Greineder signed a consent form allowing police to take his clothing and fingernail clippings. The consent form also gave police the right to look in Greineder's van and walk through his house. He also told the jury Greineder would not agree to turn over his eyeglasses to police at the station because he needed them to drive. But police photographed them at Greineder's home.

Foley also told the jury about finding the murder weapons and one glove in the storm drain near the circle at Morses Pond and the other glove in the storm drain in front of a house at the corner of Halsey Avenue and Turner Road. The storm drain was located diagonally across the street from the spot where the Greineders had parked their van on October 31.

Grundy asked Foley to describe the glove.

"The glove itself was a cotton glove. It was brown and had a knit collar up top. The palm area, the baby finger, the first finger, and the thumb were all covered with a plastic-type texture that had dots on it."

Like Chief Terrence Cunningham, Foley testified about finding the identical pair of gloves in the doghouse in Greineder's backyard during the November 12 search. Foley told the jury he went to twenty-five or thirty stores to try and find the same gloves, but the only place that sold them was Diehl's.

Foley talked about searching the Greineder home on November 1, looking for Dirk's eyeglasses, packaging and receipts for an Estwing hammer, packaging and receipts for an Old Timer knife, packaging and receipts for brown work gloves with textured palms, and the mate to the right-hand work glove that was found in the storm drain at Morses Pond. Foley said police confiscated Greineder's glasses, but the lenses had been cleaned. Foley testified that he saw what he initially thought was a $500,000 life insurance policy on the lives of Dirk and May Greineder dated October 29, 1999. He later discovered the document was only an application for a last-to-die policy that would have benefited the Greineder children after both parents had died. During direct-examination, Foley also told the jury about finding a receipt on Greineder's workbench for six packages of nails purchased from Diehl's on September 3, 1999

On cross-examination, Murphy scored some points when he asked Foley about his testimony at a hearing on July 18, 2000—testimony that contradicted the trial testimony of Detective McDermott. During the hearing, Foley said, "On November first, on the night of November first, an investigator from Wellesley, actually two investigators, looked into that car (the white Toyota Avalon) and there was a towel, a white towel, in that car that appeared to have bloodstains on it." McDermott had testified that the towel she saw that night had stains on it, but none of those stains was blood.

With that, court adjourned for the day, to reconvene at 9:00 A.M. on June 6.

In his cross-examination of Foley the next day, Murphy implied that the state police trooper didn't really have all that much experience investigating homicide cases at the time of May Greineder's murder. Foley admitted that the first homicide he investigated was in January 1999 and that he had had only a one-week homicide-training course. Through his questioning of Foley, Murphy also tried to show the jury that from the beginning police concluded that Greineder was guilty, and then conducted their investigation based on a conclusion that was premature.

After Foley's testimony was completed, Grundy called Richard Iwanicki, a chemist from the Massachusetts State Police Crime Lab. Iwanicki had searched Greineder's Toyota Avalon and found bloodstains on the passenger seat cushion and the center console. Iwanicki told the jury that he found white towels in the trunk of the Avalon that were stained with a tan substance, but it tested negative for the presence of blood. When Grundy showed Iwanicki the bloodstained white towel from the Ritz-Carlton that Greineder said he and his wife used for their nosebleeds, Iwanicki said he didn't recognize it.

After lunch, the prosecution called Dr. Robin Cotton of Cellmark Diagnostics, in Maryland, to the stand. Cotton, who also testified in the O.J. Simpson case, told the jurors that Dirk Greineder's DNA was found on the knife used to kill his wife. She said only one in 2,200 white males would match the DNA sample found on the knife and one in 680,000 would match the DNA sample taken from the bloody left-hand glove recovered in the storm drain near Greineder's van. Cotton, who testified over three days, said that, depending how good the sample was, Cellmark's DNA testing could examine up to thirteen different locations on the chromosome, or genetic code, of a sample. She said each location is assigned a number designation depending on its character, and those numbers are then compared to the values found in other samples.

Cotton said Greineder's DNA on the left-hand glove matched seven of nine test points. She told the jury that while May was the primary source of DNA on the knife—her DNA matched eight of nine determining points—Greineder couldn't be excluded as the secondary source of DNA. She said his DNA matched four of the nine characteristics of the DNA on the knife.

"The data from the knife indicates that there is a primary source and a secondary source and that the primary source is from a female and the secondary source is from a male," Cotton said.

In addition, Cotton testified that Greineder's DNA matched eight of the thirteen locations in the genetic code of the sample from the right-hand glove found with the murder weapons. She told the jury only one in 170 million white males could match that DNA profile.

Cotton, who testified over three days using numerous charts and graphs, said the only other DNA found on the right-hand glove belonged to May Greineder.

"The primary profile of that sample matches the types of Mabel Greineder," Cotton told the jury. "With regard to the secondary source, using eight out of the thirteen loci (locations), Dr. Greineder cannot be excluded as the secondary source."

The jury also heard that DNA tests did not identify any of May's blood on her husband's fingernail clippings, bolstering the prosecution's theory that Greineder wore gloves when he stabbed and bludgeoned his wife to death. Cotton told the jurors that May's DNA matched blood found on Greineder's shirt and the red backpack he was wearing, Zephyr's leash, and a Ziploc bag found near her body.

But Murphy scored some points on cross-examination. His theory that an unknown person murdered May was reinforced when Cotton testified that DNA found on May Greineder's left-hand blue fleece glove did not match either May or Dirk Greineder.

Murphy asked Cotton if the sample that came from May Greineder's left-hand blue fleece glove revealed the presence of DNA of at least three people.

Cotton responded yes.

"It couldn't have come from Dr. Greineder; is that correct?" Murphy asked.

"That's right," she said.

"It couldn't have come from Mrs. Greineder?"

"That's right."

Murphy also questioned Cotton about the fact that Cellmark had changed its standard for recording its results in the middle of testing the materials in the Greineder case. He argued that Cellmark would have had different results if it had used the same standards as the FBI, which used a higher threshold for positive tests of genetic material than Cellmark.

Murphy asked Cotton whether the test results would have been different if the sample from the left-hand brown work glove had been sent to the FBI rather than Cellmark.

"They wouldn't have gotten anything," Cotton replied.

Chapter 14

Court reconvened at 8:30 A.M., Monday, June 11.

The prosecution's first witness of the day was May's only sister, Ilse Stark.

From the stand, Stark, a petite woman with short auburn hair, tried to help the jurors understand a little bit about her younger sister. Since childhood, the two Chegwin sisters had been close, she testified. Wearing a black-and-white sleeveless dress and pearls, Stark looked straight at the jury during her testimony.

"My sister happened to be my best friend, as well as my sister, which is not always guaranteed with siblings," she told the jury.

Stark said their relationship continued and evolved as they grew older. She said they even went to New York's Hunter College together. She said May was also particularly close to Belinda, Stark's daughter, who was born while May was finishing college.

The last time Stark saw her sister was on September 22, when May had visited her at her home in Manhattan and the two shared the same bed, something they hadn't done since they were children.

Grundy then asked Stark about the relationship between May and Dirk.

"It was a relationship that I thought was very strong, although it struck me as being a different type of relationship," she said. "I would say I was much more independent and, because of that independent nature, I found that as good as I thought their relationship was, it was really different to me because they never did anything individually."

Stark said that if May needed to buy a wastepaper basket, she had to go with Dirk to pick it out.

"Whenever decisions were made for the house, no matter how major or minor—or in their life—it was something that had to be done with Dirk," Stark said.

To back up this statement, Stark told the jury that during her last visit to New York, May was horrified that her sister would purchase a couch without asking her husband for his approval. That testimony played right into the assertion Grundy made in his opening statement—that Dirk Greineder was a very controlling person.

Stark told the jury that in the past Dirk Greineder made time to visit May's family, but in the four years before he was indicted for her murder, Greineder "was not available." Nor, she said, did he visit when May's mother was dying of pancreatic cancer. She passed away in January 1999.

Stark testified that she often gave her sister money for various reasons, including air fare for May's children and to help her purchase a television and a car. Stark also gave May money for a face-lift. And Stark and her daughter gave May money so she could fly to New York to help care for her mother, rather than take the train.

Stark said the last time she talked with her sister was the Friday before she was murdered and her sister seemed "very stressed." The next time she heard from the Greineder family was on Sunday, October 31, 1999, the day her sister was murdered. Stark explained that

Britt called to tell her about May's death, but Dirk Greineder never called her. Stark said when she arrived in Wellesley the day after her sister was killed, she spoke to her brother-in-law, who told her about what happened at Morses Pond—how he left his wife to walk the dog after May hurt her back, and when he went back to meet her, he found May lying on the ground.

"He said she was still warm, so he took her pulse, and then he saw that somebody had, and I believe the word he used was 'slit' her neck, and that he jumped up and saw a jogger, started after the jogger; and in chasing the jogger, he saw a man with a small dog and asked him if he had a cell phone," she testified.

"And in the years that you knew the defendant, did you ever have any knowledge as to whether or not he carried a cell phone?" Grundy asked.

"Always," Stark responded.

Grundy's point was clear—was it just a coincidence Greineder didn't have his cell phone with him the day his wife was murdered?

Stark told the jury the first disagreement she ever had with her sister's husband was when he refused to let her go to the medical examiner's office to identify May's body.

"He insisted that Belinda go," Stark said. "He was adamantly opposed to [me going], as he was to his children going. Finally my husband said, 'You know, she's going.'"

Ultimately, Stark said, she and her husband and Belinda went to view the body and fill out the necessary papers.

She told the jurors that when they returned, Dirk told them about the simultaneous nosebleeds he and May had before they went to Morses Pond and that they used the same towel to clean up. She testified that he said when he and May got to the pond, they were both throwing a spongy ball for the dog.

"I said to him, 'I don't understand what this is all about.' And he said to me, 'It's very possible that there is DNA from the dog and myself that could be on the glove because May had—if May had defended herself, you know, you'd turn around and you'd do this"—Stark demonstrated for the jury by putting her hand up almost like a high five—"and somebody's coming at you—that there could have been the trans-ference of the DNA in that fashion.' He then indicated—went through the story of what he had told me the day before and felt that at that point—may I say what he told me, or is that . . ."

Immediately after Stark made that statement, Mur-phy asked the judge for a sidebar to discuss the information he thought Stark was about to give the jury.

Grundy explained that he thought Stark was going to talk about the fact that Greineder told her he was going to have a second autopsy done on his wife, which Grundy wanted entered into testimony.

"That conversation goes into his discussions of that with an attorney, which I would not offer. This leads to a delay in the funeral. Before they go [back to New York], they have a memorial service at the church. . . . They come back from that. The defendant sits down with this witness and says that he needs to—where he would like to borrow money from her. He could need up to half a million dollars for attorneys, investigators, experts, bail, etc. The conversation then goes into what I had previously indicated about 'The police are bas-tards. The police have it in for me,' something along those lines," Grundy said.

"Counsel," Judge Chernoff said, addressing Murphy.

"There are several layers of objection to this. The first is that all these statements, the statements about the second autopsy, the statements about obtaining counsel, asking to borrow money for counsel, were the subject of a prior motion *in limine* that this court addressed in a written order that is dated May 21, 2000."

Murphy said prosecutors had agreed to submit to the court, in written form, the defendant's statements they planned to offer at trial, at which time the judge would then decide whether the particular statements could be admitted. But, Murphy said, prosecutors had not, to his knowledge, submitted those statements to the court.

He objected to any mention of how much money his client thought the trial might cost, because it was prejudicial and had no relevance to the case whatsoever. Murphy opposed the introduction of any statements relating to a second autopsy and the fact that it delayed the funeral, because none of that was relevant.

"What has happened here, I would suggest, is very clear, which is that the Commonwealth is essentially sending the message to this jury that the defendant was not only prepared to cut his wife up the first time out at Morses Pond, but then he was prepared to pay to have somebody else do it again. That's incredibly prejudicial. It has no relevance," Murphy told the judge.

But that wasn't the reason the prosecutor wanted to introduce evidence of the second autopsy. The real reason would come out later in a sidebar during Grundy's cross-examination of Greineder.

After listening to both attorneys, Chernoff decided to let Grundy ask two leading questions. The first: "After talking to the defendant, did you learn that the funeral was going to be delayed because there was a second autopsy?" However, Chernoff did not allow Grundy to say who had ordered the second autopsy.

"I think that is relevant because the jury knows that the time issues are that she was here and she went back home and then she came back for a funeral, and it seems to me the funeral was pretty late," Chernoff said. "I think an explanation to the jury that there was a second autopsy is not irrelevant, but I wouldn't make attribution to the defendant."

Chernoff told Grundy he could also ask Stark a second leading question: "Did the defendant ask to borrow a sum of money from you?"

"Because he is going to hire a lawyer or investigators, I wouldn't let that in at this juncture," the judge said. "That may come in at a later point depending on what gets opened up in this case. If he then made statements that he thought the police were targeting him, I think that's fair game."

Murphy objected again for the record, adding that if Grundy were allowed to ask a leading question, he wanted him to say that Greineder wanted the money for legal expenses.

The judge agreed, saying Grundy could add the fact that Greineder was asking Stark for the money to cover legal expenses.

Then Grundy continued questioning Stark.

"Now, again, Ms. Stark, referring to that Tuesday afternoon after you had been to the medical examiner's office, and you were having a conversation in the living room, did the defendant also state at that time that there was going to be a second autopsy done? Just yes or no."

"No."

"And was there a conversation following that indicated that was a consideration, to have a second autopsy?"

"Yes."

"Now, you indicated that there was a memorial service for your sister as well; is that correct?"

"Yes."

"And was that Wednesday, that next day?"

"Wednesday, November third."

Grundy then asked her about a private conversation she had with Greineder at his home after the memorial service.

"And Ms. Stark . . . just yes or no, did the defendant inquire of you to borrow a certain sum of money?"

"Yes."

"Following that conversation regarding the borrowing of money, what, if anything, did he state to you with respect to the investigation into the murder of your sister, or the police?"

"He stated that they were bastards and that the reason that they were after him was because they didn't go after anybody else, and they had to show—they had to come up with somebody to solve this crime and that there had been similar crimes in the area," Stark told the jury.

"Could you describe how he came across to you during that conversation?"

"Extremely agitated and nervous."

"Do you recall after leaving that Thursday when you next heard from the defendant?"

"I didn't."

"And then there was the funeral service; is that correct?"

"As I said, we returned on Sunday and the funeral services were that Monday."

Stark said after not hearing from Greineder for a month, she called him to see how he was doing.

"I knew he was going to Europe and I wanted to re-iterate our New Year's plans. My sister and I had plans for the New Year, for them to come into New York and we would spend it together as a family and look at the fireworks that were for the year 2000. So I just wanted to tell him that everybody was still welcome," she said.

"And prior to that conversation, had you had the opportunity to speak with investigators involved in in-vestigating the death of May?"

"Yes, as a matter of fact, I told him during that con-versation that a Sergeant Foley and a Jill—I believe it was McDermott—had come by to speak to us. And Dirk said, 'You think they're your friends.' I said, 'No, I don't think they're my friends. I don't need any friends,' I said. 'I think that they're trying to do—they're the advocates for my sister.' He said, 'Well, they're not as nice as you think they are.' So I basi-cally went over what I thought were very simple questions they had asked, and he got rather agitated, so I just let it go at that."

Stark tried to tell the jury that in April she discov-ered that the Greineders had not picked up May's ashes, which were still in a storage closet at the New-ton Cemetery. She also tried to testify that she ultimately paid $2,500 for her sister's ashes, which were finally laid to rest with other deceased members of the Chegwin family in Queens, New York. But be-cause of a flurry of objections from Murphy, that testimony was not allowed in as evidence.

During cross-examination, Stark testified that Greineder told her that something bad and/or ugly was going to come up during the investigation into May's death. She said she told Greineder that she would be pounding the police's doors down to find out what they were doing to look for somebody else who might have murdered her sister.

At a sidebar after Murphy's cross-examination, Grundy tried to convince the judge to allow Stark to testify that she paid for her sister's ashes and put them in her family tomb in New York. Grundy believed the jury should hear that testimony so they could draw their own conclusions about its meaning. But on redirect, Stark was only able to tell the jury the ashes finally came to rest in Queens but not that she paid to collect them from the cemetery.

Britt Greineder, wearing a short flowered sundress—Britt often wore clothes more suited to a Boston nightspot than a Norfolk County courthouse—sobbed throughout her aunt's testimony. Colin, on the other hand, sat with his fists tightly clenched.

The next witness, Elizabeth Fisher, a crime lab technician for the Massachusetts State Police, testified that she found cotton fibers in Dirk Greineder's fingernail scrapings that were similar to the fibers found on the inside of the brown work gloves worn by May Greineder's murderer. But under Murphy's cross-examination, she conceded that cotton fibers were the most common in the world. She also admitted that she wasn't able to establish scientifically that Dirk Greineder was the person who wore the murderer's gloves. Fisher told the jury she didn't find any of Dirk's DNA under May's fingernails.

During cross-examination, Fisher testified that she examined dog hairs found on the exterior of the right-hand brown work glove worn by the murderer. Through his questioning of this witness, Murphy implied that the dog hair found on the glove could have been transferred from May's clothing while she was being murdered. The jury, however, never got to hear about the dog hair that was found *inside* one of the gloves.

Trooper Diane Lilly of the Massachusetts State Police told the jury she searched Greineder's van at the crime scene. She identified his backpack and its contents, including three balls, yellow rubber gloves, and dog leashes, which were all marked into evidence as exhibits. During direct examination, Grundy asked Lilly to identify the hammer used to bludgeon May Greineder, which he had put in the backpack before trial but was not there when she searched it at the crime scene. Grundy wanted to show that Greineder could have put the hammer in the backpack after he murdered his wife and then disposed of it in the storm drain on the paved pathway. That would explain why William Kear didn't see anything in Greineder's hands when Greineder walked quickly from the dirt path, where his wife's body was found, to the paved path, where the murder weapons and one glove were found.

Later that day, Grundy called Wellesley police officer Christopher Fritts to the stand. Fritts testified that he was assigned to watch the gate at Morses Pond from 4:00 P.M., November 1, to 1:00 A.M,. November 2. He told the jury during that time he did not see anyone put a brown work glove in the storm drain, where the murderer's left-hand glove was found.

Beth Murphy, the treasurer of F. Diehl & Son hardware store in Wellesley, testified that from January 1, 1999, to November 1, 1999, the store sold only four 2-pound Estwing drilling hammers, including one in September. There were none sold in October. Beth Murphy testified that the purchase of the hammer was made immediately after someone from the Greineder household purchased some nails on September 3, 1999. The nails were purchased at 8:55:38 A.M., and the $31.49 hammer was purchased at 8:58:05 at the same cash register and rung up by the same cashier. However, no one could say for sure Greineder was the person who made both purchases.

The last witness called by the prosecution before court adjourned for the day was Belinda Markel, Ilse Stark's daughter.

Markel told the jury that, at the time of her aunt's illness, May seemed "somewhat lonely." She said May and Dirk were spending more time apart because he was working longer hours and traveling more because he had a new job. She explained that several years before her grandmother died in January 1999, May had lost some weight and started dressing more nicely and even had a face-lift.

The day after her aunt's death, Markel said, her uncle took her into his office and told her that he and May had had intercourse the morning she was murdered, but he said that was okay, because they were married.

"I said, 'Right.' I was shocked because I had never really had that kind of conversation with him, and then he went on to tell me what happened in the park, that May had been hit in the head and her throat had been cut," Markel said.

"And did he tell you at that point in time whether or not she had been hit in the head once or more than once in the head?" Grundy asked her during direct examination.

"I believe he said multiple times."

"And did he give you any indication at that time how it was he came to believe that she had been hit in the head multiple times?"

"No."

Markel said that rather than grieving for his wife, her uncle seemed more interested in explaining how his DNA might be on the murder weapons and how fibers like those from the gloves the murderer wore could be on his pants.

"He said he was concerned that the pants that he had been wearing [and] the police kept might have fibers of gloves. He said he may have had gloves like that at some point and the fibers would be on his hands. I said that it was ridiculous because May would have washed those pants a million times between the time he had the gloves and then, so not to worry about it at that point."

"And did he indicate to you at that point in time why he had that concern or what he knew about any gloves?"

"Yes. He told me that they had searched the house the night before and they were looking for a glove, a hammer, and a knife."

"And when he told you that he may have had gloves like that, did he describe to you the gloves?"

"He didn't. He just said he may have had work gloves like that sometime before."

Markel went on to say that Greineder told her about the towel he and May shared to stop their nose-bleeds, because he was concerned that his blood and mucus were on the tissue that May had been holding and his DNA could have been transferred to the killer if May touched him.

At this point, Chernoff dismissed the jurors for the day so Grundy and Murphy could question Markel outside their presence. The subject: the second autopsy that was briefly introduced through Ilse's testimony.

During questioning by Grundy, Markel said on the morning of May's memorial service, Wednesday, November 3, Greineder called her at her hotel and told her he had been going through May's things. When he found her dilator, he realized he would have to have a second autopsy done. Greineder told her he was going to call Murphy to see if he could arrange it. However, Greineder never told his niece the exact reason for a second autopsy.

"I was planning on staying up in Wellesley until the funeral would take place. The memorial service was on Wednesday, and I'm assuming [the funeral] would be Thursday or Friday. By Thursday, when he decided they were going to do the second autopsy and that would delay the funeral, that's why I went home later on Thursday," Markel said. "Dirk called me on Saturday and told me that the second autopsy had taken place and that we would be able to have her funeral on Monday, so I drove back up on Sunday."

After giving her testimony before the judge and the attorneys, Markel left the courtroom. At that point, Grundy began arguing the relevance of allowing the jury to hear Markel's testimony about the second autopsy.

"We're speaking that within less than four days of this homicide where the defense has put out—and part of their defense is that the police were rushing to judgment, that they had targeted this individual, and that the Commonwealth's response to that is that the defendant acted defensively, at best. He contacts a cousin—excuse me, a niece, a very close relative of the deceased, and tells her that there will be a second autopsy because he has gone through May's things and found a dilator. I would suggest to Your Honor that that in no way leads to any reasonable knowledge or in-

ference as to why they now want a second autopsy [on]
an individual who this defendant had alleged to her
family members was killed by a stranger in a park,
where we have heard he has had conversations, where
he did not believe her to be sexually assaulted, that the
home or any of May's belongings were in no way involved in that crime, and that his finding of a dilator
would lead to the need to a secondary autopsy as opposed to a different need or desire as viewed by the
defendant to have that second autopsy. I would suggest
to Your Honor that it is extremely relevant as to his
state of mind at that time, not only in pursuing that avenue, but in telling the niece of the victim that it was
due to the finding of a dilator," Grundy argued.

Murphy saw things differently. He argued that the
message the prosecution wanted to send to jury members would definitely prejudice them against his client.

"I would suggest to the court that the reason, frankly,
that the Commonwealth wants to offer it is because as
they offered testimony with respect to the ultimate des-
tination of Mrs. Greineder's remains, you know, they
are essentially trying to suggest through this evidence
that the defendant was insensitive and capable of in-
flicting injury on his wife, even after she was dead."

Murphy explained that if Markel were allowed to
testify about the second autopsy, Greineder would be
forced to take the stand to explain why he decided—
with his lawyer's assistance—to have a second autopsy
done on his wife.

"[This] essentially, you know, puts the defendant in
a situation where it affects his decision making as to
whether he has to take the stand or not," Murphy said.

For Grundy, the issue was about Greineder's state
of mind.

"What this is about is this defendant stating the

May Greineder. *(Court file photo)*

An aerial view of Morses Pond taken on October 31, 1999, the day May Greineder was murdered. *(Court file photo)*

The Greineder's dog, Zephyr. *(Court file photo)*

May Greineder's blue fleece glove next to a pool of her blood.
(Court file photo)

May Greineder's body in the pathway at Morses Pond.
(Court file photo)

The murder weapons and the right-hand work glove in the storm drain on the paved path at Morses Pond. *(Court file photo)*

Right-hand work glove and bloody hammer in a storm drain at Morses Pond. *(Court file photo)*

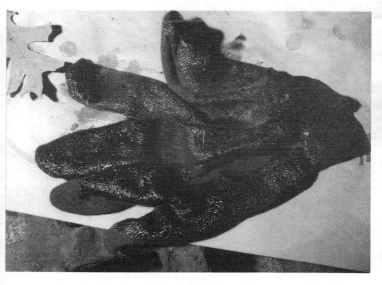

Bloody right-hand work glove found in the storm drain with the murder weapons. *(Court file photo)*

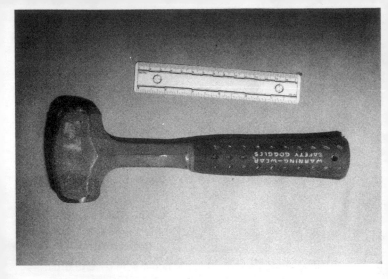

The bloody hammer used to bludgeon May Greineder.
(Court file photo)

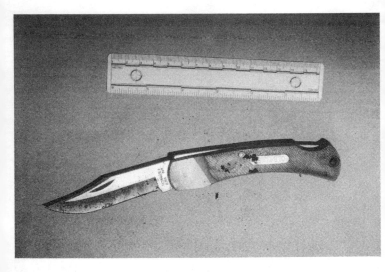

The bloody knife used to slash May Greineder's throat.
(Court file photo)

Dirk Greineder at the Wellesley Police Station the day his wife was bludgeoned and stabbed to death.
(Court file photos)

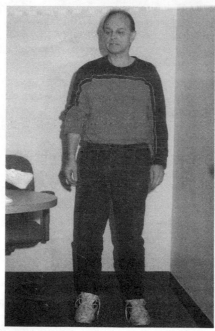

Dirk Greineder being photographed at the Wellesley Police Station the day his wife was brutally murdered. *(Court file photo)*

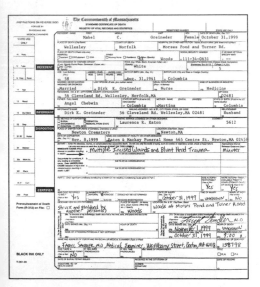

May Greineder's death certificate listing her death as multiple incised wounds and blunt head trauma. *(Court file photo)*

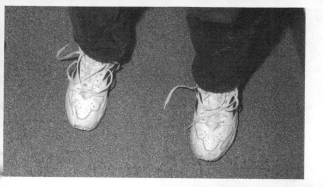

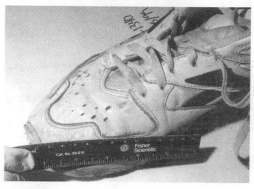

Dirk Greineder's bloody sneakers photographed at the Wellesley Police Station. *(Court file photos)*

A heel print from the Morses Pond crime scene. *(Court file photo)*

The bottom of the Reebok sneaker Dirk Greineder was wearing the day his wife was murdered. *(Court file photo)*

Blood on the left sleeve of Dirk Greineder's yellow and white windbreaker. (Court file photo)

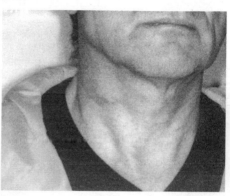

Police photographed scratches on Dirk Greineder's neck the day his wife was murdered. (Court file photo)

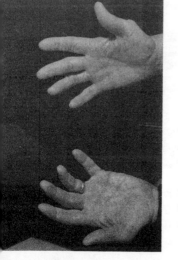

Dirk Greineder's hands, which had no blood on them even though he claimed he touched his wife's bloody body several times. (Court file photo)

Dirk Greineder's eyeglasses with blood smear and spatter on the left lens. Police photographed the glasses at the Greineder residence. *(Court file photo)*

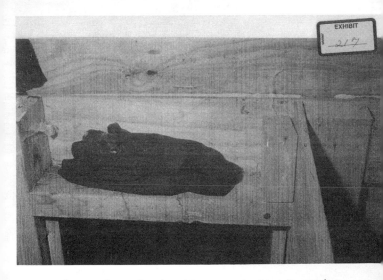

Gloves, identical to the gloves worn by May Greineder's murderer, were found in the doghouse in the backyard of Greineder's home. *(Court file photo)*

The home computer Dirk Greineder used to access pornography on the Internet. *(Court file photo)*

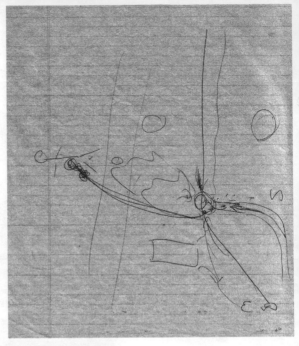

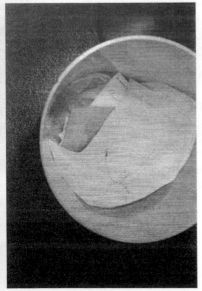

The hand-drawn map
police found in a trash can
at the Greineder home on
November 12, 1999.
(Court file photos)

Superior Court Judge Paul Chernoff questions Wellesley resident
Richard Acheson during the trial of Dirk Greineder.
(Courtesy of Associated Press)

Wellesley Police Chief Terrence Cunningham testifying at the
murder trial of Dirk Greineder. *(Courtesy of Terrence Cunningham)*

Prosecutor Rick Grundy showed the jury the photos of Dirk Greineder's clean hands during his closing arguments. (Courtesy of Associated Press)

Dirk Greineder, center, behind his attorney Martin Murphy, carrying a box, is escorted down the stairs of the Norfolk Superior Courthouse in Dedham, Massachusetts. (Courtesy of Associated Press)

words to Belinda Markel: 'I was going through May's things. I found her dilator. Now we need to have a second autopsy.' Whether or not there is, Your Honor, that statement is extremely probative of the defendant's state of mind in a sense. There is no evidence in this case that that would in any way trigger a rational individual to conduct a second autopsy, so, therefore, a reasonable inference is, is that he made these statements to Ms. Markel to have her believe for some reason that this second autopsy is necessary—that there has been some kind of sexual assault on his wife and that there is some kind of sexual overtones to this homicide. That is where the probative value comes from," Grundy told Chernoff.

But later, in a sidebar held during the defendant's testimony, Grundy would explain the real reason the prosecution believed Greineder wanted to have a second autopsy done.

During this sidebar, Chernoff said the issue was one of truthfulness.

"I suppose it's a matter of just simply that this witness says that the defendant made a statement that he found something, and it's a question of indeed whether or not he had found something. There had been searches, two searches of the premises, one a fairly detailed search because it was done pursuant to a warrant to the court. So, it seems to me that may be the threshold relevancy issue as to whether or not he said something which, in fact, was not true, that something had been found, or something existed which, in fact, did not exist."

Chernoff ultimately ruled that Grundy could bring out two things through Markel's testimony: first, that Greineder told her he was going through May's personal belongings and found her dilator; and second, that the funeral was going to be delayed because he was going to have a second autopsy conducted on his wife.

However, Grundy was not allowed to make any connection between Greineder's finding the dilator and deciding to have a second autopsy. And Chernoff ruled that the prosecution couldn't infer that the dilator was a sexual device.

Court recessed at 4:15 P.M. and was reconvened on June 12 at 8:15 A.M.

Chapter 15

When court resumed the next morning, Markel once again took the stand.

Through her testimony, the jury learned that the day after his wife's brutal murder, Greineder was worried that red marks he had on his neck from shaving, a scratch on his chest, and three or four small round bruises on the inside of his left bicep would show up on the photographs police took of him when they brought him back to the police station that Halloween morning in 1999.

Grundy now asked Markel about the dilator, the need for a second autopsy, and the reason May's funeral was postponed.

"And at some point did you receive a call from the defendant with respect to [the] funeral service being postponed?"

"I did."

"And do you recall at that time if the defendant stated to you something he had located and something he was going to do with respect to what he found that would cause a postponement in the funeral service?"

Murphy jumped up to object. It appeared Grundy was going down a road the judge had asked him to steer clear of.

"I'm going to sustain that objection."

"Well, if Your Honor would allow me to ask a leading question."

"Surely. Sure."

"Ms. Markel, did you receive a phone call from the defendant where he indicated to you that he had been going through some of May's things?"

"I did."

"And specifically that he had found her dilator?"

"Yes."

"And that, therefore, there would be—"

"Objection," Murphy said.

"No, no, sustained."

"Did he indicate at that point what he was going to do, if anything, due to the fact that he had found her dilator?" Grundy asked.

Once again, Murphy objected.

"No, the objection is sustained."

A bit confused, Grundy asked if the attorneys could approach the sidebar and Chernoff said yes.

"I realize that counsel has not had too much time to—" Chernoff began.

"Maybe I got it wrong, so I apologize," Grundy said.

"I was looking for questions that did not tie in any connection between the two. It seems to me you have already got both things out and I wouldn't allow the connection unless defense counsel opens it up with an issue of retaining counsel or having retained counsel and making arrangements for the second autopsy," Chernoff explained.

The judge explained to Grundy that he could ask Markel if Greineder told her he found May's dilator. He could also ask her if Greineder told her May's funeral was going to be postponed because he was having a second autopsy done. What Grundy couldn't do was connect the dilator and the second autopsy or make reference to the dilator as a sexual tool.

After the sidebar, Grundy did ask Markel those two questions. Her response was that her uncle told her he found May's dilator and he told her May's funeral would be delayed because of the second autopsy.

After the morning recess, the jury heard from Philip Boucher, a distributor for Norman Libretts, an importer of hardware products based in New Rochelle, New York. Boucher testified that the murderer's gloves found at Morses Pond were the same make and brand as the gloves found in the doghouse in Greineder's backyard. He told the jury that the only stores in Massachusetts, other than Diehl's, that he sold that type of glove to were in Southwick, just west of Springfield, and Great Barrington. Boucher said he did not know if similar gloves, which were made in China, were sold to other companies.

Grundy's next witness was Sandra Koch, a trace evidence examiner at the FBI laboratory in Washington, DC. Koch said the fibers found under Greineder's fingernails were consistent with the work gloves found at the scene and in the doghouse. However, she testified she could not link those fibers to the gloves Sergeant Foley purchased at Diehl's, because the dye lots were different.

After lunch, the prosecution called Trevor Williams, general manager of the Boston Sports Club in Wellesley, who told the jury that Greineder froze his membership the day before his wife's murder. Although Greineder initially requested to freeze it from November 1, 1999, to February 1, 2000, he reactivated it on November 15.

Next, Mohan Jital, custodian of records for American Express, testified that on July 8, 1998, Dirk Greineder applied for a corporate American Express card for a business called Corporate Physicians. According to the application, the company had been in existence for ten years and had three employees. (Greineder would later testify that it was a bogus corporation.) Jital said Greineder applied for a card for himself and for Thomas Young. American Express records indicated that there was a charge to Young's card on October 24, 1999, for the People2People online dating service and a charge on October 25, 1999, for another Internet site.

After Jital, Grundy's next witness was Greineder's former college roommate, Thomas Young, an attorney who lived in Maryland. Young first met Greineder in 1958, when they were freshmen at Yale University. Just classmates at first, Greineder and Young and three other classmates shared a suite of rooms in their sophomore year. When they graduated from Yale in 1962, the two went their separate ways and didn't see each other again for some seven or eight years when Greineder moved to the Baltimore area to work at the National Institutes of Health.

"When he was there, one Christmas, he called me and said, 'I'm in the area. Come to a Christmas party,' and so I did," Young testified. "I never saw Dirk again, although I have this vague recollection of exchanging Christmas cards from time to time."

Young told the jury he was never associated with Corporate Physicians and didn't know anything about Greineder using his name until Foley contacted him in March 2000.

Verizon employee Robert Maguire identified two telephone numbers Greineder called during his stay at the Sheraton Hotel in Mahwah, New Jersey—an escort service and an Internet service provider. Then

Alan Fellerman, the Sheraton controller, told the jury Greineder logged onto the Internet and purchased an adult movie for $16.95 from his room.

The last witness of the day was Robert Markwarth, the custodian of records for Fleet Bank. Markwarth said that on October 23, 1999, while staying at the Sheraton, Greineder made four withdrawals for $100 each (plus a $1 fee for each transaction). Greineder was in New Jersey to attend a meeting of the Immunology Research Institute of New England.

Deborah Doolio and Harry Page, two of the witnesses called by the prosecution the next day, June 13, testified under Judge Chernoff's order that their faces not be published in newspapers or broadcast on television. The pair was to give testimony about the defendant's sexual proclivities. Doolio ran an escort service, and Page and his wife liked to have sex with people they met on the Internet.

In Doolio's case, Chernoff made his ruling to protect her safety and the safety of her thirteen-year-old daughter. In a hearing before the judge but not the jury, Doolio said she and her daughter were in danger from two men who had physically and sexually assaulted her. She didn't want those men to find her.

In the hearing, Page, who lived in East Bridgewater, Massachusetts, told the judge his children would be psychologically harmed if people in the community knew what kind of lifestyle he and his wife were leading. In addition, he said his wife would become an outcast in her close-knit Armenian family.

Although Chernoff was less persuaded by Page's arguments, his ruling covered both witnesses.

Before Grundy called either Doolio or Page, he called Denise Parri, who worked for the Marilyn Escort Service in Brooklyn, New York. Parri confirmed that her agency sent a prostitute named Nora Lopez to Greineder's hotel room while he was staying at the Sheraton in Mahwah, New Jersey, in October 1999. Grundy and Murphy stipulated that Greineder and Lopez had sex for money, so Lopez would not be required to testify.

Doolio was the state's next witness. She told the jury Greineder responded to an advertisement she placed in the *Boston Phoenix* newspaper for her escort service, Casual Elegance. Greineder called and she met him for sex at the Dedham Hilton on June 2, 1999. She said he called her the next day and then several times in September to try and arrange another meeting. That meeting never happened because Greineder couldn't seem to decide if he really wanted to do it.

"I told the gentleman that he was indecisive and I felt confused and I told him that maybe seeing an escort wasn't to the best—the best thing to do for him until he found some peace within himself, but I would be available if he needed me or desired to see me at a future time. I remember receiving a phone call [in September]. The gentleman told me not to call again because it was not the right time. 'Now wasn't the right time,'" Doolio told the jury.

Doolio said she never talked to Greineder again.

After Doolio's testimony, Judge Chernoff instructed the members of the jury that even though they had heard about other illegal acts Greineder committed, they were not to take the commission of those acts as a substitute for proof that he committed murder. Nor were they to consider it proof that the defendant had a criminal personality or bad character. They were, however, able to consider that evidence solely on the limited issue of motive and give it the weight they felt it deserved.

The next witness, Margaret Desario, an employee of Verizon Wireless, testified that Greineder made two calls to Deborah Doolio's cell phone number— one at 4:55 P.M. on October 30, 1999, which lasted two minutes, the day before his wife's murder, and one at 10:37 A.M. on November 1, which lasted one minute, the day after his wife was killed.

Grundy's next witness, Luis Rosado, testified that while he was renovating the Greineders' bathroom on October 29, he overheard Dirk ask May if she used his computer. She said she hadn't. Greineder asked his wife that question shortly after he helped her unfreeze her computer.

Although Grundy couldn't definitively prove that May knew about her husband's use of the Internet for sex, he wanted to suggest to the jury that she might have stumbled onto his online activities if she used his computer without his knowledge.

Rosado also recalled that May Greineder burst out crying when he told her that he couldn't complete the job that day because he had the wrong set of hinges for the door to the walk-in shower.

State police trooper David McSweeney, a computer forensics specialist, testified that he examined May's computer and determined it wasn't working. He said when he examined Dirk Greineder's computer, he found two files that contained May's term paper on asthma. The document was last saved on October 31, 1999, at 12:12:12 A.M. On cross-examination, Mc-Sweeney identified various footnotes that were part of the document. Greineder would later testify that he was helping May document her source material shortly after midnight on October 31.

Cathy McGoff, the compliance manager for Yahoo! Inc., said in the week before the murder of May

Greineder, a person named T. Young set up the
e-mail address of *cosmic_jockey,* listing an alternate e-
mail of *dirk@greineder.org.* Thomas Young also applied
for another Yahoo! mail account using the screen
name casualguy2000.

Bob Gifford, who operated the Florida-based Internet porn site, Ultimate Live, testified Thomas
Young, from Wellesley, Massachusetts, purchased a
membership to the site on October 24, 1999. His user
ID was *pussyryder@yahoo.com.* Young canceled the subscription on November 10.

Under cross-examination, Gifford said up to 35,000
people a day visited the Web site, which was launched
in 1995, although not all of them joined as members.

"And the number of members you have had over
those past six years, it's in the thousands?" Murphy
asked.

"Yes, sir, it's fair to say it's in the thousands," Gifford
said.

"And it's fair to say, sir, that this is the first time that
you have been called out of state to testify in a murder
trial?"

"Yes, sir."

Peter Brennan, the keeper of the records for the online dating service People2People, said that Thomas
Young joined the service on October 24, 1999, with an
American Express corporate credit card—the card
that Greineder had applied for in Young's name. Brennan testified that Young used the e-mail address of
casualguy2000@yahoo.com. He said Young was looking
to meet a Caucasian woman thirty-five to sixty years
old, slim to a few pounds overweight, who lived within
thirty miles of Boston.

People2People member Katherine Irwin told the
jurors she communicated with casualguy2000, or

Greineder, on October 25, 1999, using the screen name bckallykat. He told her he was looking for "mutual petting and more." Another member of the online dating service, Joanne Nichols, whose screen name was daisymay828, said on October 26 that casualguy2000 responded to her ad saying he was interested in an uncomplicated, intimate relationship, but added he wasn't ready for a long-term commitment. Nichols did not write back to him.

The last witness of the day, Harry Page, testified that he and his wife, Amy, met casualguy2000 at the People2People Web site, but they continued their correspondence via Yahoo's free e-mail service. Page, who read the sexually explicit e-mails for the jurors, said he sent Greineder nude pictures of his wife, and in return Greineder sent nude photos of himself to the couple. Greineder expressed interest in meeting the Pages for group sex, but he was never able to make that happen.

Chapter 16

June 14 was a tough day for the defense.

The first witness Grundy called to the stand was Michael French, a latent-fingerprint examiner with the Keane County Sheriff's Office in Seattle. French told the jury that he tested Greineder's windbreaker with amido black—a process that can identify protein, a substance found in blood—and it tested positive.

Lieutenant Kenneth Martin of the Massachusetts State Police Crime Scene Services Section was up next. Martin began his testimony by telling the jurors that the bloodstains on Greineder's white Reebok sneakers seemed to be caused by "impact-type" spatter. Martin said the stains were consistent with someone being within inches or feet of a victim who was hit in the head with a blunt object, like a bat or a hammer. Using a laser pointer, the lieutenant, dressed in a black suit and red-checked tie, pointed out the bloodstains on a photograph on the screen in the front of the court-room. Martin explained that he looked for the "directionality" of a drop of blood as it hit a surface to determine how it actually left the body.

Using a series of photographs, Martin described how the crime scene looked when he first arrived at Morses Pond. He said there was a large pool of blood in the middle of the pathway that had drag marks going through it, suggesting May's body had been lugged through the blood.

"Looking at the victim at the scene, she was off to the side of the path, her head directed into the brush area, feet directed toward the path area," Martin said. "The area along the side of May Greineder's body on the leaves, and the ground cover about her, there were some bloodstained areas. In particular, there was actually some impact spatter that was noted on the ground beside her. The glove of the victim, one of the gloves of the victim, had come off her hand; on the palm area of the hand and also on the finger area, there was some impact spatter noted in that area as well. On the abdominal area of the victim, the victim's pants had been cut or torn open; they were slightly down above the pubic area exposing her lower abdominal area. In that area, at the scene, were observed impact spatter on the victim's abdomen. . . . As I previously mentioned, [the victim's pants] had been either cut or torn; on the edge of one of the cuts or tears, you could see some blood, as if, for example, an implement which had been bloody was used to tear them."

Martin said there was also a large bloodstain on May's shirt, as well as some impact spatter on her jacket. Some of the bloodstains on the sleeves of Greineder's yellow windbreaker were transfer stains, which could have been caused by the defendant picking up his wife and dragging her backward. Martin also said there was a "hair-type swipe" on one of the sleeves of Greineder's jacket.

"If I were to take some blood and put it into one's hair and I transfer it, one would see this stringing type of pattern which would result on the receiving surface," Martin said, pointing to photographs on the screen.

And based on impact spatters on the defendant's jacket, Martin told the jury Greineder was close to May when she was bludgeoned and stabbed. He also testified that patterns on the larger of the plastic bags found near May's body as well as on the murder weapons matched the dimpled pattern on the gloves worn by the person who killed her.

Court was adjourned for the day at 1:00 P.M., about twenty minutes after Murphy began to cross-examine Martin, because Murphy, Greineder, and a couple jurors were ill.

The next day, Murphy tried to attack Martin's testing methods as well as his expertise but failed on both counts.

Crime scene reconstructionist Rod Englert, an expert on blood spatter, didn't help Greineder's case much either.

Using a male mannequin from a tuxedo rental store dressed in the clothes Greineder was wearing the morning his wife was brutally murdered, Englert testified there were bloody grab marks on the sleeves of Greineder's yellow windbreaker. That testimony planted a chilling picture of a dying May Greineder frantically grabbing onto her husband as he beat and stabbed her to death.

Before Englert testified, using the mannequin, Murphy complained to the judge during a sidebar conference about the dummy, which was about six feet tall, bald, and had very high eyebrow ridges.

"I think it would be very difficult to imagine a more sinister-looking mannequin," Murphy said. "I know that there are mannequins available that are much less featured, and, you know, I think to dress up a mannequin in the defendant's clothes, especially one that has these facial features that make him look like a vicious killer, is incredibly prejudicial, and I think whatever this witness wants to do can be done just by an examination of the clothing itself."

Chernoff asked Grundy for his response.

"Briefly, Your Honor, the vicious killer is a mannequin from a tuxedo rental store. And it has the exact same expression as he did when he was attempting to get people to rent tuxedos. And I would suggest to Your Honor, that all the items that are on the mannequin have been offered and introduced into evidence and it's simply being used to demonstrate those items together as they would appear on an individual."

"I'm going to step down and look at it," Chernoff said before issuing his decision. "My ruling is that you can use the mannequin, but not directly right in front of the jury. You can put it behind prosecution counsel's table and the witness can step down and point things out from there."

After a bit more haggling over the placement of the mannequin, Grundy began his direct examination of Englert. Using photographs and the mannequin, the witness testified that two small spots on the knee of Greineder's black jeans, as well as a row of spots at the bottom of the left hem, were "projected stains of blood," which meant that Greineder was close to his wife when she was bludgeoned and stabbed. Englert told the jury there were also impact-type bloodstains on the backpack, the jacket, and the shirt Greineder was wearing when his wife was murdered. Some stains on the sleeves of Greineder's yellow windbreaker were transfer stains, consistent with Greineder dragging the body of his dead wife from behind.

Murphy was successful in keeping some bloodstain evidence found on the back of Greineder's windbreaker out of the trial. The prosecution claimed blood ended up on the back of the jacket while Greineder was smashing his wife's head with the hammer. But the judge ruled that Englert could not testify about the stains because neither Englert nor other experts could say for certain that the protein source found during testing was, in fact, blood.

Another piece of damning evidence for the defense was Englert's testimony regarding the pattern of small reddish brown dots found on the murder weapons, Greineder's jacket, and the left lens of his glasses, as well as on a plastic bag found near May's body. Englert told the jury the pattern was similar to the pattern on the bloody gloves worn by the murderer.

Murphy tried to attack Englert's credibility by bringing up the fact that he consulted with psychics and used hypnosis in the past. Englert, however, said he never worked on a case with a psychic and he no longer used hypnosis.

Further calling Englert's credentials into question, Murphy referenced a case Englert investigated in Indiana. Englert ruled the victim in that case, who had suffered thirty-two blunt force blows to the head, committed suicide, while the state's medical examiner, who is charged under Indiana law to determine cause of death, ruled the man's death a homicide.

"So, sir, different people can see facts of the case and come to different conclusions?" Murphy asked Englert.

"That's true."

Murphy tried to put a dent in the damaging testimony Englert gave on direct examination, but the witness always seemed to get the best of the defense attorney. No matter what question Murphy threw at him, Englert always had an answer. It appeared that the witness was controlling the cross-examination, not the attorney.

In a sidebar, Murphy tried to introduce a negative letter written by Dr. Herbert MacDonnell, the man who trained Englert. In his letter, MacDonnell called Englert a "Frankenstein monster that he created."

Grundy, however, asked Chernoff not to admit the letter because it couldn't be authenticated and because it did not speak to Englert's professionalism but was expressing a personal vendetta that Mac-Donnell had against his former student.

"I think the documents are hearsay," Chernoff said. "This witness, however, is an expert witness. His reliability is up for grabs and so you can ask him whether or not he's ever been the subject of peer review within the community of his peers and whether or not there has been one or more individuals who have, in a peer review, commented negatively [about] him."

"And, Your Honor, I would ask that it be specifically directed toward his professionalism because, as Your Honor notes, that last letter, it's quite interesting and humorous, but it's a little psychotic, too, and it says, you know, this is a personal opinion," Grundy said.

Again, Chernoff said the letter was hearsay and could not be admitted as evidence, but Murphy could ask Englert whether MacDonnell ever said anything negative about his work.

When Murphy asked Englert if his peers ever criticized his methods and practices, Englert said he wasn't aware of any criticism.

"Well, in particular, sir, you're aware that you've been subjected to criticism about your methods and practices by Professor MacDonnell, the person from whom you learned this trade; is that correct?"

"He has never addressed that with me. I've only

received from him in letters, and from him, compliments about good work. I have never received criticism about any type of work. He's never told me that, but I've heard things, but he's never addressed it nor cited any particular case in that area," Englert responded.

"But you are aware that Professor MacDonnell, the pioneer in the field and the man who taught you, has expressed criticisms about the quality of your work in this field?" Murphy continued.

Englert told the jury that it seemed whatever issue MacDonnell had with him was personal, not professional.

Reminding the jurors not to discuss the case with anyone or pay attention to any media reports about it, Chernoff adjourned court for the weekend a little before 4:30 P.M.

When court reconvened on Monday, Grundy called Stanton Coleman Kessler, the chief of staff for the Massachusetts Medical Examiner's Office, to the stand. Kessler told the jurors he was called to Morses Pond at 2:00 P.M. on October 31, 1999, but didn't perform an autopsy on May Greineder's body until the next day.

Kessler described the condition of the body for the jurors. He said she had seven bruises on her legs, some that were fresh and others that were old. Kessler told the jury May suffered a total of ten wounds, including two blows to the head and numerous stab wounds. The fatal wound was a rapidly fatal, large, gaping wound on the left side of May's neck that measured five-and-a-half inches by two-and-a-half inches and was four inches deep.

"The wound is straight in to the neck. It goes directly in. It doesn't have lateral movement and it cuts the underlying vertebra, the fifth cervical vertebrae," Kessler said.

"In the process of going inward, it cuts the main draining veins of the brain, the jugular veins, the main draining veins of the face. It cuts the neck muscles. It cuts some of the muscles that hold the neck and the back together, and it goes all the way in and cuts a portion of the thyroid cartilage, which is deep in the neck. This is a wound that could have had one or two thrusts—I can't determine that—it depends on whether the person is moving around or not. It is horizontally oriented, and it is a lethal wound," Kessler told the jury. "This is a very, very large wound, and it is associated with, in my opinion, movement of the decedent."

Kessler also described a blow to the back of May's head that could have been made by a two-pound drilling hammer. He said that wound would not have rendered May unconscious or unable to deal with what was going on. In addition to those wounds, May was stabbed twice in the chest. The stab wound just above her left breast, which was one and three-quarter inches wide and five inches deep, sliced through the pulmonary artery and went through her lung.

"This was, again, a penetrating stab wound, a little bit downward, straight in," he said.

"And that wound, sir, untreated, would be a fatal wound; is that correct?" Grundy asked.

"Yes."

Kessler added that because he found only about four teaspoons full of blood going through May Greineder's heart, he determined that she was already dead or in a state of shock when she received that wound. Kessler said May was also stabbed a little below her left breast.

He said the knife that made the one-and-a-half-inch wide wound went in two inches and actually made a "tool mark" showing the pattern of the knife on May's ribs. However, there was very little bleeding associated with this wound, meaning May was most likely already dead at this point.

Kessler determined an abrasion on May's back was caused when she was dragged backward by her shoulders. May was also stabbed twice in the back of her head and three times on her forehead.

Kessler also testified that May didn't have any defensive wounds on her hands, indicating, "She was taken by surprise. She didn't react to her attacker. She knew her attacker, didn't expect to be attacked, was unable to react to any of those situations."

When Murphy cross-examined Kessler, he asked if the absence of defensive wounds could mean that May was already unconscious when she was being stabbed.

"It could be, or it could be any of the other instances that I suggest," Kessler responded.

During cross-examination, Kessler told the jury that May's carotid artery was not severed, which contradicted what Grundy said in his opening statement.

Throughout Kessler's graphic testimony, the three Greineder children remained in the courtroom to support their father. But more often than not, they listened to the talk of their mother's injuries with their heads bowed down.

The prosecution's last witness was Lorie Gottesman, a document examiner at the FBI crime lab. Gottesman said two heavy-duty, one-gallon Ziploc freezer bags recovered near May Greineder's body came from a box of Ziploc bags found in the Greineders' home. She said she could tell by examining the striations on the bags that they matched the seven other bags left in the box.

But Murphy countered that even though Gottesman had extensive knowledge of plastic bags, she still couldn't say who brought the bags to Morses Pond. Greineder would later testify under cross-examination that May might have brought the bags to collect berries for the birds without his knowledge. However, he testified during direct examination that he didn't see her bring the bags.

"Ms. Gottesman, is it fair to say that one thing that all your extensive knowledge about plastic bags doesn't tell you is who brought them to the scene?"

"That's right," she responded. "I'm just examining the bags."

The prosecution rested. The defense was now set to begin its case.

Chapter 17

The first witness for the defense was Dirk Greineder's eldest child, thirty-year-old Kirsten.

Dressed conservatively in a gray blazer and patterned blouse, and wearing a braided gold necklace, Kirsten Greineder proved an effective witness for her father, and the jury seemed interested in what she had to say. Appealing and sympathetic, Kirsten was cool under pressure. It was clear putting her on the stand was a strategic move by Murphy. If Kirsten could tell jurors what her father told her happened on the day her mother was murdered, he, most likely, would not have to take the stand in his own defense.

Kirsten began her testimony by talking about her childhood. Even after hearing the medical examiner talk about her mother's injuries in graphic detail, Kirsten remained composed.

Kirsten was born in New York City and spent a few years as a toddler in Bethesda, Maryland. However, she grew up mainly in Wellesley, Massachusetts, and graduated from Wellesley High School in 1989. She attended her father's alma mater, Yale University, and graduated in 1993. From 1993 to 1998, she attended Harvard Medical School, taking a year off after her third year to do a Fulbright Scholarship in Heidelberg, Germany, the country where her father was born. After

Harvard, Kirsten went to the University of Michigan Hospitals in Ann Arbor to do her residency.

"I truly had a wonderful childhood. It has really been as I have gotten older that I have realized how blessed I was," she told the jury. "I had two parents, or I continue to have parents, who loved me, supported me, and allowed me the opportunity to do everything I wanted and supported me in all my educational pursuits, my athletic pursuits, and let me have fun. I had a great, fun childhood. I played. I enjoyed. I had a truly rich childhood, with also two wonderful siblings who were intermittently involved in my life."

Kirsten explained that when the Greineder children were young, they were avid swimmers. In fact, they had learned the competitive swim strokes by the time they were eight years old and they were all on competitive swim teams.

"We would swim on weekends and meets," she testified. "And it became a family event because meets are very long and grueling experiences and both of my parents actually went to all of my meets, which is a fairly unique feature. My parents actually got certified in stroke techniques, in becoming starters and so forth in order to participate."

But as the children got older and went off to college, family activities revolved around weekends and vacations when they could all be together.

Kirsten said when she and her siblings were young they often went to Morses Pond to swim. When they got older, they would often accompany their parents to Morses Pond on the weekends to walk the dogs.

"Our dogs quickly became people in our family," she said, laughing. "They are an integral part of our family. Both of my parents had been dog lovers since I was a child. Their first child was actually another

German shepherd named Wotan, so the dogs were an integral part of our family life, inasmuch as animals can be."

Apparently, Kirsten had been coached well by Marty Murphy. Her statements about her parents' love for their dogs would help explain her father's excessive concern for Wolf and Zephyr almost immediately after finding his wife's stabbed and bludgeoned body at Morses Pond.

Using a series of photographs, which were entered as exhibits, Kirsten then detailed the various routes the Greineders would take on their walks in Morses Pond and how the family would interact with their dogs on those walks. Through Kirsten's well-choreographed testimony, Murphy was able to elicit information that otherwise would have to come from the defendant.

The Greineders' eldest daughter also told the jury about her mother's bad back and her nosebleeds, which had been so severe that she encouraged her to have some blood tests done to rule out cancer.

As for May's back, Kirsten said, her mother had intermittent episodes of such severe pain over the years that she had to stop what she was doing and lie down.

"In the spring of 1997, when I was in Germany, my family took a big family vacation to Spain for three weeks and she had had such severe back pain at the time that we almost had to cancel the vacation," she told the jury. "And the back brace was actually part of what got her through that."

Although May was supposed to wear her brace as much as possible, she didn't always do so. She was a nurse and it was difficult to wear it with her white coat, her daughter explained.

"She was supposed to wear it to walk and anytime she was active . . . but she didn't always wear it because she was stubborn and forgetful," Kirsten said, looking at the jury. "She didn't like to be dependent on anything to do whatever she wanted to do. She saw that the back brace was making her dependent and she didn't like that."

Although May Greineder didn't like being dependent, she often relied on her husband to help her with computer-related matters, according to Kirsten.

"She was in school at Massachusetts General Hospital and she did use a computer for school," Kirsten told the jury. "She turned my sister's bedroom into a mini office for herself. There was a computer there that she used."

Kirsten told the jury her mother refused to become computer savvy. She said she tried to get her mother to read the e-mails she sent from Germany, but May refused. So Kirsten asked her dad to print out the e-mails for her mother because her mother didn't even have a printer in her office.

"They'd be on the kitchen table in the morning for her," Kirsten said.

This testimony confirmed Dirk Greineder's statements to police that he often printed out his wife's school papers for her because she didn't have a printer. According to Greineder, the couple's relationship was as strong as ever, and he was even helping her with her school project the night before she was murdered.

Under direct examination, Kirsten provided the jury with a bit more insight into the workings of the Greineder family.

She explained that when she moved to Ann Arbor to do her residency, her parents went with her to help her set up her apartment.

"When I moved to Ann Arbor, we took two cars,"

she said. "My parents moved all my stuff out and stayed with me for five days. . . . It was a big move with the first child to leave the New England area."

Kirsten said her mother was sad that her daughter was leaving New England.

"And I was sad to leave my parents. I was worried about what happens to Mom and Dad when all the kids were out of the house," she testified. "And I was actually very reassured because they had gotten Huntington tickets. They were going to the Huntington Theater. They were going to the symphony. They were enjoying activities together on top of the typical movies and other activities."

Kirsten also talked about her wedding and how her mother was helping her plan her big day. Kirsten and Aleks Engel became engaged on October 16, 1999, and for the last two weeks of her life, May was helping to plan the nuptials. After her father was arrested, Kirsten and Aleks decided to set their wedding date for August 4, 2001, because they assumed Dirk Grei neder would be acquitted and would be able to walk his first child down the aisle.

"I was doing very little, but she was doing a lot," Kirsten said about her mother's involvement, eliciting a smile from her father.

Kirsten said she subsequently became aware of a large book that her mother had put together of things she had done to prepare for the wedding, including calling about fifty different places where the wedding could be held, as well as contacting florists and photographers.

Kirsten then told the jurors about how coming back to Wellesley, she first heard her mother was dead and her father's explanation of the events leading up to her murder.

"I remember him describing that they had gone on a walk. She had twisted her back throwing a ball to Zephyr. They had had a discussion that Zephyr needed a walk and needed to be exercised, so he went on ahead and she was going to meet him and walk slowly just to the circle. They had split up in the sand pit. He had come back and hadn't seen her where they were supposed to meet. And so Zephyr tore ahead of him. He followed her and saw my mom lying on the ground. His initial thought was, sure, her back is hurt. You know, she may just be lying on the ground. Zephyr was licking her face. He came up to her and that's when he knew something was terribly wrong," Kirsten told the jury, trying hard to hold back the tears.

"And he said to me, 'Kirsten, I was shaking.' He says, 'I was shaking so much, I couldn't even tell if she had a pulse.' I remember that was the thing that struck me because our relationship has been somewhat of doctor to doctor, to some degree. And he says, 'I couldn't even do it. I couldn't even get her pulse. I knew she felt a little warm. I tried to pick her up so I could do something, and then I ran back to get help because I knew I couldn't do it. I needed to help her.' The next thing I remember, from what he told me, was he got the cell phone in the car, made a call, came back. He was brought back part of the way by a police officer, had trouble getting out of that car, and was very, very, you know, anxious about that because he wanted to get back to my mom," she said.

For the most part, Kirsten was almost too composed on the stand—at one point, she even checked her watch. Her behavior was not what you would expect from someone talking about the brutal murder of a loved one. Although Kirsten kept talking about what a great dad she had and how upset he was the day her mom died, she glossed over the fact that her mother had been brutally murdered. She described her mother as "stubborn," "forgetful," and unwilling to learn about computers. When she talked about May planning her wedding, Kirsten portrayed her mother as a "take-charge" individual—but that portrayal didn't come across as a positive attribute. In fact, throughout her direct testimony Kirsten didn't mention any of her mother's good qualities.

Kirsten then told the jury about what happened after she got to her parents' house and about the police coming to talk to her father and search the house in the early-morning hours of November 1.

"Did you and your dad talk about what the police said?" Murphy asked.

"It was predominantly my brother and I, who have studied molecular biology, and we had a discussion about how quickly you can process information, you know, stuff you would collect from a crime scene in order to generate DNA evidence. There was a prolonged discussion, particularly among my brother and myself and my father [at the Ganses']."

"And what do you recall saying about DNA to your dad and your brother?" Murphy asked.

Kirsten told the jury that they discussed how quickly they felt that DNA could be obtained and questioned whether it could be obtained within the sixteen-hour period since May Greineder was murdered. In addition, the three Greineder family members discussed where DNA could be found and the potential for misinterpretation and misunderstanding about how DNA from May could be found on Dirk and vice versa.

Here, Kirsten was actually helping the prosecution. She confirmed the family was already talking about

DNA transfer despite not even having the results of any tests. The prosecution contended that Dirk Greineder knew that his DNA was all over the murder weapons and needed to have an explanation for that fact.

Kirsten told the jury that while the family was at the Ganses' during the first police search, they talked about whether they should hire an attorney— a discussion that continued the next day, Tuesday, November 2.

Kirsten also explained how troubled her family was to learn that police had expanded the investigation to include their dogs.

"On Tuesday, Aleks and I went to the funeral home to make arrangements, and when we came back, [the police] had taken the dogs. My family was very upset. They both had areas of their fur shaved off and they had blood sticks. We also became aware of the search of my dad's office," she said.

During her direct testimony, Kirsten also refuted her aunt Ilse's statement that her father had forbidden her to go to the medical examiner's office to view her mother's body. In her testimony during the prosecution's portion of the trial, Ilse told jurors that Dirk Greineder had prohibited Kirsten from going to the ME's office.

Kirsten testified that on Wednesday, November 3, the family continued talking about the ways in which DNA could be transferred from one surface to another, such as gloves, balls, and clothing, and the potential for DNA to be obtained that might make her father look responsible for her mother's death.

"It was a very, very scary time," Kirsten said.

The poised young woman also told the jury that at some point during the two days after her mother's murder, the family discussed the nosebleeds her father and mother both had before they went to the pond on Halloween morning.

"There had been a towel that had been used for those nosebleeds," Kirsten said. "We all had typically white towels in our cars. They were typically for stains, you know, things you spill, like coffee or something in your car. They were always in the side doors or down on the side."

Once again, via Kirsten, Murphy was able to get Dirk Greineder's version of the events leading up to his wife's murder on the record without having to put him on the stand.

And Kirsten said on November 8, 1999, she bought foil loaf pans at Roche Brothers to make banana bread. Police found the receipts and the wrappers for those pans and said they matched the ones found near May's body.

Murphy also asked Kirsten to talk about why the family hadn't bothered to pick up her mother's ashes, even though six months had passed since her death.

Kirsten responded that her mother was cremated, according to her wishes, after a service that was held at the Newton Crematory. Kirsten testified that the family then discussed the disposition of May's ashes, but couldn't agree on what to do with them.

"Was there any discussion in your family about whether your mother's remains ought to stay in Boston or go to New York?" Murphy asked.

"Yes, there was."

Kirsten explained that her aunt and cousin lived in New York and her grandmother, grandfather, and her mother's brother were all in urns in a crematory in Queens, New York, and her aunt and cousin wanted May's ashes to be placed there.

"We all felt that we wanted my mother to stay nearby to us," Kirsten told the jury.

"And, Kirsten, do you recall the day that your dad was indicted and arrested?"

"Yes."

"And do you remember what day that was?"

"February 29, 2000."

"And after your dad was arrested, was there a decision made among the family about what should happen with your mother's ashes?" Murphy asked.

"The agreement was by six months after my mother's death, we were going to make a decision, and that would give us a little bit of time with breathing room and the crematory was willing to hold onto her ashes for free for a year. So for that reason, we decided six months. Obviously, February twenty-ninth was only four months, a little under four months. So at that point, given the new added issues that we were dealing with, my aunt approached me and asked if she could take the ashes to New York. We, at that point, said that even though initially that's not what we wanted, we felt at this point, given the circumstances we were dealing with, that that was appropriate," she explained to the jury.

"Nothing further, Your Honor."

Now it was Grundy's turn to question Kirsten.

First he asked her about sketches of Morses Pond that were found in a wastebasket at Greineder's home nearly two weeks after the murder.

Kirsten said although she knew about the maps, she had never seen them before they were introduced as evidence at trial. She said while she knew the weapons that had been used to kill her mother were found at Morses Pond, she did not know exactly where they had been found.

Grundy also questioned her about the disposition of her mother's ashes.

Kirsten told the jury that the debate over what to do with her mother's remains mostly took place during the first month and a half after her death.

"I recall saying to my father on February tenth . . . 'You know, we're getting to four months. We have got to think about what we are going to do here, and we have got to come to some agreement.' And we were beginning to make the process and we were interrupted by the events of February twenty-ninth."

"During that four months, your aunt Ilse had indicated to you on numerous occasions that she was concerned that her sister was in a potter's field; is that correct?"

After admitting she didn't know what a potter's field was, Kirsten said her aunt mentioned a couple of times that she wanted to take her mother's ashes to New York, but she and her siblings, as well as her father, felt that her mother wouldn't have wanted her remains to be in New York.

"Well, your aunt's concern was the fact that they were being held by nonfamily—relatives being held by a business; isn't that correct?"

"They were in what essentially is storage, from my understanding."

"And her concern was that they be taken somewhere other than storage?"

"I agree. They needed to, ultimately, and those four months were a very difficult time. And when you're dealing with many issues, we had addressed it. We had discussed it as a family and we had decided that at six months we would make a decision because that would be a time when those of us that actually wanted to have something to visit would want to do it, and it was a decision we made as a family to wait."

Kirsten testified that she was not sure if anyone ever told her aunt and cousin that the family had decided to wait six months before making a final determination on the disposition of her mother's ashes.

"I am not aware of whether I told them exactly a date, but I told them that ultimately we would make a decision," she said. "There was not a great deal of animosity over this issue. This was an issue where we disagreed, and as a family, we were going to come to a decision."

"And Ilse offered to pay the bill so that the ashes could be released and you could do what you wanted, including holding on to them until a decision was made?"

"No. There was no bill to be paid until we made a decision as to where to put the ashes," Kirsten responded.

Grundy then questioned Kirsten about a trip she and her family and her fiancé made to Denmark at Christmastime to visit his family. He also asked about another trip the family was planning to San Diego and Las Vegas before her father was arrested.

His point—the family could make decisions and plan trips, but they couldn't make a decision to take May's ashes out of storage.

When Grundy brought up May's chronic back pain, Kirsten said she knew that two days before her death, her mother had slipped on a step and exacerbated her back problems.

"In fact, that's why she didn't go for a walk the following day was my understanding," she said.

Grundy jumped on that statement because Greineder told police that May didn't go for a walk the Saturday before she was murdered because she was working on her school project.

"When you say that you understand that's why she didn't go for a walk, somebody told you that?"

"Yeah, one of my siblings."

But the only way Britt or Colin would have known that was if their father had told them. Although Kirsten was trying to tell the truth, she was at a distinct disadvantage, because she only knew the version of the truth her father wanted her to know.

Grundy began to question Kirsten about her German and Spanish heritage.

Kirsten testified that she traveled to Germany three times—she spent a month there in 1987 between her sophomore and junior years in high school, returned in 1992 before starting her senior year of college to work in Munich at a pharmaceutical company, and went back again from 1996 to 1997 on a Fulbright Scholarship. She also spoke German and Reich German (the language of the Third Reich), but said she spoke only limited Spanish. And Kirsten told the jury that her home contained German literature—children's literature as well as adult books, including a German version of *Mein Kampf,* which belonged to her father.

The jury listened as Kirsten talked about her father's family and the fact that they never really accepted her mother because they thought she was from a different walk of life and from a different world and never accepted the way she was raising her family.

"And for that reason over time, we separated ourselves from our grandparents, my grandmother and grandfather," she said. "My uncle we have never really had any contact with."

Despite this fact, she said Greineder's ailing mother,

who lived in Connecticut—his father had passed away years earlier—and Juergen, his brother, who lived in a suburb south of Boston, attended May's memorial service on November 3. But they did not go back to the Greineders' Wellesley home after the service.

Grundy then asked Kirsten about her mother.

"Your mom was a very strong woman, wasn't she?"

"My mother was a very strong, loving, and caring woman."

"And she was brilliant, wasn't she?"

"She was a very bright woman, yes."

"And as a nurse, she was often told that she was smarter than the doctor she was working for."

"At times, I believe, she was told that."

"And she was pursuing that knowledge just six weeks into her nurse practitioner's course; is that correct?"

"Yes. She was about two months into her nurse practitioner's course."

What was Grundy's reason for asking these questions? It certainly wasn't obvious from his cross-examination of Kirsten, but later something Chief Cunningham said made it a lot clearer. Cunningham said that the paper Greineder was helping his wife with the night before she was murdered challenged his theory on childhood asthma. Although she didn't prove his theory inaccurate, the chief said her research did draw into question some of his findings.

Just that year, Greineder had published the results of a one-year study looking at the effects of an asthma outreach program on emergency ward and hospital use by children with asthma. The researchers determined that children who received both one session to educate them about asthma and additional telephone calls to nurses and/or visits to health care providers, if necessary, lived longer (and their care cost less) than those children who received just the one education session.

As of this writing, it's unclear exactly what May's research showed, because police wouldn't release a copy of it.

Grundy showed Kirsten a white towel that had been entered into evidence and asked her if it was the same type of towel the members of her family kept in their cars to clean up spills.

"It looks similar," she responded.

Then he showed her another towel with a crest on it—the one her father had taken from the Ritz-Carlton and said he and May used to stop their nosebleeds—and asked her if it was the type of towel the family carried in their cars.

"We sometimes had larger towels in the trunk, but specifically, no. . . ."

"And you never knew your father to have this on the floor of his car; is that correct?"

"I would have known my dad had white towels in his car."

"And, again, I'm showing you a specific towel of this size with a crest on it. You didn't have any knowledge of your father having that on the floor of his car?"

"That specific one, no."

"And I believe Mr. Murphy asked you if there was a conversation about what to do with that towel; is that correct?"

"Yes."

"You didn't give the towel to Mr. Murphy, did you?"

"I did not," Kirsten answered.

"And you don't know when and how that occurred; is that correct?"

"I know that we discussed, after he had decided

that he had picked Martin Murphy as his attorney, that we discussed it as a family—that being myself, my siblings, and my father—and we decided that the best thing to do with this towel was to give it to him. The following morning, it was my understanding that he gave it to him."

"And, again, you don't have any knowledge as to when that was handed over personally; is that correct?" Grundy asked.

"Specifically, I know within probably a day."

"Were you there?"

"I was not there," Kirsten replied.

"And you didn't see it?"

"I did not see it."

"And you have heard testimony that that was provided to the Commonwealth in April; is that correct?"

"I was not aware of when it was provided to the Commonwealth."

Grundy moved on to Kirsten's testimony before the grand jury on November 10, 1999.

"Do you recall indicating at that time that your father told you that your mom slipped when she was coming down the pit?"

Kirsten said she wasn't sure, so Grundy gave her a copy of her grand jury testimony to refresh her memory.

"And is it fair to state that you indicated your dad told you, 'Mom slipped when she was coming down the pit'?"

"Yes, and I have heard that story so many times that I have to confess my memory today is most likely of that particular phrase. What was said is definitely affected by the story I have heard so many times."

"Sure. And on November tenth, when you had an opportunity to indicate that story, you stated there was a conversation. Your dad indicated there was a conversation about continuing on the walk. 'They continued on some, and then after that initial slip as she was coming down the pit, she then tossed the ball and wrenched her back a bit more.' Is that correct?"

"Yeah. On [page] 173 I said that, yes."

This was the first time this version of the story was ever mentioned.

"In the grand jury, you indicated that as your father told you the story, one of the first things you asked him was: 'Why didn't you have your cell phone with you?' Is that correct?"

"Somewhere in that first conversation, yes, I asked him why didn't he have his cell phone with him."

"And you actually told the [grand] jurors that, at page 177, that 'it was on a rare occasion that he didn't have a cell phone with him. He almost always carries his cell phone. He was charging it.'"

"My dad usually has his personal cell phone with him, in addition to the cell phone we have in the car."

"Okay. Did you know your dad to have more than one portable cell phone?"

"We have more than one in the family, but he has his own personal one."

"Doctor, when you were forced to come to the grand jury, you took an oath and you testified to a group of strangers about probably the most traumatic incident in your life; is that correct?"

"That's true."

"And you testified truthfully and honestly, didn't you?"

"I did, to the best of my ability."

"And at one point in that testimony, you were asked to describe the relationship with your parents; is that correct?"

"Objection, Your Honor," Murphy said.

"That's true." Kirsten answered Grundy's question before the judge had a chance to rule on Murphy's objection.

"And do you recall exactly what it was that you told them at that time?" Grundy continued.

"One moment," Judge Chernoff said.

"Objection, Your Honor," Murphy said again.

"Why don't you come to the sidebar," Chernoff told the two attorneys.

Murphy was the first to speak.

"Again, Your Honor, he is just asking the witness to read her grand jury testimony. You have to establish a contradiction before you impeach, or you have to establish a lack of memory before you use it to refresh her memory," Murphy argued.

"I believe my question, Your Honor, was if she recalls exactly what she told the grand jurors on that subject. She indicated that she didn't and I referred her to a particular page and paragraph," Grundy responded.

"My point is, Your Honor, and I don't mean to interrupt, but the question can't be: 'What did you tell the grand jurors?' The question has to be: 'What are the facts?'" Murphy said.

"I think you're right," the judge told Murphy. "You can ask her what her memory is as to what the relationship is between her parents. If she doesn't remember, you can refresh her recollection with her grand jury minutes. If it is something contrary to the grand jury minutes, you can impeach her with her grand jury minutes."

"Your Honor, may I be heard on one other matter, please?" Murphy asked.

"Yes."

"I move for a mistrial as a result of Mr. Grundy's

invocation of the fact that the defendant has a German version of *Mein Kampf* in his house. I did not make an objection because I did not want to draw attention to it at the time, but I think it is incredibly prejudicial. It is not relevant at all. The only possible reason for asking that question is to paint my client as a Nazi."

Murphy went on to say there was case law that specifically addressed that point.

"There was a specific holding by the [Massachusetts Supreme Judicial Court] that the kind of reading material one possesses is not admissible to show that someone subscribes to the set of views set there, so I move for a mistrial on that basis. I think it is incredibly prejudicial to have my client cast as a Nazi in front of this jury and it is going to require a whole lot of explaining when the defendant testifies. That should never have been permitted, never inquired of, and I would ask for a mistrial. In the alternative, I ask that the court instruct the jury that any evidence about the possession of a book in the defendant's home is not relevant, that it was improper to ask the question, and it should be stricken from their consideration in this case," Murphy said.

The judge then asked Grundy to respond to Murphy's contentions.

"Again, Your Honor, it was in line with the whole line of questioning begun by the defense with respect to culture and upbringing and how they were brought up in that home," Grundy told the judge.

Grundy wanted to include the reference to the Nazi book to show Greineder was a control freak. In his closing, Grundy called May's murder the ultimate act of control.

"It seems to me what you should be able to do is

elicit from her—and I would let you even do it in leading questions and then I would give you an opportunity to speak with her first about what books were in her bookcase. I'm sure there must have been a number of other adult books in German. I didn't know where the question was going when it came, or I would have done something about it. It's a very limited probative effect—probative value—I thought it was to show that there were both adult and children's books in the German language. It's of minor relevance but I would certainly give you an opportunity on redirect examination to direct her attention to other adult books and I would also give a special instruction to the jury on how irrelevant it is [about] what children's or adult books were in the bookcase," Chernoff responded.

"And again, Your Honor, if this was part of the upbringing in her house, it's not irrelevant to the extent that the defense has decided that it was relevant as to what a marvelous upbringing they had and all the phenomenal things that they were exposed to; it completes the picture," Grundy said.

But Murphy didn't agree.

"That was begun because of the prosecution, through Belinda Markel and Ilse Stark, deciding to introduce, essentially, negative character evidence, so they started this. That doesn't allow them to get Hitler as a—you know, essentially that's what we have got in the case, we have got Hitler now," Murphy said.

"Well, I would like to know what the negative character reference was," Grundy responded.

But Chernoff had heard enough.

"My ruling is this. I will give you an opportunity to speak with her before redirect examination. We will take a stretch break and you can find out from her what other adult books were in the bookcase that were in the German language and you can bring that out before the jury. At some point, I will say, 'It's all irrelevant anyway,' and I'll deny the motion for a mistrial."

"Thank you," Murphy said.

Grundy then continued his cross-examination of Kirsten Greineder, asking her about the relationship between her parents.

"My parents had a wonderful, close relationship that was based on a partnership in raising three children to whom they were very committed and centered their lives around," she said.

Grundy then asked Kirsten if, in November 1999, she was aware that either of her parents had been unfaithful to the other.

She responded that she wasn't aware of it at that time. She said when she went to the Wellesley police station to ask police to watch the family's home during her mother's funeral, she was asked about her parents' marital fidelity by a Wellesley police officer.

"At that time, I said that the possibility of any extramarital affair between my parents was completely out of the question, that my parents were devoted to each other and to the three of us."

"And that was the truth as far as you knew it, correct?"

"Correct."

"And it remained the truth, as far as you knew it, for the next four months; is that correct?"

"That's correct."

That testimony showed that Kirsten didn't really know what was going on between her parents, and if that was the case, maybe she didn't really know to what lengths her father would go to protect his lifestyle. If, in fact, Greineder killed his wife, maybe it wasn't so he could continue his double life, but, rather, so he could keep it secret. Maybe May had threatened to out him, or even divorce him—ruining his reputation and throwing his life into turmoil. And maybe he just couldn't let a woman, any woman, have the upper hand.

"Your father never indicated to you anything other than that in the four months subsequent to you mother's death; is that correct?"

"My father never indicated anything specific. He said that there was something that he was not proud of in his life and he said that at this point it was better that we didn't talk about it, and the conversation ended there."

Kirsten told the jurors that she only learned about her father's secret life after he was indicted for the murder of her mother.

"And after, in fact, that indictment occurred, the following day you talked to your father on the telephone; is that correct?"

"I'm sure I did."

"And you asked your father how long had that been going on, didn't you?"

"Yes. I think I did."

"And he told you approximately a year?"

"I actually recall in that conversation my dad curtailing the conversation very quickly because he said it wasn't an appropriate time to be having that conversation, because we couldn't really talk on the phone about these issues. But I recall asking him how long it had been going on and I recall—I actually don't recall the length of time he told me. I remember the conversation being ended very quickly by him."

"And, Doctor, you then asked your father if your mother knew; isn't that correct?"

"I actually remember that, and I remember him not answering me because he said—"

"Your father told you, 'I think so,' didn't he?" Grundy interrupted.

Murphy rose to object, but the judge overruled his objection and let Kirsten answer the question.

"On that phone conversation, my memory of that phone conversation is my dad curtailing the phone conversation very quickly."

"Do you recall?" Grundy asked, continuing to press the witness for a direct answer.

"At this point, I recall never knowing exactly the answer to that question. I don't know, so—"

"Do you recall telling other people present that your father said, 'I think so,' in response to your question as to whether or not your mother knew?"

"I don't recall it."

"Thank you, Doctor," Grundy said, ending his questioning of the witness.

The judge now called a five-minute break.

Once the jury had left the courtroom, the judge and the two attorneys spoke at the bench about the *Mein Kampf* reference.

"Your Honor, I thought hard about it, but there is nothing I can do about the Hitler thing that won't make it worse in my estimation and so I'm not going to ask any questions on redirect. I would ask the court to give an instruction now that says that none of this has any relevance to the case and I think it was a completely improper question, and I renew my motion for a mistrial," Murphy said.

"And, Your Honor, I object strenuously to that where they laid the groundwork to set the scene of the environment with which these children were raised, and they chose to cast it in a certain light that was different than that cast light, and I would suggest that Hitler's name was not mentioned by me. It was a question with respect to the literature that was in the home that was broached on the direct examination of that woman as to her training and culture and the readings in that home," Grundy told the judge.

"I never said anything about training, culture, or readings," Murphy shot back.

"I'm going to instruct the jury. Thank you," Chernoff said, ending the discussion.

When the jurors had taken their seats in the jury box, Chernoff said, "I was thinking over our five-minute recess just now, you know, what people have in their bookcases, whether they are children's books or non–children's books, are absolutely irrelevant to the issues here in this case and I think that is not an appropriate area for examination by any lawyer in this case. So, anything that you have heard in that line just simply is irrelevant and should be put aside, and focus on the real evidence in this case. Thank you."

Chapter 18

After a brief bench conference regarding the time that court would end for the day, Murphy stunned everyone in the courtroom by calling his client to the stand. When his name was called, an audible gasp arose from the spectators. But, in reality, Murphy had no choice but to have his client testify. The only way the jurors would understand who this man was and why he did the things he did, was if they heard it from him.

Greineder, still sporting his wedding ring, had lost more than thirty pounds since his arrest. His face looked haggard and drawn and his clothes didn't fit quite right. After talking the stand, Greineder first told the jury about his early life, where he grew up and went to school. He then spoke about coming to America, going to college, meeting May, and ultimately marrying her. He took the jurors through his life, through continuing his education, his jobs, his growing family, and their move to Wellesley. The jury heard how the Greineders raised their family and how the defendant worked himself up to the position he held as head of the allergy department at Harvard Pilgrim Health Care.

After getting through this relatively easy testimony,

Greineder was forced to face his deviant sexual behavior head-on.

Greineder told the jury it all began in the mid-1990s, when his relationship with his wife changed. Around that time, she seemed to lose interest in sex progressively and also developed some discomfort and pain, which then led to a cessation of the couple's sex life. It was something she wanted, he said.

The defendant said about a year later, he began to buy little booklets of sexually explicit letters published by *Penthouse* magazine. Soon after, he started calling the sex phone lines that were advertised in those booklets. The doctor said he then graduated to surfing the Web for pornography. He said he would look at pictures as well as enter various sex-related chat rooms, where he would use a variety of screen names, including Ryder, Tom, and Jeff, to sign on and talk with other members. Sometimes he would arrange to communicate with these people via e-mail in order to have more private conversations.

Greineder said these activities would occur in clusters—maybe he would engage in them frequently for a period of one or two weeks and then not again for several months. During this time, he was working at Harvard Pilgrim, as well as in the allergy department at Beth Israel Hospital in Boston. Throughout this testimony, Greineder kept his head down, apparently too humiliated to look at the jury or even his attorney.

The members of the jury heard how much the doctor's family meant to him.

"I felt very blessed to have the family that I had. I thought we really couldn't do much better with that one exception, which I have mentioned, but that really wasn't, in a sense, the overriding feature. There was so much mutual warmth and growth in that family that it just was—I just felt really blessed to have what I had," he said, now making eye contact with the jurors.

"Can you explain to the members of the jury, Doctor, how it is you can say that you felt happy, when you were going on phone sex numbers and going on pornographic Web sites? Can you explain that?" Murphy asked.

"I can try and it's hard, simply because it seems so silly. What the family meant to me and means to me is so much more, and, you know, my wife was the most wonderful person I have ever met. She made me a better person. She helped my family become what we became. I was a better doctor because of her, and I was a much better father because of her. And, in hindsight, it seems so silly, I guess, immature, but it didn't seem central. . . ."

During this part of his testimony, Greineder seemed to break down crying; the problem was, there didn't appear to be any tears.

Greineder explained that his family was the most important thing in his life and said he always made his career decisions around his family. He said he changed to clinical medicine because it was warmer and he had more contact with patients. He said his wife encouraged him to make that change and showed him how to be a warm clinician.

"So how do you explain what you were doing?"

"It wasn't central. It was a side activity. I was, I guess, gratifying a secondary need. I did it and I'm not proud of it, but if I had to choose, that would have been easy."

At this point, court recessed for the day and the defendant stepped down from the witness stand. When Greineder returned to the defense table, his attorney put his hand on his client's shoulder as if to say, "Good job."

All in all, Greineder did seem to do pretty well. He was nervous and embarrassed when he talked about his sexual activities and emotional when he talked about May and his family. Murphy put him on the stand so the jury could see that there was absolutely no way this world-renowned physician and upstanding member of the community could have committed such an evil, cold-blooded act as murdering the mother of his children. There was no question that Greineder had to talk about his secret life. And he had to give the jurors an explanation about what drove him to sex on the Internet and to prostitutes—an explanation that maybe they could accept. After all, it wasn't as if he had a girlfriend on the side—someone he loved and wanted to be with.

But the important question was: Did the jury believe him?

The next morning, June 19, Murphy began questioning his client where he had left off the previous day.

"Did there come a time, Doctor, when you made a decision to contact a prostitute?"

"Yes."

Greineder talked about his February 1998 rendezvous with Elizabeth Porter in the Crowne Plaza hotel in Natick. He told the jurors he brought champagne to make their meeting less awkward. He said he met her again a week later at the Copley Westin Hotel in Boston.

Greineder claimed that before February 1998 he had never had sex with anyone other than his wife, but between that date and October 1999, he had sex with other women eight times. Two of those women, he said, were not prostitutes, but people he met in Internet chat rooms.

Greineder explained that he first used Tom Young's name as a screen name to get in those chat rooms because his own name was just too unusual. Then, when American Express solicited him for a corporate card, he got one in his name and one in Young's name as well, which he sometimes used to rent hotel rooms when he met with the prostitutes.

Murphy then asked his client about his use of Viagra. Greineder said he wrote himself a prescription for the drug when he first heard about it in April 1998. He thought it might help him overcome the awkwardness he felt when he had sex with prostitutes. He wrote himself a second prescription on June 2, 1998, the day he was to meet escort Deborah Doolio. He had forgotten his original prescription at home and decided it would be easier to just write a new one.

Greineder also explained why he signed up for the People2People dating site.

"I felt I had a very uncomfortable and crass encounter in Mahwah, New Jersey, that I would really call a New York experience, and I felt that this just wasn't something I wanted to do again, and I was just looking to see if there was some other avenue that would be a little less commercial," he said.

"And what were you seeking through People2People, Doctor?"

"A sexual encounter—a short-term, isolated sexual encounter."

"Now, on the Saturday before your wife's murder, Doctor, did you call the escort that came in here in court and testified?"

"Yes, I did."

"And why did you do that, sir?"

"I felt that the People2People avenue was even less desirable than the escort prostitute approach, if you wish. It was clear that it was likely to lead to more entanglement and more complications than I was willing to get involved with. And I began to recognize that if I wanted just a quick sexual encounter, that probably my best bet was actually a commercial prostitute; pay for it, have no strings attached, and be done."

"Sir, did your wife know about your activities?"

"I'm not sure."

"Did you ever discuss them with her?"

"No. We never discussed that."

"Did anything ever happen that caused you to believe she may have realized that something was going on?"

Greineder, who told the jury that his wife was an incredibly intelligent and intuitive person, said that in the summer of 1998, shortly after the couple returned from Michigan, May was cleaning out the bathrooms and found a bottle of Viagra in his shaving kit. She then called Dirk at work to ask if he had an explanation for the medication.

"And did you give her an explanation, Doctor?"

"I couldn't think of anything, other than to say— than to tell her that I had bought them to experiment with, and this is, of course, when Viagra was new and there was a lot of noise about it on the Internet—I mean, in the news and the TV, and I said nothing further."

Greineder said during that conversation, as well as the next day, May apologized to him for prying into his private affairs. They never talked about that subject again.

"I never really knew what she knew, but I felt that she probably had some idea," he told the jury.

Greineder said he never considered asking his wife for a divorce because he couldn't imagine living without her.

"My wife was a wonderful person. She was truly the best person I have ever known. And life with—I still wanted a sex life, and obviously I was pursuing that—but life with May was so much more than a sex life, it was about caring, it was about little things, like doing a crossword puzzle on Sunday mornings with her because she wanted to after we walked the dogs. It was going out in the snow and cleaning off the bird feeders in our pajamas and our slippers so that the birds could have their breakfast before we would if it had been a fresh snow.

"But the bigger things—driving to New Haven in the middle of the night when the kids got hurt or supporting each other through her mother's illness. And it was cutting up fruit every morning for twenty-five years and having her help me organize and pull off a departmental dinner when I became allergy chief at the Brigham. And, most importantly, May was all about family, raising the kids, and making sure that I helped her with the kids. We did it together, changing diapers and reading college essays, helping each other be stronger and better.

"May cared enough to make sure that she doesn't just make our life easier, but she made our life better and she expected all of us to care enough to do the same, that we should make our lives—demand enough of each other to make our lives better, to make each other stronger, and to support each other. And in that way, I think she was the most incredible person I have ever met and had the most impact on me of any person I have ever known. She is more important to me than my parents and for all that I love her more than anything. I just can't imagine living without her to this day." Greineder all the while kept his head down, never looking at the jury.

Greineder told the jury that after having some trouble settling the estate of May's mother, who died in late January 1999, the couple decided to do some estate planning of their own. So, in early 1999, Greineder visited an estate-planning attorney, Jeffrey Schlossberg. Greineder said he did the groundwork because May wasn't interested in getting involved until it was absolutely necessary. One of the things Schlossberg recommended was that Greineder sell the house to his wife to make their estates more equitable. Doing so, he said, provided the couple with a significant tax advantage. Greineder took this advice and sold the house to May, for a nominal amount, sometime in the summer of 1999. Schlossberg also recommended that the Greineders take out a $500,000 second-to-die insurance policy, which meant the Greineder children would get the money only after both parents died. The money would have helped the children pay off the taxes on their parents' estate. Although the Greineders filled out the application for this policy, it was never executed. Police initially thought this was a $500,000 life insurance policy on May's life and, as such, was a motive for murder. However, once they determined the true nature of the policy, they backed off that claim.

Greineder also said that he had a $500,000 term life insurance policy and May had a $200,000 policy in place since the early 1900s. Greineder told the jury that, despite renovating part of their home and buying some new furniture in 1999, and planning for his daughter Kirsten's wedding, at the time of his wife's death, he was not under any financial strain.

The jurors next heard about how the Greineders spent the day before his wife's murder—she stayed home to work on her school project while he went to walk Zephyr at Morses Pond.

"Doctor, when you went to the beach at Morses Pond that Saturday morning, did you bring this hammer with you?" Murphy asked, holding up the hammer.

"No."

"Before this trial started, had you ever seen this hammer before?"

"No."

Murphy continued asking Greineder about whether he had brought the items found at the crime scene to the pond the day before his wife's murder. With each question, he held the item up for Greineder to see.

"On Saturday, October thirtieth, when you went to Morses Pond, did you bring this knife with you and hide it?"

"No," Greineder answered, looking straight at Murphy, not the jury.

"Before this trial started, had you ever seen this knife before?"

"No."

"On Saturday, October thirtieth, Doctor, did you bring this loaf pan to Morses Pond?"

"No, I did not," he answered, looking down at his feet and rubbing his left eye.

"On Saturday, October thirtieth, Doctor, did you bring this lighter fluid?"

"No."

"On Saturday, October thirtieth, Doctor, did you

bring two brown work gloves to Morses Pond and hide it [*sic*]?"

"No, I did not."

"And on Saturday, October thirtieth, Doctor, did you bring latex gloves to Morses Pond and hide it [*sic*]?"

"No."

"And on Saturday, October thirtieth, Doctor, did you bring this white plastic bag to Morses Pond to use to hide things you were planning to use to kill your wife?"

"No."

"On Saturday, October thirtieth, Doctor, were you planning to kill your wife?"

"No," he said in a loud voice, shaking his head back and forth.

Greineder then explained to the jury what he did after leaving Morses Pond that Saturday morning, while his wife was doing her schoolwork. That afternoon, he admitted, he called Deborah Doolio, a prostitute he had seen once before. And that evening, he said, he helped May with her school paper.

Greineder next recounted for the jury everything that happened while they were getting ready to go to Morses Pond on Halloween morning, 1999. He began with preparing breakfast.

"When you were making breakfast for your wife, were you planning to kill her that day, Doctor?"

"No, I was not," he said, shaking his head and looking straight at his attorney.

"When you were eating breakfast with your wife, were you planning to kill her?"

"No."

Greineder talked about trying to get Zephyr into the van, then told of the double nosebleeds and the towel he had taken from the Ritz-Carlton Hotel in Atlanta that they both used to stop the bleeding. A towel he had used numerous times to put on his lap if he was having coffee so he wouldn't spill any on his clothes, to wipe his face and hands after he had eaten. A bloody towel the doctor said he threw back in the Toyota Avalon after they had used it. A towel police never saw when they searched the car on November 1. A towel Greineder found after that search and gave to his attorney on November 5. A towel Murphy didn't turn over to police until two months after Greineder's arraignment.

"Doctor, again, when you went to the pond on Sunday, October thirty-first, did you bring this hammer with you?"

"No, I did not."

"This knife?"

"No."

"These two brown work gloves?"

"No."

"This loaf pan?"

"No."

"This bottle of lighter fluid?"

"No."

"These rubber gloves?"

"No."

"And, sir, did you bring Ziploc bags?"

"No, I did not."

"And did you bring this plastic bag, exhibit 172?"

"No."

"Did you see your wife bring any of those items?"

"No."

"Can you tell us, Doctor, whether—"

"I'm sorry, I didn't hear that last question," a juror said.

"Did you see your wife bring any of those items?" Murphy asked his client again.

"No," Greineder responded, quickly turning to face the jury, but still keeping his head down.

Murphy asked his client whether he ever before saw his wife bring any Ziploc bags to Morses Pond. Greineder said sometimes she would bring them to gather different kinds of berries to bring home to feed the birds. But, he said, he did not see her bring any Ziploc bags to the pond that Halloween morning. However, Greineder said, he remembered seeing some Ziploc bags on the path at some point that morning.

Looking at photographs of Morses Pond, Greineder took the jurors through the couple's walk at Morses Pond—walking into the forest area, throwing the ball for Zephyr, and to the raised section over the sand pit, then walking down the path into the sand pit. Greineder said he heard May slip on some gravel and somehow hurt her back. He told the jury his wife said she had been trying to throw the ball into the gravel pit and that's when she probably slipped.

"So my impression was that she had hurt her back throwing the ball and standing on the gravel," he explained.

After trying to figure out what they should do, Greineder said his wife told him to continue walking the dog to the beach and she would walk back by herself and meet him at the flat rock by the edge of the circle. At first, Greineder said no, but then he decided it wasn't such a bad idea.

"I walked down the path out to the circle and, as always, took an immediate right past the pumping station," he said.

"Was your wife with you when you walked down that path?"

"No . . . I was ahead of her. I can't say exactly where she was, because she was traversing the meadow, which is actually a goodly distance."

"Did you walk down that path that morning with your wife and kill her on that path, Doctor?"

"No, I did not."

Greineder said he moved on, throwing the ball for Zephyr, and when he got to the circle, he took a right and headed toward the beach. However, he said, he never got to the water because Zephyr seemed distracted by something. So he decided to go back and find May. But she wasn't at their meeting place. As Greineder started to call May's name, Zephyr ran back into the path they had just left.

Throughout this testimony, Greineder's eyes were focused on his attorney. He never looked at the jury.

At this point, court recessed for a midmorning break. After the recess, Greineder continued his testimony.

Greineder told the jurors by the time he arrived at the rock to meet his wife, they had been separated for about ten minutes. He said he followed Zephyr down the path and that's when he found May lying on the ground. His first thought was that she was lying down because her back really hurt. He described trying to rouse her and then trying to take her pulse.

"I leaned over to take it on her left side, and that's when I saw there was a lot of blood and something there, and so I quickly went to the right side, not wanting to disturb what I didn't know. And I took her pulse on the right side, which is not what I normally would do, coming from that side."

"And were you able to get a pulse, Doctor?"

"I couldn't. I was shaking so hard—my hand, I couldn't control it. I couldn't feel a pulse, but I really wasn't sure that I was able to do anything with it."

This part of his testimony was actually beneficial for the prosecution. Although Greineder said he saw the blood on his wife's neck when he first found his wife lying in the pathway, he told Detective McDermott at the scene that he didn't see the wound until after he made the emergency call to the police and went back to his wife a second time.

Greineder said he tried to pick his wife up several times—although he told police at the scene he only tried to pick her up once—but was unable to do so. Finally he grabbed Zephyr's leash from around May's waist, hooked it on her collar, and took off to get help. He said he ran to the pumping station, but no one was there. At this point, he and Zephyr were at the edge of the circle. He said he looked up and thought he saw some movement go down the paved pathway.

"So I followed that movement, which I thought was a runner, into the path, and I was sort of looking," he said, without ever looking over at the jury box. "And I get into the path—I don't know how far I ran in, not too far—and I didn't see anything anymore, and that was clearly not the way to go. So I turned around and came back, expecting to run up the access road and get help."

"When you went down that path, Doctor, did you dump a bloody right-handed glove, a knife, and a hammer in a storm drain?"

"No."

Greineder said when he came out of the path and turned to go up the access road, he almost bumped into William Kear, the man with the little dog, and he asked him if he had a cell phone. Greineder said for some reason he forgot to take his cell phone with him that morning, although he did have his pager. When Kear said he didn't have a phone, Greineder asked him if he would go and make a call, but Kear didn't move. So Greineder then went to his van to call police. On his way, he ran into Rick Magnan, who was jogging and asked him if he had a cell phone. When Magnan said he didn't, Greineder continued on to his van as fast as he could. When he got to the van, he put Zephyr inside and started dialing the police, only he said he called his house first, by accident.

Before the police arrived, Greineder started running back to his wife. When Officer Fitzpatrick came, he got into his police car and the pair went back to the spot where he left his wife.

"What did you do when you got there?"

"It is still hopeless. I still hoped. I tried to take her pulse again, I think. I know I looked in her eyes and I couldn't even tell if the pupils were moving and it was too hard. So then I pulled up her shirt, thinking I would hear a heartbeat that might—if I just put my ear to her chest. So I put my ear to her chest and, I mean, I saw the wound. That didn't seem to matter. I couldn't get a heartbeat. I knew she was gone, but it just—I didn't believe it. I suddenly realized that Fitzpatrick was right behind me, and for some stupid reason I was looking down and there was her belly all exposed and there she was exposed in front of this stranger. And I pulled up her pants, or tried to. I didn't get them very far. It just didn't seem right that she should be out there like that."

The defendant said the next thing he remembered was two or three firefighters, or EMTs, arriving, and Fitzpatrick telling him to back away so they could do their jobs.

Greineder said he remembered backing up on his knees, ending up with his knee either in, or right next to, the pool of blood in the pathway.

"So what happened then, Doctor?"

"I heard somebody say something about putting up some tape and somebody, I think, grabbed my elbow and got me up and walked me out of there. I thought it was Fitzpatrick—I have heard that it wasn't—and walked me out to the circle area."

Greineder had just provided the jury with an explanation for how his heel mark ended up in his wife's blood. He had never mentioned before that he had backed up on his knees in the blood and that someone grabbed his elbow and got him up and walked him out of there.

Greineder testified that he stayed in the circle area with Fitzpatrick, separated from everyone else, until Detective McDermott arrived on the scene, patted him down, and then questioned him about what had happened.

"Do you recall asking Officer Fitzpatrick if your wife was dead?"

"I do. Everybody was in there. Nobody was coming out. Nobody was telling me anything, and I knew she was dead. But it just seemed like nobody was behaving the way they should. . . . And then I think—I don't know if I asked him then or later, if I was going to be arrested."

"Why did you ask Officer Fitzpatrick at some point that morning whether you were going to be arrested?"

"I suddenly realized that he had been told to keep me separate. I had been searched, and no one was talking to me."

"And by that point, Doctor, had you asked to use a cell phone to call your daughter?"

Greineder said at that point all he wanted to do was call his daughter Britt, who lived nearby. Kirsten was in Michigan and Colin was in New Haven.

"And I wanted to call Britt and I wanted to get out of there and I couldn't do that."

He told the jury despite his repeated requests to use a cell phone, he was not allowed to do so.

"I kept being told, 'Wait until the state policemen get here.'"

Finally Sergeant Foley arrived and Greineder asked him if he could use his cell phone.

"And he said: 'Well, just answer a few questions and we'll get around to that,' or something like that."

The jury heard that Foley questioned Greineder for some twenty or thirty minutes, during which time Greineder said he kept insisting he had to call Britt, but Foley kept insisting that there were only one or two more questions.

"Did you mention your dogs at all?" Murphy asked.

"I was trying to get out of there. I felt we had family things to do and I understood that there was going to be an investigation. I understood my wife's body had to stay there. That's sort of what I was complaining about when I asked Fitzpatrick about, you know, what was going to happen. But I felt we had family things to do. The kids had to be notified. We had to come together. I didn't know how I was going to tell the kids and even the dogs had to [be] part of that. We all had to come together and see how we were going to deal with the whole thing, and so I probably did mention the dog. Besides, there was a reason to let me out of there, and Zephyr was locked in the van. And by now, two hours had gone by. And I'm thinking, my God, we're going to kill her, too."

"Did there come a time, Doctor, when you went to the police station?"

"Finally it seemed like we were due to leave. Still, no permission to use a cell phone. There was a cell phone right in the car when I got in Foley's car. We were in the front seat, but he wouldn't let me use it. He said, 'No, no, call from the police station.' At this point, I thought, all right, we're leaving. Let's just go."

When he got to the Wellesley police station, Greineder said he was finally allowed to use the telephone to call his daughter. As he was making the call, the police suggested he ask Britt to stop at his house and bring him a change of clothes, because they wanted to keep the clothing he was wearing.

"With that, I suddenly realized that they thought I might have done this," Greineder said.

So Greineder called a friend, Terry Segal, who happened to be an attorney, because he felt he needed someone to help him deal with the situation. When Segal came, he advised Greineder to sign a release allowing police to take his clothes, as well as search his house and van.

When Britt arrived at the station, the police told her about her mother's murder before they allowed her to see her father.

"She came tearing in. She obviously knew and I think she asked me, 'What happened? What happened?'"

The defendant said while Britt and Segal were there, the police photographed him with his clothes on and without any clothing. They also clipped his fingernails. Then he changed into clothes that Segal's wife had brought to the station. Police wanted to keep Greineder's glasses, but he told them he needed them to drive and do his other daily business.

During this time, Greineder said Britt started making calls to notify the other family members.

Finally the group left the station, headed for the Greineders' home. Greineder said he went in Terry's car and the police followed in several cars. Britt drove to Morses Pond in her car to get Zephyr.

Greineder told the jury about the walk-through police did at his house. He said that afternoon, after the police had left, family members started arriving—first Colin, then Kirsten and Aleks. He testified that after the family went to bed, police came back with a search warrant to search the house. According to Greineder, after the police entered his house, Sergeant Foley told him to go into the living room and sit down because they had to talk. So he and Foley sat down on the sofa side by side; he said there were other officers standing in front of the sofa.

"[Foley] said to me, 'I need your help. We found some weapons.' I think he said weapons; he may not have said weapons. I know he enumerated: 'We have found a hammer and a knife and a right-hand glove and I want your help in telling me where the left-hand glove is.' And I don't know if I said anything or just looked at him, but I didn't know what he was talking about. And he said, 'If you could tell us where the left-hand glove is, it will be a lot better for your family.' I still don't recall saying anything. And then he went on to say, 'We found them in a storm drain right off the path that you went in, and I have got the time-line all figured out. I know what you did, and if you tell us what happened and help us find the glove, it will be a lot easier for your family.'"

Greineder went on to say that Foley told him the police had his DNA.

"And that sort of hit me like a ten-ton truck," he told the jury.

"What were you thinking when he said, 'We've got DNA'?"

"I mean, I'm not a forensic scientist. I'm not an expert in this field, but I know a fair amount about DNA, and this wasn't even a day after this happened. And there is no way, there is no way that he would have DNA, but that scared me."

While this conversation was going on, Greineder said, some other police officer was reading him his Miranda rights in the background. Greineder said he knew at this point he needed some help, so he called Terry Segal, who then called Nancy Gans, and then the entire family all went across the street to the Gans home.

In the meantime, Greineder said, police were searching his house, looking for a textured-palm work glove, an Old Timer knife or its packaging, an Estwing hammer and/or packaging, store receipts for any of those items, and any bloody clothing and bloody instruments.

"At that time, Doctor, did you know whether you had any work gloves with textured palms?" Murphy asked.

"I did. I knew I bought some somewhere along the line."

"Did you know where they were?"

"No, I had no idea."

"Now the jury has heard testimony about the police finding a pair of brown textured work gloves in your doghouse. Doctor, did you hide those gloves in the doghouse to prevent the police from finding them?"

"No."

"How did they get there?"

"I really don't know. I could only make assumptions."

"Well, can you tell us, sir, whether you can think of any activity that you would perform in the backyard that would lead you to leave those brown work gloves in the doghouse?"

"Objection, Your Honor," Grundy said.

"You may have the question," Chernoff told Greineder.

"Surely. Cleaning the doghouse, sweeping out the doghouse, I would definitely have used those gloves putting up the hoses and cleaning up in the backyard, maybe doing a little bit of raking; like I know I didn't do much, I would use those gloves or some gloves. So, whatever—many chores in the backyard, I would be putting on some gloves."

"And how would they end up in the doghouse?"

"The doghouse lid, I think we have seen, folds up, and when it is up like that, I would prop it up . . . so it doesn't fall on our heads, his head—and you can get in the doghouse and sweep it up and when you climb out, there is a ledge right over the entrance to the doghouse. There is a little two by four and I guess that's where I had seen the photos of where they were found, and I assumed I put them down there at some point after I finished cleaning."

"Do you have any memory of doing that, sir?"

"No, I do not."

The defendant said it was 3:00 A.M. by the time the police left and the family was able to return home. The next morning, he said, May's niece Belinda arrived with her three children. And shortly after that, May's sister, Ilse, and her husband, Murray, arrived. He told the jury one of the things he talked about with Belinda was whether he and his wife had sexual intercourse the morning of her murder.

"I'm pretty sure that what I told Belinda was, 'Can you believe it? Almost the first question the policeman asked me was had I had intercourse with my wife that morning.'"

This, of course, was not how Belinda testified she remembered the conversation. She said her uncle told her he and her aunt had had intercourse that morning, but it was okay because they were married.

"Do you remember telling Belinda anything else on that subject?" Murphy inquired.

"And I said, 'Of course not.' But, you know, at the time, on the one hand, I could sure understand the question, but it still was almost the first thing he asked me, and I said [to Belinda], you know, 'Can you believe that?' but I told her that we had not."

The defendant testified he decided not to tell Belinda or other members of his family the details of his wife's injuries because he thought it might upset them.

That morning, Greineder said, he surveyed the house to see what condition it was in and to make a list of the items the police confiscated during their search. He said he went through the home. "And as I went through the house, I went to the garage. And the first thing that struck me when I got into the garage is that all our gardening and work gloves that we owned were spread out on the floor and on the hood of the Toyota. They had been in a cabinet right in front of the cars, near the nose end of the cars, and the drawers had been pulled out and the gloves taken out and all spread out all over the floor and the hood. The other thing I noticed, I'm not sure that I noticed that on Monday morning or on Tuesday morning, but Monday or Tuesday I got in the car, the Toyota—the van we didn't have, the van was impounded. The police had that, so it was our only car at that point, but Britt had her car, and I got in the Toyota and I realized that the bloody towel was still on the passenger seat, where I had left it the day before. And also on the passenger seat was that dried brown circle of blood that we have seen photographs of here."

"And, Doctor, is that the circle of blood that you saw when you looked in your car after the search was conducted?" Murphy asked, showing his client a photograph of the stain.

"That's correct."

"Do you remember how that spot got there, Doctor?"

Greineder explained that about a month or two before she was killed, May had had a nosebleed while they were out driving one evening and it dripped between her legs. Greineder said he didn't realize it at the time and then just never got around to cleaning it up. He said when he saw it the morning he found the towel, he figured he'd get into trouble if he cleaned it up.

"When I saw it that morning, I really didn't know what to think, I almost cleaned it up."

"Why didn't you?"

"I thought: My God, if I touch this, I could get into trouble. I mean, they searched my house. I don't know. I know it is innocent, but I had already decided I better leave it. I hadn't cleaned it up before, I better leave it now."

"Doctor, after you came back from the pond on October thirty-first, can you tell us whether or not you had any supply of your wife's blood around the house?"

"No."

"Did you create the bloodstain on that seat between October thirty-first and November twelfth?"

"No. I wouldn't have been able to."

Murphy asked Greineder about the two sketches of Morses Pond that police found in a yellow wastebasket when they searched his house on November 12.

Greineder explained that he made those diagrams for Murphy on November 5 to describe the area before they actually went to walk around it. Greineder also said on that same day he gave Murphy the bloody towel he claimed he and May used to stop their nosebleeds the day she was killed.

Greineder said he gave it to his attorney because he was concerned that it might contain evidence that would be pertinent to the case and he was very concerned that the police had not found it the night of November 1.

"I felt that it would probably, or possibly, lead to a misunderstanding because I couldn't believe that they hadn't seen it," he said.

Murphy questioned Greineder about his discussions with his family concerning DNA. Greineder said he talked about DNA with Kirsten and Colin, both of whom were trained in molecular biology and had personal, practical experience with DNA reactions.

"Did you express any other concerns about DNA in these discussions with your family?"

"Being a biochemist and molecular biologist of sorts myself, and having read a lot of the literature about it, I knew DNA was transferable and that tiny amounts of DNA could be analyzed for it. . . . The amount of DNA required to get a positive reading in the laboratory, in a scientific laboratory, is exceedingly small, and I felt concern that when two people live together—there had been a bleeding episode involving us the same day—and there could be DNA contamination at the scene, or at—you know, of us— that could lead to misinterpretation of the data, just knowing that this level of sensitivity of the DNA analysis is great. I didn't know that—I wasn't a forensic DNA specialist, but I knew that we could measure tiny amounts."

"And did you express those concerns to members of your family?"

"I did, and I was not at all reassured by the kids who confirmed that their expected impression also was that it didn't take much."

The receipt for the six boxes of nails bought at Diehl's hardware store—the ones bought a couple of minutes before the purchase of a two-pound drilling hammer—was the next topic Murphy addressed with his client.

"In the course of this case, Doctor, have you learned that one of the things that the police seized in your house on November twelfth was a receipt for the purchase of nails at Diehl's?"

"I have become aware of that."

"Tell us, Doctor, whether you remember, one way or the other, whether you bought six boxes of nails at Diehl's on September 3, 1999."

"I cannot recall. I don't know."

"Could you have?"

"I—it's conceivable. I do not remember buying six boxes of nails, but I really have no memory of such an event."

"Have you bought nails before at Diehl's?"

"Oh, yes."

"Doctor, have you ever bought a two-pound drilling hammer at Diehl's?"

"No."

"Do you think that would be something you would remember?"

"Oh, I think I would remember that."

"Did you buy this two-pound drilling hammer at Diehl's on September 3, 1999?" Murphy asked, holding up the hammer.

"I did not."

"Are you sure?"

"I'm very sure."

"Did you buy this knife anywhere before October 31, 1999?" Murphy asked, holding up the knife.

"I did not."

"Doctor, before October 31, 1999, did you form an elaborate plan to kill your wife?"

"I did not."

"On October 31, 1999, did you go out to Morses Pond with gloves and a hammer and a knife and a loaf pan and other gloves and lighter fluid with the intention of killing your wife?"

"I did not."

"On October 31, 1999, Doctor, did you want to kill your wife?"

"I did not."

"How did you feel about your wife, Doctor, on October 31, 1999?"

"I loved my wife, and I loved her on October 31, 1999."

"How did you feel about your family, Doctor, on October 31, 1999?"

"It was the most important thing to me in my life, more than work, more than fame, more than money."

"Doctor, did you kill your wife?"

"I did not."

"I have nothing further, Your Honor."

And with that, Murphy concluded his direct examination of his client. Murphy had done the best he could to tear down the building blocks of the prosecution's circumstantial evidence. Despite the fact that he rarely looked at the jurors when he answered his attorney's questions, court observers thought Greineder came off sincere and believable. He looked legitimately horrified and afraid when he talked about finding his wife's body and then knowing police were zeroing in on him as her murderer. However, while he appeared to cry at the appropriate moments of his testimony, the tears just didn't seem to flow.

Throughout his direct testimony, some jurors looked straight at him, while others kept their heads down, taking notes. What were they thinking? Did they find him credible and his story plausible? The answer would come soon enough.

Chapter 19

Dr. Dirk Greineder came off pretty well during questioning by his attorney—acting cool and calm and showing emotion at just the right moments—but if he thought he was going to escape unscathed under Grundy's cross-examination, he was in for a rude awakening.

As soon as Murphy finished questioning his client, Grundy jumped up from his seat and started peppering the defendant with questions, often not even waiting for Greineder to answer one question before he fired off another.

The first series of questions was designed to show that while he claimed to love his wife, Greineder left the heartbreaking and unpleasant task of notifying the family of May's death to his younger daughter, even though he had no problem calling a prostitute the day after his wife's gruesome murder.

"Doctor, on October thirty-first, you had Britt call Kirsten to inform her of the death of her mother; is that correct?" asked Grundy.

"Yes, sir."

"And you had Britt call Colin to inform him of the death of his mother?"

"I don't recall exactly how we tried to reach Colin. He was not in his room when we called him."

"And you had Britt call Belinda Markel to inform her of the death of her aunt?"

"I don't think so. I don't recall who called, but I believe that fell to me. But, again, I can't remember."

"Are you telling this jury that you called Belinda Markel to inform her of the death of her aunt May?" Grundy asked.

"I know I talked to Belinda about the death of her aunt."

"My question to you, sir, is: who called her to inform her?"

"I don't remember."

In fact, Markel testified that it was Britt who called her home first and left a number for her to call, and when she called that number, she reached Greineder.

"And who called May's older sister to inform her of the death on October 31, 1999?" Grundy continued.

"To the best of my recollection, Britt, a member of my family," Greineder answered, never looking at the jury.

"And on October 31, 1999, you loved May?"

"I loved May, and now."

"And Britt was making those calls. And on November first, you loved May, too; isn't that correct, sir?" Grundy said, his voice dripping with sarcasm.

"I love her now."

"And you called who on November first?"

"I called Ms. Doolio."

"Thank you."

"To cancel—"

"Can we take a lunch break, Your Honor?" Grundy asked, paying no attention to the defendant's last comment.

After lunch, Grundy zeroed in on the lack of blood

on Greineder's hands, again pelting him with one question right after another.

"I'm showing you, sir, exhibit eighty-five, exhibit eighty-four, and those are your hands as they appear as they were photographed at the Wellesley Police Department within an hour, or, excuse me, within two hours after finding your wife; is that correct?"

"No, that's not correct."

"And, I'm sorry, showing you, sir, exhibit twenty-six, is that a picture of how your hand appeared and that jacket appeared, again at the time that you were photographed at the Wellesley Police Department?" Grundy asked, not paying any attention to Greineder's previous answer.

"Yes, but it was not at the time you said."

Grundy continued this line of questioning, reminding Greineder that he told Sergeant Foley he had not washed his hands after he had touched his wife's bloody body.

"Sergeant Foley asked you if you washed your hands, and you said, 'No.' He asked you why there was no blood on your hands, and you stated you didn't know. He asked you if you had washed your hands, and you stated, 'No, the police have been with me the whole time.'"

Realizing Grundy's tactics were confusing his client, Murphy stood to object.

"Objection, Your Honor. May we have one question at a time?"

"I would prefer that," Greineder said.

"Why don't you break it up into two parts?" Judge Chernoff told Grundy.

"Sure. Do you recall telling Sergeant Foley that you hadn't washed your hands because the police had been with you the whole time?"

"I believe I do."

Grundy then hammered Greineder for changing his story about the number of times he tried to pick his wife up when he found her lying in the pathway. During direct examination, Greineder said he tried to pick his wife up several times. However, until that point, he had always maintained he only tried to pick her up once. The prosecution believed that Greineder changed his story in order to explain the blood spatter on his clothes and sneakers.

"And today we hear that you actually tried to pick your wife up a number of times; isn't that correct, sir?"

"That's correct."

"You never told police that prior to today, did you, sir?"

"They never asked."

"Your statement was, 'I tried to pick her up. She was deadweight.' That was it, correct?"

"That's the statement I gave to them at the time."

"And your statement to this jury right now is: 'They never asked if I tried to pick her up anymore.' Is that correct, sir?"

"That's correct."

"And you didn't think that would be important to tell them?"

"What was important to me was trying to pick her up."

"And when you were feeling put upon by the police and they were asking for your clothes, including that jacket, you still didn't think it was important to tell them you tried to pick her up a number of times; is that correct, sir?"

"I didn't tell them about it; that's correct."

"And the question is: you didn't think it was important to; is that correct?" Grundy asked, never letting up on the defendant.

"I didn't feel we were talking about that kind of subject at that time."

Grundy continued.

"Well, how many times did you try and pick up your wife, sir?"

"Three times, although the middle one was not a very substantial effort."

"And it's fair to state that the first time you ever mentioned that to anybody was here today at trial?"

"Objection, Your Honor."

"The objection is sustained," Judge Chernoff said.

"Did you mention that, sir, to any investigators prior to today?"

Again, Murphy objected, and the judge agreed with him again.

Grundy tried to ask his question a different way, without leading the witness.

"Again, sir, when you spoke to investigators about the death of your wife, did you ever mention that you had tried to pick her up more than once?"

"Only on the day of the murder," Greineder responded, contradicting his previous testimony.

"Oh, you did tell them that?" Grundy pointed up the inconsistency.

"No, I was never—we never discussed anything about the murder except the day of the murder."

"And your testimony today is that during this process of trying to pick her up numerous times, you noticed what you called that wound. Is that correct?"

"Essentially, yes."

"And prior to this date, you told a number of people that you didn't see the neck wound until you went back the second time; is that correct?"

"I don't believe that's correct."

"You didn't tell anybody that?"

"I believe that I mentioned that I took her pulse on the side that I would not normally use because I saw the wound on the left side of her neck and I did not want to disturb that. When I talked to them, I didn't say that part, but I said, 'I took her pulse on the right side because I didn't want to disturb the wound on the left side.' "

Foley, however, testified that Greineder told him that he didn't see the gaping wound on his wife's neck until he went back to the body after having called police for help.

Grundy, who had no patience with Greineder's attempts to avoid answering his questions, tried again.

"And, again, sir, I would ask you to listen to the question. Did you, in fact, tell people that you did not see the wound on the left side of May's neck until you returned to her a second time?"

"No, that's not correct."

Grundy tried to ask the question again, in such a way as to trick the doctor into giving a different answer. Even though Greineder didn't bite, the damage to his credibility had already been done.

"And, sir, as you testify here today . . . it's your testimony that returning the second time you then checked her left carotid artery; is that correct, sir?"

"That is not correct."

Grundy then asked Greineder about all the things he touched after he tried to pick up his wife's bloody body, including his car phone and the handle of Officer Fitzpatrick's patrol car. Those items had one thing in common—none of them had blood on them because his hands did not have blood on them.

Grundy also attacked more new information Greineder provided during his direct examination.

"Sir, did you tell Sergeant Foley that you were on your knees and you backed up into this pool of blood with the investigators looking on?"

"I cannot recall my exact words, but I believe that's roughly what I said then, and this morning."

"Oh, you believe that you actually told an investigator who has testified here in court during the course of your trial that you were on your knees and you backed up on your knees into a pool of blood?"

"No, I'm sorry. You have managed to make me misspeak," Greineder responded, clearly weakening under Grundy's blistering cross-examination. "I remember backing up; I don't remember whether I told Sergeant Foley that."

"And you never said that before you heard Deborah Rebeiro talk about your heel mark, did you?"

Murphy jumped to his feet to object, but the judge allowed Greineder to answer the question.

"You didn't ever say that until you heard Deborah Rebeiro talk about your heel mark in that blood?" Grundy rephrased the question.

"Objection to 'ever'," Murphy said.

"All right. You can lay a foundation for time," Judge Chernoff said.

"Do you understand the question, sir?" Grundy asked the defendant.

"I don't remember whether I told anybody about backing up on my knees."

Grundy pelted Greineder with more questions about inconsistencies in his testimony. Grundy pointed out that although Greineder testified under direct examination that he didn't realize his wife's injuries weren't caused by an accident until he returned to his wife with

Officer Fitzpatrick and was on his knees in a pool of blood, he told the Wellesley police dispatcher that "someone attacked her. It's definitely an attack."

During his cross-examination, Grundy painted Greineder as an uncaring husband, one who was more interested in getting home to take care of his dogs than staying at the pond to help police find out what happened to his wife.

Greineder said he told police at the pond that he needed to get home to his dogs as an excuse because he "wanted to get out of there and that was another reason to get out of there," although he explained that caring for his dogs was not his main concern. He said what he really wanted to do was call his daughter Britt, but police wouldn't let him and he became frustrated with the whole situation.

"And you were frustrated and you were angry at the police and you wanted to care for your dog and call Britt, and I believe your statement was you wanted to get out of there, correct? Was that your statement, sir?" Grundy asked.

"That was my statement. May I explain it?"

Grundy ignored him and went right to the next question and a new subject—the plastic bags police found at the scene of May's murder—bags that the FBI later identified as coming from the Greineder household. In his direct testimony, Greineder explained that sometimes his wife took plastic bags to the pond to pick berries to put in the bird feeders. He also said the couple had planned to put up the bird feeders that weekend. But he admitted under questioning from Grundy that May never mentioned anything to him about picking berries for the birds on the morning she was murdered.

Soon Grundy was grilling Greineder about the virtually simultaneous nosebleeds he and his wife had in the garage before they went to the pond.

"Sir, not only with respect to investigators, but when you spoke to your own niece, Belinda, the term you used was, 'We had simultaneous nosebleeds that morning'; isn't that correct?"

"I believe that is likely true."

"And you never told Belinda that the dog jumped on you and caused the nosebleed, did you, sir?"

"I don't believe the dog jumped on me at all."

"Well, didn't you just tell the jury that you were wrestling around with the dog, trying to get it in the car, and that's how your simultaneous nosebleed occurred?"

"Since every word that I have said you're asking me to be very precise about, I did not say the dog jumped on me. I said the dog's head bumped my nose."

"And, again, sir, you never told your niece Belinda that . . . you had simultaneous nosebleeds?"

"They were minutes apart."

"My question, sir, is: did you tell Belinda that you had simultaneous nosebleeds?"

"No—yes."

"And it's fair to say that as you testify to this jury today, charged with murder, you realize that sounds ridiculous and you changed the story?" Grundy asked, obviously wearing the defendant down.

"No, that's not true."

And to prove his contention that the defendant did not always answer questions truthfully, as well as to get into his secret life of pornography and prostitutes, the prosecutor brought up the doctor's use of Internet screen names.

"For instance, sir, you indicated in response to Mr. Murphy's questions that you used certain names on the Internet, and you told Mr. Murphy that you used the name Ryder?"

"That's correct."

"But that's not what you used, is it, sir?"

"I did."

"What was the name that you used, sir, that had Ryder in it?"

"I used Ryder and variations on Ryder."

"What kind of variations, sir?"

"Why don't you prompt me?" Greineder asked, trying to bait Grundy.

"Pardon me."

"I know I used Pussy Ryder on some occasions," Greineder finally answered.

"What else?"

"Casual Guy."

"Two thousand," Grundy added.

"Yes."

"The ad that you responded to from Ms. Doolio had a caption, 'Casual Elegance'; is that correct?" Grundy asked.

"I never saw that ad."

"You never saw that ad?"

"Not in the *Phoenix*. I never read the *Phoenix*."

"And Ms. Doolio would be the individual who testified last week that in a conversation in September, she told you to call her when you were ready to see her; is that correct?"

Greineder testified that he didn't believe that he had called Doolio in September.

"And could you tell the jurors: was there something that you expected would occur in the year 2000 that would make you a casual guy?" Grundy continued.

"No. Would you like to know why I used that name?"

Grundy ignored his question and moved on to talk

about Elizabeth Porter, the prostitute Greineder met with in February 1998. The prosecutor focused on all the lies the defendant told Porter when they were together. The implication was obvious—this was a man who could lie easily when it suited his purpose. So why should the jury believe anything he told them now?

"Sir, you indicated you met with a prostitute in February of 1998; is that correct?"

"That's correct."

"And her name was Elizabeth, wasn't it?"

"It was."

"And your first name to her was Tom; is that correct?"

"That's correct."

"And that was a lie?"

"That's correct."

"And you told Elizabeth you were a researcher from California; is that correct, sir?"

"Actually, I said a researcher from Baltimore. She remembered wrong. . . . I told her I was a researcher from Baltimore, since Tom Young, I knew, was in Baltimore."

"Your friend Tom Young, who you wanted people to think you were in case trouble happened. . . . So, I guess, it wouldn't have mattered if he was in California versus Maryland; it's all a lie, right?"

"It wasn't true."

Grundy questioned Greineder about his conversations with Elizabeth, asking him if he told her he stopped having sex with his wife because she was old and soft, and whether he told the prostitute that he was getting a divorce from his wife.

Looking down, not at the jury, Greineder said he told Elizabeth that he and his wife were no longer intimate and he might have told her they were divorcing. "I told her . . . that I hadn't had sex with [my wife] for

a long time, and I was so embarrassed that I was need-
ing to hire a prostitute to have sex that I did tell her
that I was separated and I might have used the word
'divorced,' but it was because I was so embarrassed that
I should need to use a prostitute while I was married,
standing there with my wedding ring. I felt terribly—"

"And then you went back to Elizabeth to have sex
with her again, despite your embarrassment,"
Grundy said. "You took your ring off and you made a
point of saying to her, 'Look, I don't have my wedding ring on anymore,' didn't you, sir?"

"I did."

"And, sir, you got over your embarrassment to the
point where you would Internet naked pictures of yourself with full-frontal nudity to strangers, correct, sir?"

"In response to their pictures."

On the topic of his relationship with his wife,
Greineder told the jurors that the couple's problems
started when May told him she was no longer interested in having sex because it was painful. He said
that was the one difficulty they couldn't seem to re-
solve. However, he admitted that they hadn't gone to
counseling to try and work through it. He explained
they had seen a counselor earlier in their marriage,
and although they thought it had been helpful, they
decided they didn't want to do it again.

Grundy also brought out the fact that in the years
before her death May had had a face-lift, lost weight,
and started buying new clothes and wearing sexy lin-
gerie. This was the prosecutor's way of implying that
she was trying to win back her husband's affection because she knew he was seeking pleasure elsewhere.

During his cross-examination, Grundy questioned
Greineder about how May hurt her back the morning
she was killed. Grundy wanted to know which story the

defendant told was true. Did she slip on the gravel in the sand pit and injure her back, or did she hurt herself throwing the ball to Zephyr? And if so, did she throw the ball underhand or overhand? Did Greineder see her throw her back out, or did he hear something, turn around, and realize she was injured?

Greineder admitted it was possible that he told different stories to different people.

"I remember the dog running for the ball, the ball being in motion around the same time. I probably did assume the day at the pond that she had been in the act of throwing when she hurt herself."

"So if you had said at any point prior to today that you saw her slip, twist her back, and throw the ball, that would be incorrect, but we've got it right now; is that correct?"

"Objection, Your Honor," Murphy said.

"No, you may answer it," the judge told Greineder.

"My best recollection is that she was throwing the ball, but most likely, that I actually saw the ball more than I saw her throw it," he explained.

"And this was after she had already slipped on the gravel and hurt herself?"

"I don't believe I said it was after."

"You didn't say that you heard the gravel slip?"

"I did hear the gravel slip."

Grundy then reminded Greineder that May had hurt her back a few days before they went to the pond together. And he questioned why Greineder would leave his wife alone and continue walking his dog when she was so obviously injured.

"But whether she had hurt her back two days before or not, and whether she had thrown a ball and you saw it, whether she was slipping and falling, you decided to leave her in the sand pit instead of going in the exact same route that you were both going, help her through that path, help her through the gravel, help her up the incline, get to the rock, take the dog to the water, and go up the paved surface. That was the decision you made, correct?"

"I guess. Most of the time, given time, she could resume movement as long as she was careful and slow," Greineder said.

"Careful and slow through the gravel, through the sand, up the incline, out to the rock, where you were both going anyhow, to the paved surface?"

"Mr. Grundy, it's the worst decision I ever made in my life."

"Perhaps, perhaps not."

"Objection, Your Honor," Murphy said.

"I'm going to strike both the answer and the comment," Judge Chernoff said.

Grundy continued, "The question, sir, again was: through the gravel, the path, the incline, to the rock?"

"That's what I asked—what she told me she wanted to do," Greineder said.

Grundy now launched another attack at Greineder regarding exactly what he saw that made him go down the paved pathway, where the murder weapons were ultimately discovered.

When Grundy asked him about going down that path and whether or not he saw Bill Kear and his little dog walking down the access road, Greineder said his eyes were focused on movement and the person he thought he saw running into the pathway.

Grundy's contention was that Greineder didn't see Kear when he went into that paved pathway to dispose of the murder weapons. But when he came back out and realized Kear had seen him, he had to make up a reason for going there.

"Let's talk about that movement, sir. Had you ever termed what you alleged to have seen in that paved path we're looking at right now as 'movement' before, or is that a new term?" Grundy asked as he displayed a photo of the path on the screen at the front of the courtroom.

"I believe I told Officer [Detective] McDermott that I saw a shadow move. I believe that's the phrase I used. I saw a shadow move and thought it might be a runner. That's my best recollection."

Grundy then asked the defendant if he told Kear that he saw a shadow, a jogger, or movement when he came out of the paved path and asked to use Kear's cell phone.

"No, I did not."

"And you didn't tell Bill Kear that he should get the hell out of there because it's dangerous—your wife had just been attacked?"

"I wasn't in the slightest thinking about danger at that moment."

"You didn't say anything to Mr. Magnan about a shadow, a jogger—that you thought you saw movement; is that correct?"

"That's correct."

"You spoke to the police, specifically the dispatcher, Shannon Parillo, and you told her specifically that there is a jogger, being Mr. Magnan, and there's another guy with a small dog, correct?"

"I am not sure."

"And those were the only two people—"

"I need to have my memory refreshed," Greineder interrupted the question.

"And those were the only two people you mentioned; is that correct?"

"I think. Wasn't her question, was anybody there with me? I think that—I'm not sure, but I—"

"And you didn't mention it to Shannon Parillo or anyone else that you saw, correct?"

"No."

"No shadow."

"No."

"No movement."

"No."

After a five-minute break, Greineder continued pounding Greineder with questions about whether he told anyone at the scene that day that he saw a shadow, or movement, or a jogger go down that paved path. It didn't matter what answer Greineder gave to Grundy—the defense attorney was never satisfied. He just kept asking the same question over and over again, in different ways, trying to confuse the defendant. Grundy knew it was difficult to remember what lie you told to which person.

"Sir, to recap, I believe upon finding your wife, you spoke to Bill Kear, Rick Magnan, Shannon Parillo, the dispatcher at the Wellesley police, Mr. Magnan again, Paul Fitz[Patrick], and I believe that's where we left off; is that correct?"

"I believe so."

"You subsequently speak with a firefighter by the name of William DeLorie; is that correct?"

"I do not know his name and I do not know which one I spoke to."

"Can you say whether or not, sir, you told him about a shadow, jogger, movement down that paved path?"

"I don't believe I did."

"And there is no mention, as you stand within your estimate of fifty to sixty feet of that path, as you stand there with, as your testimony goes to this jury, an officer assigned to not let you leave, with your question to him being, 'Is she dead? Am I going to be arrested?' and you don't mention to Officer Fitz[Patrick] movement, shadow, jogger?"

Murphy stood to object because Grundy had asked his client more than one question at a time, but Judge Chernoff allowed Greineder to answer it.

"I knew the path was empty when I entered it, and at that moment I wasn't concerned about the path; I was concerned about what had happened and I wasn't yet, I think, really thinking about anything else except what had happened," Greineder responded.

Grundy continued to hurl questions at Greineder about the movement he claimed caused him to go into the paved pathway.

"And you see movement. And by the time you get there, whatever this movement is, is gone."

"I looked down the path, and I can't see anyone."

"But you go down the path."

"I enter into the path; that's correct."

"You go down the path, sir, you don't enter it. Your testimony was that you went down the path. You have got a man with a little dog thirty feet away from you." Grundy refused to let up on the defendant.

"I haven't seen the man."

"Objection, Your Honor. Can we have a question, not an argument?" Murphy said.

Grundy continued right where he left off, without waiting for the judge to rule on the objection.

"Is this just after you held your wife and slashed her throat?" Grundy asked, seething.

Again, Murphy jumped up to object.

This time, the court agreed.

"Let's stop and let's start with a question," Chernoff told Grundy.

"Was this after you just tried to pick your wife up
three times, sir?" Grundy asked sarcastically.

"Shortly after, exactly."

Grundy then resumed questioning Greineder
about how far he went into the path and how long he
stayed there.

"I went down the path a number of, what I would
call, body lengths, turned around when I realized I
didn't see anyone, slipped a little, and then came back
as fast as I could. As I stopped to turn around, I slipped
on a leaf and then came back out. I also haven't told
anybody that, because I didn't think it was terribly important."

"Well, that saves me some questions, sir. The first
time that slip has ever been mentioned," Grundy said,
implying that the defendant was continuing to change
his story to fit the evidence. Saying he slipped on a leaf
while he was in the paved pathway would help him explain why he was out of sight for twenty or thirty
seconds, as Kear testified.

Before ending his cross-examination for the day,
Grundy clashed with Greineder over the inconsistencies in his statements about a back rub he said
May gave him the morning she was murdered. At the
scene, police noted that Greineder had a couple of
scratches on his neck. The prosecution believed that
Greineder made up the story to explain why his wife
might have his skin under her fingernails, but ultimately none of his DNA was found under her
fingernails.

"Did May give you a back rub that morning, sir?"
Grundy asked.

"Scratched my back."

"You told Detective McDermott she gave you a back rub, right? Did you tell Detective McDermott that?"

"I used the word 'back rub,' but I misspoke."

"And did you testify to the jurors today she scratched your back?"

"It was more of a scratch."

"Are you sure it was a scratch, sir?"

"She often had an itchy back. I scratched her back, and naturally she scratched mine, where my scar is."

"Sir, do you recall Detective McDermott specifically asking you after you told her that May gave you a back rub and, therefore, 'you would find my skin under her fingernails,' did she ask you: 'Did you give May a back rub?' And you said, 'No.'"

"I didn't give her a back rub."

"You scratched her back?"

"My memory is that I also did that. I think that's how—"

"Excuse me. And you told Detective McDermott, no; is that correct?"

"I don't remember saying that. I don't remember. I might have. I don't remember."

"Anyhow, it's not true, is it?"

"No. To the best of my memory, she scratched my back and—okay. Actually, I rubbed her back with my fingertips. She liked to scratch; I liked to rub. That's the difference, because her skin is very sensitive and she wants me to scratch, but I always rub it, so that I don't scratch. But it's just basically, and not an itchy—it's rubbing to control, not a back rub massage, but just getting-rid-of-my-itchy-back kind of rub."

"So, it's not your itchy back; it's your wife that has the sensitive skin, right?"

"That's right, and she liked—she would scratch

and say, 'That's what you should do to me,' and I said, 'No, I won't do that.'"

Grundy had heard enough of Greineder's ramblings.

"Sir, were you lying to Detective McDermott, or are you lying to the jury?"

Greineder didn't say a word; he just shook his head no. This was the first time he was at a loss for words. Standing for nearly seven hours in ninety-five degree heat in the courtroom had taken its toll on the normally composed doctor.

Chapter 20

When Grundy resumed his cross-examination of Greineder the next day, June 20, he continued to press the defendant on the inconsistencies in his statements to the jury and those he made right after the murder.

"Sir, I believe yesterday you testified that, in fact, you had attempted to pick your wife up three times, as opposed to the one time that you had initially told the police. Is that correct?"

"That's not actually precise. I never quantified to the police. I told them I tried to pick her up. They never asked further and at that particular moment it didn't seem to me to be that important. I was more focused on my wife, rather than on, I guess, stains on myself," Greineder said, responding more confidently than he had the previous day.

"Right. And now you're focused on the stains on yourself. Correct?"

"No."

"But now you do remember that, in fact, you tried to pick her up three times?"

"I always remembered that. It's not something that was discussed."

"And what you said to the police was 'I tried to pick her up. I couldn't. She was deadweight.'"

"That's correct."

Grundy then asked Greineder to explain exactly how he tried to pick his wife up. The prosecutor even squatted down on the courtroom floor trying to act out the defendant's account of the events. Again, Grundy's contention was that Greineder changed his story about the number of times he tried to pick up his wife in order to explain the blood spatter on his clothes and shoes. Greineder claimed he was splattered with his wife's blood when her body fell back to the ground.

"Tell us now, today, as you remember, how did you position yourself to first try and pick up your wife, exactly?"

"It's difficult to do that. I know I was kneeling."

"On both knees or one?"

"I'm not completely sure. . . . I cannot remember whether I tried to pick her up with bringing up my other knee. Again, my usual habit would be to pick up something with one knee down and one knee up, because that's just what I've learned to do with my legs. I really don't remember . . . how I positioned my feet—whether I had one knee down or both. I assume I had at least one knee up, because it's sort of hard to get up from both knees."

Grundy continued to press Greineder on the exact position of his body when he tried to lift his wife—acting out each pose as the defendant described it.

"Did her entire body come off the ground?" Grundy asked at one point in his cross-examination.

"No."

"How much of her body came off the ground?"

"It wasn't terribly high. The upper part of the body came off the ground. Even then her head started to drop back. I don't think it was very high because—on that side—because I remember being frightened by the way her head was moving."

"And you saw the neck wound. Right?" Grundy asked, once again drawing attention to Greineder's varying statements about when he first saw that wound.

"Yes. I had seen the neck wound."

"I apologize," Grundy said. "Do you recall telling people that you did not see the second wound—the neck wound—until the second time you returned to her?"

"I don't believe that—my best recollection is that I told somebody, and I can't really say who, that I saw the neck wound when I first took her pulse on the right side. . . . I avoided the left pulse because I was aware of the injury and I wanted to stay away from this. . . . I'm fairly confident that at that moment I knew the wound was on the left side. I would not have taken her pulse on the right. I would not have specified the right side in my statements to McDermott and Foley, if I had not been aware that—I mean, that's what makes me realize that I was conscious of the wound when I took her pulse on the right side. I would have otherwise taken it on the left," Greineder said, keeping his head down. Not once did Greineder look at the jury while talking about the events surrounding his wife's murder.

"So again, sir, the question is—yes or no—do you recall telling Detective McDermott that 'I didn't notice the wound to her neck until the second time I returned'? Yes or no, sir?"

"I do not recall telling her that."

"But do you recall, in fact, telling Sergeant Foley that 'I checked her right carotid artery for the first time and then, upon returning, I checked the left carotid artery, where I do a better job.' Do you recall that, sir? Yes or no."

"I remember saying something about doing a better job on the left side. And I can't be more precise than that."

Grundy kept bombarding Greineder with very specific questions about how he tried to pick up his wife. By asking for such an incredible amount of detail, the prosecutor hoped to trip Greineder up, make him misspeak. Grundy knew Greineder would have a hard time describing every aspect of what he did, because he was lying. At times, the defendant looked angry and exasperated; at other times, he came off as stubborn and obstinate.

Grundy next questioned Greineder about his relationship with Terry Segal. He wanted to show that the two men weren't particularly close and the only reason Greineder called him from the police station the day May was murdered was because he was a lawyer. Greineder did look at the jury when he talked about Segal.

Grundy also asked Greineder about the blood on the glasses he wore at Morses Pond the day his wife was murdered. Greineder told the jury he knew there was blood on the left lens of his glasses, but he didn't know how that blood got there.

Jumping from one topic to another, Grundy asked the defendant with whom he communicated over the Internet the night his wife was killed. Greineder responded that he "really couldn't say." Grundy then interrogated Greineder about why he turned to sex over the Internet and about a woman with whom he exchanged e-mails for a period of time in 1998. Grundy wanted to show that maybe the defendant was having a relationship with someone who was not a prostitute.

During their investigation, Wellesley police found an e-mail Greineder had written to a woman the

night of his wife's murder, saying he wouldn't be able
to speak with her for a while because of a tragedy. Police believed she lived in Portugal and had met
Greineder at a medical conference. They also believed that he was having an intimate sexual relationship with her. But they were never able to track
her down.

"Sir, you indicated that when you started using the
Internet for the different purposes you've described
during this trial, you ended up having a back-and-
forth with someone who then suggested to you that
you communicate by e-mail instead of in different
chat rooms. Is that correct?"

"In 1998, I believe, that's correct."

"Who was that person, sir?"

"I have no recollection."

"What was her screen name?"

"I have no recollection of that either."

"No idea whatsoever?"

"It was in 1998. I remember that person and I exchanged some e-mails for a period of a few weeks.
And I don't remember the screen name."

Grundy then grilled Greineder about why he was involved in phone sex. The prosecutor wanted to know
if it was because his wife was no longer interested in a
sexual relationship with him. The defendant stumbled
over his words.

". . . I testified that I started doing it after, not because of . . . ," Greineder said.

Hoping to catch Greineder off guard, Grundy continually switched from one subject to another.

He next asked Greineder when he cut up the credit
cards police found in his work area. Greineder said he
cut them up either Saturday night or Halloween morning before he and May went to the pond. But police

didn't find them during their first walk-through of the Greineder house. They only found them when they came back with a search warrant on November 1. Greineder said he didn't know why police didn't see them the first time they walked through his house.

Grundy quizzed Greineder about May's paper that was on his computer—the paper he claimed he helped her with the night before she was killed. During his direct examination, Greineder initially didn't recognize the paper. Grundy's point was that Greineder wasn't familiar with the document because he never really worked on it with his wife.

Grundy now turned his attention back to the almost simultaneous nosebleeds Greineder said the couple had in their garage right before they headed out to Morses Pond. Grundy used his questioning to ridicule the defendant for even telling such a story and to ask him about the bloody towel he said they used to stem the bleeding.

The prosecutor then asked Greineder if, on the day after his wife's murder, he told his niece Belinda that May's funeral would be delayed because he wanted to have a second autopsy done on her. Greineder danced around the question, initially saying he wanted the second autopsy done because he had found May's dilator. Ultimately, though, he admitted that he had talked about a second autopsy with Belinda before he ever mentioned finding a dilator. During her testimony, Belinda Markel told the jury her uncle said May's funeral would be delayed because he wanted to have a second autopsy done. The issue of a second autopsy—whether Greineder found May's dilator or not—never made much sense to the media or to court observers. But people speculated that when Greineder found his wife's dilator, it reminded him that it was painful for his wife to have sex. So he figured if he had a second autopsy done, it would reveal her condition, adding credibility to his statement that it was his wife's decision to stop having intercourse.

But according to the trial transcripts of a sidebar the attorneys had with the judge during this part of Greineder's testimony—the defense attorney objected to Grundy's line of questioning here and asked to be heard at the sidebar—the prosecution's reason for continuing to press the defendant on this matter became abundantly clear. During the trial, the public and the jury were not privy to what was said during the sidebar, so no one knew then exactly what Grundy was driving at with this part of his cross-examination.

First, it's important to remember that when police conducted a search of Greineder's house, as well as the Toyota that was in the garage, police never found the bloody towel Greineder said he threw on the seat of that car after he and May had used it for their nosebleeds. Jill McDermott said she saw a towel in the car during that search, but it did not have blood on it, only coffee and other stains, so she didn't take it as part of the search. However, Greineder said, when he got into the Toyota on the Monday or Tuesday after his wife's murder, the towel was still on the seat where he left it. During his direct examination, he said he gave that towel to Murphy on November 5, when the two met to discuss the case. But Murphy didn't turn the towel over to police until two months after Greineder's arraignment in February 2000.

In addition, during questioning by his attorney, Greineder said the same day he found the towel he noticed a small circle of blood on the passenger seat that he claimed was there on November 1 when police first searched his car. But again, police didn't see that spot until their November 12 search, at which time they took a sample of it. That blood belonged to May.

During direct-examination, Murphy asked Greineder if he had a supply of his wife's blood lying around the house after she was murdered and if he created the bloodstain on the seat of the car. Greineder responded he "did not" to both questions. He said the blood spot on the seat got there a few weeks before May's death.

"While driving in my car somewhere, I believe we were going somewhere in the evening because I remember May had a pants suit on, or something like that, or a better pair of slacks—it wasn't jeans. She got a nosebleed while we were driving in the car and it dripped between her legs and made that stain. We went on our business. But later, about that time, I realized the stain was there and I just never got around to cleaning it up. And when I saw it that morning, I really didn't know what to think. I almost cleaned it up."

"Why didn't you?" Murphy asked.

"I thought: My God, if I touch this, I could get into trouble. I mean, they searched my house. I don't know. I know it is innocent, but I had already decided I better leave it. I hadn't cleaned it up before, I better leave it now."

Grundy, however, believed that there had been no nosebleeds and no bloody towel. He believed Greineder made that story up, that's why police didn't find the towel during their first search. And he also believed that he did, in fact, have a supply of his wife's blood, which he put on a towel, along with his blood, to create the evidence he needed to prove his story.

And where did Grundy think Greineder got his wife's blood? From the doctor who performed the second autopsy, which is what he told the judge during the sidebar.

Grundy's questioning of Greineder before Murphy asked for the sidebar went like this:

"You had a full autopsy done on your wife. Is that correct, sir?" Grundy asked.

"I don't know what was done."

"You don't have any idea?"

"I did not discuss—"

"Did you receive a report?"

"I don't believe I ever have."

"And you didn't speak with anybody about it—just yes or no?"

"Not in detail."

"And you're aware, sir, that blood was taken from your wife?"

The defendant didn't answer; he just rolled his eyes. Still he didn't look at the jurors.

"Objection, Your Honor. May I approach sidebar?" Murphy asked the judge.

"Yes," Chernoff said.

"Again, it's the same objection, Your Honor, that I made in motions *in limine* prior to the time the trial started. Any probative value that this has is substantially outweighed by the prejudicial effect. This was, as the defendant testified, arranged by me. And I was the one who contacted Dr. McDonough. And [Grundy has] now put me in the untenable position, if this area's going to go—of being in a position with respect to the client. I thought I would renew my objections into going into details of this," Murphy said.

"Where are you going with this?" Judge Chernoff asked Grundy.

"The question, Your Honor, asked on direct by Mr. Murphy, was if you had any access to any of your wife's blood subsequent to her death."

"Where are you going with your questioning here, if permitted?" the judge asked again.

"As to whether he has knowledge whether or not blood was taken from her," Grundy said.

"Are you really, legitimately suggesting that you think Dr. McDonough from the medical examiner's officer took blood and gave it—" Murphy asked, incredulously.

"Absolutely," Grundy responded.

"You can't legitimately have a good-faith basis to believe that the deputy chief medical examiner of the Connecticut Medical Examiner's Office took blood from the victim and gave it either to me or the defendant?" Murphy asked again.

"I don't know. I haven't been able to speak with Dr. McDonough," Grundy said.

Having heard enough, the judge said, "I'm going to sustain the objections to this question." And the sidebar ended.

But Grundy didn't give up, again asking Greineder if he knew blood had been taken from his wife.

"And again, sir, you were aware that that was done. Is that correct?"

"I was aware that it was done," Greineder answered.

"Objection, Your Honor," Murphy said.

"Sustained," Chernoff said.

Grundy went on to question Greineder about the fact that he left his wife's ashes in storage at the crematorium for four months, before her sister finally paid the bill, collected the ashes, and brought them to New York.

"Her ashes were in storage at the crematorium," Greineder said.

"In a cardboard box?" Grundy asked.

"I believe so. I'm not exactly sure."

"You're not exactly sure, because you never went to see them. Correct?"

"That's correct."

Although he couldn't make the trip to pick up his wife's ashes, Greineder did travel to Denmark at Christmastime with his family, and before he was arrested, he had planned to attend a medical conference in San Diego and then stop off in Las Vegas for a family vacation on the way back.

Grundy questioned Greineder about the textured brown work gloves that police took from his doghouse during their search on November 12. After that search, Greineder was concerned, because those gloves were missing. Grundy's point was that Greineder was upset because they were exactly like the gloves the murderer wore to kill May.

After that, Grundy asked the doctor why he had filed an emergency motion on November 19 to have his computers returned to him. The police had taken his computers, as well as his son's laptop, during the November 12 search.

The defendant said it was because they contained vital information related to his work as well as confidential patient information. The prosecutor pointed out that there was also a vast amount of pornographic material on those computers—material Greineder didn't want anyone to know about. And didn't tell anyone about until after he was arrested.

"How would it have affected your job if it was known that you were running around with prostitutes, doing the things you were doing on the Internet, meeting strangers?" Grundy asked.

"I would assume it was not a favorable outcome."

"How do you think it would have affected your ability to get grants?"

"I don't know, the honest truth."

But Greineder had already lost a major grant he had applied for with another doctor.

"How do you think it would have affected your ability to go around the country with IRINE (Immunology Research Institute of New England) and lecture?"

"Objection, Your Honor," Murphy said.

"Objection overruled."

"The real answer is I don't know."

"It probably wouldn't have been a good thing," Grundy said.

"Probably not favorably."

"And yet what you were doing in that marriage you testified to this jury was a side activity. Correct? Was that your testimony, sir?"

"It was—"

"Sir, was your testimony to this jury that it was a side activity?"

"May counsel give the witness time to think?" Murphy asked the judge.

"Yes," Chernoff responded.

"I may have used the word 'side.'"

"Gratifying a secondary need?"

"I believe I used that phrase."

"Secondary to the vow of marriage?"

"Secondary to the importance of the four people most important to me in my life."

"And you were concerned because if something happened to that marriage, it was going to affect the relationship with your kids. Correct, sir?"

Greineder didn't answer right away.

"It was going to affect the relationship with my wife, May, and my kids," he said finally.

As this line of questioning continued, an obviously frustrated and nervous Britt Greineder, sitting in a first-row bench, kept shaking her legs and, at one point, took off her shoes and twisted her feet around on the floor. Her brother, Colin, put his head down in his hands, as if to block out the scene in front of him. In the courtroom, you could hear the proverbial pin drop. Everyone sat quietly, listening to the doctor's testimony.

Grundy pressed on, reminding Greineder that he went out of his way to keep his secret life hidden from his family and coworkers. And reminding the jury, in so many words, that most likely May found out about his "side activities" and threatened to blow the whistle on him. And maybe that's why he killed her.

Now Grundy again asked Greineder more explicit questions about the prostitute named Elizabeth he met at the Crowne Plaza in 1998.

"This is the woman who you indicated you bought champagne for. Is that right?"

"I bought champagne for that occasion. Yes."

"And you told the jurors that you were so embarrassed, that's why you bought the champagne. Right?"

"I was embarrassed," Greineder answered.

"And you brought roses?"

"The second time."

"And you asked to rub the roses on her body?"

"I believe—yes, I believe I . . ."

"You brought the—"

". . . used those on her."

"You brought a group of creams and oils?" Grundy questioned.

"She had told me to bring—"

"No. Did you bring a group of creams?"

"No, not a group of creams and oils," Greineder responded.

"Did you bring a cream?"

"Not a cream."

"What did you bring?"

"One bottle of Neutrogena oil."

"You asked her to take a shower with you, and she wouldn't, correct?"

"She actually took a shower."

"You asked her if you could take a shower with her and she would not. Is that correct, sir?" Grundy repeated.

"I believe so."

"She said you could watch her. Correct?"

"I believe so."

"And you did that?"

"Yes," Greineder answered.

"You tried to see her again. She never returned your calls. Is that correct?"

"I did call her subsequent."

"And without getting any more graphic than necessary, you asked to perform certain acts on her that she did not allow you to. Is that correct?" According to police, Greineder offered to perform oral sex on her and she refused.

"That's correct," Greineder replied.

"And this is a side activity, but you love your wife, don't you, sir?"

"I'm not proud of what I did."

"I'm not asking you that, sir. I'm asking you: it's a side activity; it's not a big deal; it didn't interfere with the love you had for your wife and your marriage, correct?"

"I loved my wife."

"It didn't interfere with that marriage and the love you felt for her at all?"

"I loved my wife. I—that's all I can say," Greineder stated.

At that point, the judge called the morning recess. After the recess, Grundy started in where he left off.

"Sir, at the same time that you were involved in these side activities you indicated that there were, as in anyone's life, financial transactions being conducted in your home."

"I believe so."

Grundy pointed to the renovations that were being done at the time to the bathroom and kitchen of the Greineder home—renovations that cost over $60,000. He also noted that the couple purchased a new $15,000 dining-room set.

"And in May of 1999 the house went to May. Correct?" Grundy asked.

"That's correct. Approximately. I'd have to ask Mr. Schlossberg."

May Greineder was also planning to spend a large amount of money on her daughter Kirsten's wedding, something Grundy didn't bring up. According to police, the price for just the hall at the fancy Boston hotel May wanted to rent was $60,000. The entire wedding would have cost well over $100,000, and Greineder had no say in any of those financial decisions.

One police officer said May was spending money like it was going out of style. She even had granite countertops and brand-new appliances installed in the kitchen. Police said this was out of character for her. She was usually so frugal and spent money wisely. And Greineder wasn't worth all that much—maybe $500,000, police said. Initially he even asked May's sister, Ilse, to loan him money for his trial—which cost over $500,000.

The prosecution theorized May found out about

his "side activities" and planned to leave him—
ruining his reputation and leaving him with nothing.

Grundy brought up Greineder's emergency call
to Wellesley police the morning of his wife's murder.
Greineder always claimed he first called his home by
mistake before calling police. But Grundy showed
him his cell phone bill and asked him if he saw a call
to his home on that bill.

"I do not," Greineder replied.

Another lie for the prosecution to hang its case on.

Grundy again brought up Greineder's involvement
with prostitutes and pornography, questioning the
defendant about his relationship with Deborah Doolio and his visit with a prostitute while in New Jersey
the week before his wife's death. He also asked him
about the naked picture of himself he sent to the
Pages over the Internet.

"Sir, with respect to Ms. Doolio, you didn't speak to
her when you called her after several months. Isn't
that fair?"

"That's correct."

"And you didn't speak to her the day after, November first, after your wife's murder, did you, sir?"

"That's correct."

"You didn't owe her a call on November first, did
you, sir?"

"Excuse me?"

"You didn't owe her a call, did you, sir?"

"No, but I left her a message on the thirtieth."

"And in going through your list of things to do, you
wanted to take care of that on November first?"

"Yes."

The jury heard that Doolio wouldn't let Greineder
perform any sexual acts on her other than straight
vaginal intercourse. The jury also heard about the

frenzy of sexual activity Greineder engaged in while at a medical conference in Mahwah, New Jersey, in the week leading up to his wife's murder. These activities included surfing the Internet for escort services in the early-morning hours, seeing a prostitute, then watching a porn movie almost immediately after the hooker left. And when he got home, he renewed his membership to a pornographic Web site, UltimateLive.com, and joined the dating service People2People, to meet other people for sex.

Grundy's implication was that Greineder was a man obsessed with sex and not one merely fulfilling a "secondary" need.

The prosecutor cross-examined Greineder about the receipt for nails he bought at Diehl's hardware store and the hammer that was purchased two and a half minutes later. The defendant said he didn't purchase the hammer and he didn't even remember buying the nails.

Grundy asked Greineder a number of questions about whether he was being truthful about certain issues, including how many times he picked up his wife, the receipts for the nails, why he told Elizabeth Porter he was divorcing his wife (Porter testified to the grand jury that Greineder said May was old and soft, but he denied it), the simultaneous nosebleeds, the back rub or back scratch, why he went down the paved pathway, and how far he went.

To each question, Greineder answered, "I am."

"Isn't it true, sir, that your side activities, gratifying a secondary need, had become a large part of your life, that kept you up all hours of the night, and you were getting in deeper and deeper in activities that were far from what one would term normal sexual intercourse?"

"Not really. I was certainly up late that night, but I arrived at the hotel very late and—"

"Was that separate from other nights, sir? I mean . . . would it be unusual for you to be on the Internet at three A.M.?"

"Three A.M., yes. Five-thirty A.M., no."

"And, sir, it would have been devastating to you, your career, your children's thought of you, if any of this was known, wouldn't it have, sir?"

"It would have been upsetting."

Without skipping a beat, Grundy asked Greineder whether he knew anything about the gloves worn by May's murderer or the lighter fluid found at the scene.

Greineder said he did not.

"I'd like to ask you one more time, sir, just as Sergeant Foley did. It's now unlikely that you tried to pick up your wife three times, and tell me why we don't see any blood on your hands?"

"I don't know."

"It's because you had gloves on, isn't it?"

"I did not," Greineder answered.

"You had gloves on and you killed your wife?"

"I did not, Mr. Grundy."

"Can you tell me why you had fibers under your fingernails?"

"I'm sorry. Can you repeat the question?"

"If you did not have gloves on, can you tell me why you had fibers under your fingernails?" Grundy questioned.

"I believe fibers under the fingernails are a common occurrence, but I certainly—"

"But you never had gloves on?"

"Not that day."

"Fibers consistent with those gloves found in the storm drain?"

"And consistent with the gloves in my doghouse," Greineder added.

"Which you noticed missing after November first, sir?"

"Which I was aware I did not know the location of after the November first search."

"Is it fair to state, sir, that you had bathed since you had gloves on, according to your testimony. Correct?"

"I had . . . Sorry."

"Bathed."

"Bathed?"

"Yes."

"I may or may not have showered Saturday night. I do not recall when I last wore the gloves in the doghouse. And I know I didn't shower that Sunday morning. So, I'm afraid I really can't specifically answer your question."

"So you had no idea whether or not—what's first in time: washing your hands, taking a shower, or having those gloves in your doghouse on?"

"Oh, I certainly have washed my hands in the interim," Greineder answered.

"Thank you, sir."

And with that Grundy ended his cross-examination.

On redirect, Murphy asked his client if he knew where he got the red, white, blue, and aqua fibers found under his fingernails. Greineder said he didn't know.

"Did you ever hear about red, white, blue, aqua, fibers in the gloves at this trial?"

"I don't think so."

The jury also learned that Greineder chose the Internet handle CasualGuy2000 because CasualGuy was already taken, and since he needed a variation on the name, he chose 2000 because it was almost the year 2000.

"Let me ask you, Doctor—I guess Mr. Grundy has this idea that you killed your wife because you thought somehow that if she had discovered your sex habits, things would go badly for you in the public eye. Let me ask you this—between October 31, 1999, and February 29, 2000, how did things go for you in the public eye?"

"I did not feel that in the public eye they went well at all."

But Murphy's question didn't take into account one thing—Greineder never thought he'd get caught.

Greineder also told the jury that he called Doolio the day before his wife's murder because he wanted to keep his sexual liaisons on a more professional level than they would have been had he continued trying to meet partners through People2People.

"When you made that call, were you planning to kill your wife?"

"I wasn't planning to kill my wife."

Greineder said he called Doolio back the day after his wife was killed to tell her not to call his cell phone because his children were using it and he didn't want her to talk to them.

"Doctor, when you called her, did you ask to set up another date?"

"No, I did not."

"What message did you leave?"

"I said I did not want to see her again. I don't know if I said anything else. I might have said there'd been a family crisis. I'm not sure."

"Did you tell her, 'I've done what I've been planning to do. The coast is clear'?"

"No."

"Did you want to kill your wife because she found out about your Internet activities?"

"No."

"Would killing your wife make you financially better off, Doctor?"

"No, not at all."

The jury listened as Greineder said he told police at the pond he tried to move his wife's body but didn't tell them how many times he tried to pick her up, because they didn't ask. He also told jury members none of the police officers ever asked him to show them the route he took after he split up from his wife. And he said police never tested his hands for the presence of blood.

As he ended his redirect, Murphy asked his client to tell the jury what had happened the day May was murdered.

"The worst thing in my life," he said.

"What was that?"

"May was dead."

During his recross-examination, Grundy again focused on the lack of blood on Greineder's hands, even though he said he checked his wife's carotid artery and tried to pick her up several times.

In addition, both Grundy and then Murphy, on further redirect examination, asked whether Greineder had really left a message for Doolio when he called her on November 1. He maintained that he did.

"Did you make a hang-up call, or did you leave a message?" Murphy asked his client.

"I left a message."

"Nothing further, Your Honor."

And after three grueling days on the witness stand in over ninety-degree heat, Greineder stepped down.

Chapter 21

On June 21, Murphy called DNA experts to the stand to support his "transfer" theory about how Dirk Greineder's DNA ended up on the knife that was used to murder his wife, as well as on the gloves the murderer was wearing. Murphy contended that DNA from Greineder could have been on his wife's face because of the towel they shared when they had almost simultaneous nosebleeds and that Greineder's DNA could then have been transferred from her face to the killer's gloves and the knife.

These witnesses also questioned information presented by the prosecution's DNA experts.

Dan Krane, an assistant professor of biology at Wright State University in Dayton, Ohio, testified that Cellmark changed its testing standards in the middle of testing evidence from the Greineder case, thereby slanting the results.

"This is not a simple interpretation," said the professor, referring to the many different 'peaks,' or markers, that correspond to different individuals' DNA. "We're discussing samples . . . in which mixtures were involved."

When Krane applied the lower of Cellmark's two standards, he said, he found evidence of DNA on May Greineder's left-hand blue fleece glove, her fingernails, and her stomach that might have come from some unknown person.

"It's not just a single individual's DNA profile, but rather a number of individuals that are present in these DNA samples," he testified.

On cross-examination, Grundy questioned Krane's qualifications, saying he was not an accredited forensic scientist. Grundy also slammed Krane over his contention that Greineder's DNA could possibly have been transferred to the knife and gloves from a source other than the actual killer, even though he never did any of the transfer testing himself.

After more questioning from Grundy, Krane admitted to the jury that the quantity of unidentified DNA found on the evidence was so small that it was unlikely that there was an unknown person involved in May's murder.

Murphy also called Marc Scott Taylor, who ran Technical Associates, Inc., a small DNA testing laboratory, in Ventura, California, to the stand to refute the prosecution's DNA theory.

During a hearing without the jury present, Judge Chernoff said he would allow Taylor to testify at trial but would not allow him to testify in depth about the tests he conducted.

Taylor, a former actor who appeared with Jack Klugman on the 1970s television show *Quincy, M.E.*, told the jurors he believed the defense's transfer theory was possible, because he had done a series of tests that duplicated such a transfer—although he was only able to replicate one such transfer.

On cross-examination, Grundy attacked Taylor's qualifications.

"You don't consider yourself an authority on the transfer of DNA, do you?" Grundy asked.

"I'm not sure who would be considered an authority," Taylor responded.

Grundy was also able to get Taylor to admit that just because DNA transfer was possible didn't mean it was probable.

The next day, the defense called blood spatter expert Stuart James to refute prosecution evidence tying Greineder to the murder scene.

James, who examined numerous photographs of the crime scene and the evidence, testified that the stains on Greineder's sneakers could be misinterpreted as impact spatter, but they also could be what he termed satellite spatter. James said satellite spatter described "small bloodstains which have resulted from small droplets of blood which have rebounded from a surface after the passive falling of a single drop or multiple drops falling into each other.

"These are the types of spatters that are in the size range of medium- and sometimes high-velocity impact which can be misinterpreted, depending on the situation," James told the jury.

But, in a blow to the defense, James couldn't definitely rule out impact spatter.

When Murphy asked James how those bloodstains got on Greineder's sneakers, he said, "Either impact spatter due to significant impact through a source of wet blood, or satellite spatter from passive drops falling onto shoelaces and the edge of the toe of the shoe."

According to James, the bloodstains on Greineder's jacket, shirt, and pants could also have been caused by satellite spatter. But, again, he couldn't rule out impact spatter either. James said the bloodstains could have been caused by Greineder trying to lift his wife's body. He said blood could have dripped from May, hit Greineder's sneakers, or even the leaves on the ground next to his shoes, and bounced back up, landing on his clothing and sneakers.

But during cross-examination, James said the bloodstains could have been caused by Greineder lifting his wife under her shoulders and dragging her backward.

James also helped the prosecution when, during questioning by Greineder's attorney, he praised the investigative work done by Lieutenant Kenneth Martin of the Massachusetts State Police Crime Scene Services Section.

Murphy asked James whether he agreed with Martin's assessment that the murderer's glove left a particular imprint on the knife used to slice May Greineder's throat.

"And, sir, based on the work that Lieutenant Martin did, do you have an opinion, to a reasonable degree of scientific certainty, as to whether the pattern evidence on the questioned knife, which is before the members of the jury now, is consistent with having been deposited there by the evidence glove that is depicted in that photograph?" Murphy asked, showing him a photograph of the glove.

"Yes, I have an opinion."

"And what is that opinion?"

"That based upon my review of this—and I have only seen it here recently—that I agree with the type of comparison that was done here," James replied. "I think it is the scientific approach, and I would agree that you have a consistent pattern from something like that glove, not necessarily that particular glove . . . but a glove of that type producing those transfer patterns. It was nice work."

When Grundy got his turn to cross-examine the witness, he used passages from a forensics manual

James edited to challenge his interpretation of the evidence.

"Did you visit Morses Pond, sir?" Grundy asked.

"No, sir, I did not."

"Sir, this is a passage from one of the books that you edited, 'The examination of the crime scene, whether pristine, recent, or old, should be viewed as the single greatest opportunity the bloodstain analyst will have to obtain information. Regardless of the age of the scene, whenever possible, the bloodstain pattern analyst should visit the crime scene. The actual crime scene frequently holds a wealth of useful information for the analyst.'"

James tried to explain why he didn't visit the crime scene at Morses Pond.

"That statement obviously applies to crime scenes that have some semblance of being protected, where you cannot compare that to a crime scene outdoors in a park a year and a half to two years later that has undergone four seasonal changes with changes in foliage, et cetera. Those types of statements essentially do not apply. But if the scene is inside, then certainly it would," James said.

Grundy was not about to let James off the hook.

"Can you show me where that very, very important proviso you have just chosen to offer to the jury is included in your instructional manual, sir, that that piece of advice that I have just read applies only to indoor crime scenes," Grundy asked.

"Well, I think it is obvious."

"Excuse me, sir. My question is: can you point out where that is included in your book?"

"Well, it is not."

Murphy's last witness of the day was Gerard Belliveau, a private investigator who photographed areas of Morses Pond for the defense. Belliveau testified about various items, including an aluminum loaf pan he found at the park on November 9, 1999. Through Bellieveau's testimony, Murphy wanted the jurors to know that because many people use the area, anyone could have discarded the items found on the path near May's body.

Court was adjourned for the weekend at 3:15 P.M.

Chapter 22

Britt and Kirsten smiled at their younger brother as he strode confidently to the witness stand. It was Monday, June 25, Colin's twenty-sixth birthday.

Under direct examination by Murphy, Colin told the jury his mother was the person he felt closest to in the whole world.

"She was a wonderful person," he said. "It's hard to just sum her up with adjectives. There are so many. But she was warm and she was caring. She was funny. She was fun to be with if you were a little kid. She was fun to be with if you were an adult. And she was—I would say she was like the center of our family."

Through Colin's testimony, the defense was hoping that the jury would think that Greineder was innocent because his son would never testify for him if he had killed his mother—the person he was closest to in the world. Like his father, Colin had a tendency to look down, rather than at the jury, when he answered Murphy's questions.

During his testimony, Colin said he used to think of his parents as a WWF (World Wrestling Federation) tag team.

"They had their strengths and they had their weaknesses and they knew how to use that and how to take advantage of that and when to call upon each other," he said.

As Dirk Greineder's only son, Colin looked to his father's relationship with his mother as a model for his own relationships. On the stand, Colin painted a picture of a loving family—one steeped in tradition and routine, whether it was his parents watching their favorite television show, *Law & Order*, on A&E, attending a Friday-night movie together, or having cut-up fruit and muffins or cereal for breakfast. And walking the dogs on weekend mornings and coming home and doing the crossword puzzle together.

It seemed Colin's trip down memory lane was meant to raise one question in the jury's mind—how could this man, this wonderful father, take away the mother of the children he loved so dearly?

But Colin's impression of the relationship between his parents suffered when he accidentally discovered pornography on his father's computer sometime in 1997 or 1998.

It happened one day when Colin was using his father's computer and he decided he wanted to erase the history of a particular Web site he had visited. So he went to the history folder to erase the site from the computer's memory and, in doing so, he discovered a number of porn sites his father had apparently been frequenting.

"And what did you do when you saw those sites?" Murphy asked.

"I—I felt embarrassed," he told the jury. "I felt embarrassed and I was just sad. I was just sad for—I don't know. I just—like it's hard to explain what I did, why I did it. I went—but I just wanted to know what was on the computer, you know. And so I did a search of the computer for pictures, movies," Colin explained, "and I found a folder that had pictures."

"What kind of pictures?"

"Sex—pornographic pictures."

After Colin found the porn sites and pictures, he wanted to confront his father, but ultimately he couldn't muster up enough courage to do it. But he continued keeping track of the sites his dad visited. And finding those sites made him pay very close attention to his parents' relationship.

Then in the summer of 1999, Colin asked his mother if she was happy in her marriage. He told the jury that she said she was happy, but she added their sex life could be better.

Colin's testimony seemed to contradict his father's testimony directly. Greineder told the jury it was May who stopped having sex because it was too painful. But now, through Colin, the jury heard that May wanted more of a sexual relationship with her husband.

"I think I probably just stood there for a second or two and there was like—and I got myself together to say, 'Well, have you talked to Dad about it? Is this something you've talked to Dad about?' She said, 'Oh, yeah. Yeah, we've talked about it. But I think your dad has his own way of dealing with that now.'"

Colin talked about how his parents would always help their children move into their new apartments or dorm rooms. In fact, Colin said they helped him move into his new apartment in New Haven at the end of August 1999. During that move, Colin testified that he was home in Wellesley and he went looking in his toolbox for some nails to hang pictures and posters with, but he didn't have any, so he went to his dad's workbench and took his nails. He said he told his mother that he was going to replace them.

Colin said he went back to New Haven to finish the move and then came back to Wellesley, at which point he went to Diehl's and replaced his father's nails and left them on his workbench.

"I'm showing you what's been marked as exhibit 236. That's a receipt from Diehl's for nails?" Murphy asked.

"Mm-hmm."

"And that's dated September 3, 1999 at eight fifty-five and thirty-eight seconds?"

"Yes."

"Colin, can you tell the members of the jury whether you know for sure that that's a receipt that you obtained when you bought nails?"

Colin gave a long, rambling answer to Murphy's straightforward question.

"No, I can't. I mean, I can tell you that these look like the nails that I . . . I remember that the nails I—I was saying, were to hang pictures and to run telephone cords and whatever. In particular we had—my dad would frame pictures and then run wires over the back. So we put—these walls have, like, plaster, so it's hard to hold anything big, significant on it. I mean, if you want to do that, you've got to put in a backing, and then put the screw into the backing. So what we did— what we found worked was to, you know, use little nails. And then it didn't—you know, it was just enough. . . . Those look like the ones that I bought."

Murphy then projected a picture of Greineder's workbench on the screen in front of the courtroom and asked Colin if he recognized anything on it.

"Sure, these are the nails that we used. These are— actually, the red ones are the tacks. And the green ones, I believe, are the one-and-a-quarter and eighteen ones. And then there's some boxes."

Colin said the green nails came in small, cylindrical tubes with an octagonal cap.

"And again, Colin, can you tell the members of the jury if you're sure that those nails are the nails you bought the first week in September?" Murphy asked.

"No. I mean, I can't tell you that those are the specific ones. I mean, I left them on his workbench. And those are the nails, but—"

"Do they look like the nails you bought?"

"Yeah."

Did Colin really buy nails for his father the first week in September, or was he lying to protect him? If he were telling the truth, then maybe a complete stranger really did buy a two-pound Estwing drilling hammer three minutes after someone in the Greieder household—maybe Colin—purchased those nails. And if that were the case, then maybe that hammer wasn't the murder weapon. That was something the jury would have to sort out during deliberations.

During cross-examination, Grundy also asked Colin about the nails.

"And, sir, with respect to the nails that you bought . . . you have a memory of, instead of going to the store and buying nails, you took them from your father's workbench?"

"I have a memory of taking them from my father's workbench. Yes."

"And then replacing them?" Grundy asked.

"Yes."

"And do you recall, sir, the specific sizes or—that you took to replace?"

"That I took—I mean, I was trying to buy the same

nails that I'd taken. And, like I said, there were smaller nails and some tacks, I believe, that we used."

"Do you recall, sir, the exact sizes that you bought or that you had taken from the bench? Or did you jot it down somewhere?"

"No," Colin answered.

"They are little, cylindrical?"

"Yes."

"And that's what you bought, sir?"

"I remember—I have a memory of buying those nails. Yes. Or nails like that."

"In that cylinder?" Grundy asked.

"I think there were other ones. There might have been other ones, too. I mean, we bought—there were multiple nails."

And with that, Colin Greineder's testimony ended and the defense rested.

Right before lunch, the prosecution called Britt Greineder to the stand.

Grundy wanted to ask Britt about statements her father made to her regarding what happened when he first found his wife's body. Greineder told various law enforcement officials differing stories about when he actually first saw the gaping wound on his wife's neck. So Grundy wanted Britt to reaffirm her grand jury testimony, which was that her father didn't see her mother's neck wound until he returned to her body with police.

But calling her to the stand was a disaster. Britt, who was very emotional, testified that she didn't remember what she said to the grand jury, even though Grundy read her grand jury testimony back to her.

Under cross-examination, Britt said even though she was reading her grand jury testimony, she just couldn't testify to anything she said that day because she had been very upset.

Grundy then recalled Sergeant Martin Foley to the stand to refute Colin's testimony about the replacement nails he bought for his father at Diehl's. Grundy showed the trooper a receipt from Diehl's for six types of nails that Foley had taken from Greineder's workbench during the November 12 search.

"And, sir, did you then have an opportunity to correspond those nails listed in that receipt with the packages that were in the tool bench area," Grundy asked Foley.

"Yes," Foley said, then pointed out the various nails on a photograph being displayed on the projection screen.

"And that would be a total of six boxes of nails. Is that correct?"

"Yes, sir."

"And none of those were in cylinders. Is that correct?"

"No, sir."

Colin had testified that the nails he bought from Diehl's were in a cylindrical package. Grundy wanted the jury to know he may have been lying for his father.

Murphy objected to Grundy's line of questioning and at a sidebar told the judge it was completely inappropriate.

"We don't know when these nails were bought. We don't know what the price is. You know, this is not—he's not a competent witness on this point," Murphy told the judge.

"I think the question is how do we know this is how the nails would have appeared back in September of

1999, that that's how they were packaged?" Chernoff asked Grundy.

"Well, one of them is from '99, Your Honor," Grundy responded.

"How do you know it's from '99?" the judge asked.

"The labeling. But, beyond that, Your Honor, I would suggest that it has a probative value to the extent that they're the exact same size nails, from the same store. Just with respect to their packaging," Grundy told the judge.

"But we don't know when they were packaged," Chernoff said. "It seems to me that the one that has the '99 marking on it is something that's got some probative value here."

And the sidebar ended.

On cross-examination, Foley admitted he did not seize any of the nails himself but merely photographed them.

Grundy then recalled Greineder's niece Belinda Markel.

Before Grundy could question the witness, Murphy asked for a sidebar.

At the sidebar, Murphy told the judge he didn't know what Grundy was going to ask Markel, nor did he know that she was going to be recalled and wasn't prepared to question her.

In addition, Murphy said during the morning's testimony, the clerk's office had been sending him messages about someone calling the courthouse to say she saw someone at Morses Pond the morning of May's murder. The person said she told the police about it and sent a letter to them, but no one ever followed up on it.

"You know, I simply think I ought to put that on the record. It obviously comes very late in the day. But in the event that the Wellesley police do have this information—essentially what she is saying is that she and her business partner were at Morses Pond on the day of the murder; that someone came and—someone came and ran into their yard, or ran by them some way. I've just gotten a cryptic message that she wrote a letter to the Wellesley police and that information has been in the possession of the Wellesley police and they've never followed up. I obviously don't know any more about it than the fact that the call has come into the clerk's office. I think there have been two urgent calls today. So I would request that if that information is available at the Wellesley police that a search be conducted. And it, to my knowledge, has not been produced. And I think I ought to put that on the record."

"Aside from that, are we ready to go with this witness?" Chernoff asked.

"Yes," Murphy said.

"Okay," said Chernoff, who would deal with the information that had come in to the clerk's office after lunch and outside the presence of the jury.

Grundy then questioned Belinda Markel about a telephone conversation between Kirsten and Greineder that took place after he had been arrested for murdering his wife. Markel testified she was at the Greineder home and heard Kirsten ask her father if he thought her mother knew about his sexual activities. Markel said when Kirsten got off the telephone, she told her what her father said.

"And what did she indicate to you the defendant stated?" Grundy asked.

"He said he thought so."

On cross-examination, Murphy asked Markel if she

thought her aunt knew that her husband had been unfaithful to her.

"Is it fair to say that during the week in the summer of 1999, based on your interactions with your aunt, and the things she said to you, you reached the conclusion that your aunt believed that your uncle had been unfaithful to her?"

"I reached the conclusions that she had suspicions that he was unfaithful. Yes."

Murphy's point was that if May had known for some time that her husband was unfaithful, why would he have to kill her to keep her from finding out about it?

After Markel's testimony, both the prosecution and the defense rested their cases.

Everything seemed to be going according to plan.

But just as the attorneys were to give their closing arguments and the trial was to go to the jury, the proceedings unexpectedly came to a screeching halt.

Several minutes before Judge Chernoff released the jury for lunch, he was informed that a Wellesley woman had written to the Wellesley Police Department a couple of days after May Greineder was brutally murdered saying she saw a strange man in her yard that Halloween morning in 1999. The woman, Jacqueline F. Swerling, forty-eight, lived on Ingleside Road in Wellesley, about two and a half miles from Morses Pond. However, she claimed she never received a response to her letter from the police. Because of that, she faxed a letter to Marty Murphy at the courthouse the day the trial was to end.

When the members of the jury returned from their lunch break, Chernoff shocked the packed courtroom when he told the panel that something had come up that he had to deal with that afternoon. He apologized for the delay and told the jurors the case would continue the next morning. He then dismissed them for the day and sequestered them in the Dedham Hilton, not far from the courthouse.

After a brief recess, the judge told counsel that he felt it was appropriate to question Swerling, as well as Wellesley police chief Terrence Cunningham, about the matter at that time, rather than at another time.

Chernoff called Chief Cunningham to the witness stand first. After questioning him about how mail was delivered to, and distributed within, the Wellesley police station, Chernoff handed Cunningham a letter, apparently dated November 2, 1999, and asked him if he ever saw it before, or if he heard that it was delivered to the station. Cunningham said no to both questions.

The judge then asked Cunningham if he had ever heard of Jacqueline F. Swerling and her partner, Richard Acheson, and if he had ever received any correspondence from either of them. The chief said he knew their names, but he had never received any letters from them.

But Cunningham did know the couple from an incident that occurred in 1998. It seemed Swerling called Cunningham about a month after Wellesley police officers had transported her to Newton Wellesley Hospital to be committed to the mental-health unit for observation. When police first arrived with a commitment order signed by a Norfolk County judge at the request of her psychiatrist, Swerling wasn't home, so they left. A short time later, Acheson called police headquarters to say she had returned. The reason Swerling telephoned Cunningham later was to complain that the officers had forcibly removed her from her home.

"I believe the officers' reports reflected that she actually went voluntarily, even though there was a pink paper that had been issued. So they didn't have to restrain her at the time to take her down," Cunningham testified.

In addition, Cunningham responded to Swerling's home in 1997 when someone called to say she had tried to commit suicide. At that time, paramedics rushed her by ambulance to Newton Wellesley Hospital for a medical, as well as a mental-health, evaluation.

Cunningham told Chernoff that over the years the police had been called to Swerling's home at least twenty or twenty-five times from 1993 to 1999 for various reasons, including three possible suicide attempts, domestic violence issues, and because someone had filed a missing person's report. She had also been stopped twice for drunk driving, he said.

Cunningham testified that the only time he spoke to Swerling's partner was after she called to say police had forcibly removed her from her home.

"When he and I spoke, he indicated to me that he was aware that Ms. Swerling had some serious issues and that he was trying to get her some help," Cunningham testified.

Jacqueline Swerling took the stand next.

She told the court that on the morning of October 31, 1999, a person in jogging gear, who appeared "in a total daze," was blocking her driveway.

"We were trying to get into our driveway at the time," she testified. "He was not even aware that we were there, trying to get into our own driveway. It was when Rick . . . Rick wanted to get out of the car and approach this man, but he had had a heart attack recently and was recovering from that, so I was really concerned about his health and wanting to keep himself calm. So I simply said, 'Toot the horn and get the guy out of the way.' So we did."

Swerling told the court that the person in front of her driveway turned to face her. When he did, she could see he was sweating and he was holding his right side.

"He was in a daze and he didn't say anything to us," Swerling testified. "Then he just slowly walked out of our yard and then we let him go. I mean, we didn't want to approach this guy. He didn't say anything to us. In a daze, he just kind of like walked up Manor Road. He wasn't jogging. I mean, he was kind of like limping; and he just went on his business and we pulled in our driveway and let it go."

Swerling said the incident really nagged at her and she became very upset when she found out about the murder of May Greineder.

"I told Rick, 'I think it is really our responsibility at least to let the Wellesley Police Department—to put in writing everything very clearly, what we saw, as soon as possible," Swerling told the court.

Seeming a bit confused, Swerling said she thought she might have faxed her letter to Wellesley police, as well as mailed it to them. She also said she could have called the police department to tell them about the person in her driveway. Swerling said although the incident had been bothering her and Acheson for some time, she did not check to see if police had actually received her letter.

"I can't tell how many times I wanted to find the name of the attorney for the family, the Greineder family. I mean, I just—there's been so many times that I've wanted to do it," she said. "I either got so tied up with something else, or I let it go because I said, well, you know, maybe—we didn't want to get involved. It was that kind of thing, the publicity part of it. You know, we just let it go. We figured if the Wellesley Police Department didn't get back to us with this information, we felt, well, they already had enough of the information already, you know, that was plenty, you know, obviously, and that what we had to say was not relevant. And that's how it went."

"What I want to ask you is: why didn't you go further on this, after you did not receive an initial response?" Chernoff asked.

"Because at one point they had already accused Dr. Greineder. And we felt that they probably had enough evidence, and that when they read my letter it wasn't relevant," Swerling told the court. "So, I kind of sat on it for a long, long time. But it doesn't mean that I didn't think about it, and I wouldn't have my doubts. It never left my mind that there was a doubt, ever. I mean, just because of this situation in front of my home, you know.

"But today, the reason I'm doing it today is because, like I said, it's been bothering me for a long time. And I don't think it would be very fair that some of the—I haven't been following this case, by the way, and I've rarely been reading about it. So I don't even know what all the evidence is. But I will tell you one thing, that I've just been—you know, I had an operation last week. So I've been tapping in and out, peeking in and out on this case. And I was thinking about some of the testimony. And I thought, 'Geez, half this testimony doesn't have half the knowledge of what I have on this piece of paper that I wrote that morning of the murder.' I mean, you know, nobody ever checked on that. I find that so hard to believe, you know, and that's the part that bothers me. It may be a little intimidation, too, you know, to call the Wellesley Police Department and ask them, you know, 'How come you never got back to me on this, by the way?'"

Judge Chernoff asked Swerling if she had ever had any "negative contact" with the Wellesley Police Department.

She responded yes, because she was a recovering alcoholic. But she stressed that fact had no bearing on what she was telling the court about the jogger or her letter to the police.

"And to this day, I still want to know why the Wellesley Police Department didn't call me," she told the court. "I'd like to hear that part of it, if anybody is out there that wants to answer that question—why they never called me. I'd like to know."

Later that afternoon, Swerling's partner, Richard Acheson, took the stand, outside the presence of the jury.

First off, Chernoff asked Acheson about the letter Swerling allegedly sent to the Wellesley police.

Acheson explained that Swerling had written the letter about the jogger several hours after the couple returned home and saw him blocking their driveway.

"I believe she faxed it to police," he said. "We discussed it and discussed it, in detail, with each other. And she eventually got on her computer and composed a letter and printed it and then faxed it. I read it—when it was printed—before she sent it."

Acheson told Chernoff that he distinctly remembered Swerling faxing the letter on October 31, 1999, because she had to call the police first to get the station's fax number. He couldn't recall whether she mailed it as well.

But when Chernoff pointed out to Acheson that the letter from Swerling was dated November 2, the

Wellesley man admitted maybe he didn't remember the exact timing.

"Seeing November second there, then that must have been the day," Acheson said. "But that's irrelevant to what we saw. . . ."

Acheson said the couple hadn't had any further conversations about the letter until two weeks before Greineder's trial was scheduled to end.

"She was still curious why no one had ever contacted us about it," he said. "And she has feelings of civic duty. And I said, 'Well, you know, there is a life involved here. And if you feel that you should—need to come forward, then go ahead and do it.' . . . In her mind, there was still some doubt as to the nature of who actually did this, because of what we saw. And, in the meantime, she had an operation. . . . She knew that today was the last day of testimony and I think that's why she contacted you folks this morning."

Acheson told the court that he and Swerling tried to walk their dogs at Morses Pond around 9:30 A.M. on October 31, 1999, but were turned away by police. So they decided to walk their dogs at a nearby school, returning home a short time later. When they arrived home at approximately 10:00 or 10:30 A.M., Acheson said the pair saw a man in their yard, staring at a shed that was in the backyard.

"And the only other thing I recall is that he was sweating profusely, as though he had been running quite a bit. And he had shorts on," Acheson testified.

"Did he say anything to you?" Chernoff asked.

"No. No. I tooted the horn, and he turned around and just started walking away. And then we pulled in the driveway and went in the house with the dogs," Acheson said.

Acheson told the court he had never before seen the man.

The judge then asked Acheson if he had ever had contact with Wellesley police in the twelve years he had lived on Ingleside Road with Swerling.

"Well, they have been at my house, which I believe Jacqueline told you about, because she was having problems with alcohol," he said. "And we had to call nine-one-one a few times. But she's fortunately recovering now."

After he finished speaking with Acheson, Chernoff asked the attorneys if they had any questions.

Grundy said no.

Murphy, however, asked Acheson if he had any doubt that Swerling faxed the letter to police at some point.

"No, I don't," he responded. "I'm certain that's how it was transmitted to the police."

"Were you present when she called the police and asked for their fax number?"

"Yes."

"Were you present when she faxed it?"

"Yes," Acheson said after a long hestitation.

"Nothing further, Your Honor. Thank you," Murphy said.

After sensing Acheson's indecisiveness, Grundy decided to question him.

"Sir, I noticed you were extremely hesitant when giving that last answer. Can you tell me what it is you needed to think about to get that specific recollection of being present when it was faxed?" Grundy asked.

"I remember sitting in the office while she was composing it. And I was apparently home working the day when it was composed."

"But didn't you just say a moment ago, sir, it would

have been the same day when you got home from the pond?"

"Well, I didn't notice the letter—on the letter that it was dated November second. I had thought, and this is because of hindsight, that she had composed it and sent it on that same day. And apparently it was Tuesday. But I find it irrelevant to the content of it."

"So, your memory was that it occurred on the thirty-first, and now you actually recall it being on a Tuesday," Grundy said.

"No, I don't."

"But you do recall being present when it was faxed?"

"Yes."

With that, Grundy sat down at the prosecution's table.

Judge Chernoff, however, had a few more questions for the witness.

"Is there anything you think that I or the lawyers have left out in asking you what you know about these events?"

"I guess we just thought there was some doubt in our minds that Dr. Greineder could have done this, when we know about this person, who, based on our location, and—from the pond—and this person, and the timing, and so forth, that there was just some doubt in our minds that this person, who we had never seen before, could be an unknown assailant."

The judge then asked Acheson if he knew any of the people involved in the case, including the police, attorneys, or members of the Greineder family.

Acheson said he didn't.

Acheson and Swerling were then asked to appear at court at 8:45 A.M. the next day for more questioning, unless they received a telephone call by 8:15 A.M.

But they didn't have to show up on Tuesday, because after listening to the testimony from Swerling and Acheson, as well as Cunningham on Monday, Murphy decided not to call either of them as a witness.

All that was left now were the closing arguments.

The jogger that Swerling and Acheson saw the morning May Greineder was killed went to the Wellesley police station on Tuesday, June 26, 2001, to identify himself and tell police he had **no**thing to do with her murder. The man, Patrick Libby, twenty-seven, told police he was the mysterious jogger Swerling saw in her driveway.

"I know I was that person," Libby told WBZ-TV, channel 4, in Boston. "I'm absolutely certain in my mind. I just wanted to clear the record that there was no bad games going on or anything like that."

Libby told the Associated Press he was standing by Swerling's home because he had lived there as a boy. He said he left when Swerling and Acheson saw him in their driveway because he didn't want to disturb anyone. Chief Cunningham told the news service that Libby contacted police Tuesday evening and he personally interviewed him about his interaction with Swerling and Acheson. Cunningham said Libby was "shocked" that he had played such an unexpected role in the Greineder case.

"This allays fears in the neighborhood that there may have been an unidentified stranger associated with the homicide case," Cunningham told the AP. "I think this was a public service to the residents of Wellesley."

Chapter 23

Standing in front of the jury on Tuesday morning, June 26, 2001, Marty Murphy began his summation.

"May it please the court, counsel, members of the jury. I want to begin with a thank-you. We have all been here for a long time, longer than any of us anticipated. I know that this has been a tremendous sacrifice personally and professionally, and Dr. Greineder and I thank you for that tremendous personal and professional sacrifice. It's a sacrifice, but it was an important sacrifice to make because the decision you are about to make is as important as any you will make in your life. The issue you have to decide is whether the Commonwealth has proved beyond a reasonable doubt—whether the Commonwealth has proved to a moral certainty—that the defendant, Dirk Greineder, deserves to be branded with a label that is as horrible a label as one can possibly imagine—the label of being the murderer of one's own wife—the murderer of the mother of one's own children," Murphy said.

"We watched you and we know how conscientious you've been. We know how carefully you've listened to the evidence. We know the notes you've taken, but this is it—now is the time and I want to begin by asking you three questions that go to the heart of what is at issue in this case. Three questions about the Common-wealth's evidence. Three questions about whether they have sustained their burden of proof. After five weeks of testimony, after hearing from seventy witnesses and see-ing four hundred seventy-three exhibits, has the Commonwealth given you any reason to believe that on October 31, 1999, Dirk Greineder wanted his wife dead?

"After five weeks of testimony, after hearing from sev-enty witnesses and seeing four hundred seventy-three exhibits, has the Commonwealth given you any evi-dence that anything happened in the weeks, days, and hours before the morning of October 31, 1999, that gave Dirk Greineder a reason to kill his wife?

"After five weeks of testimony, after hearing from seventy witnesses and seeing four hundred seventy-three exhibits, has the Commonwealth given you any evidence, any real evidence, to make you believe with-out any reasonable doubt that the man sitting with me at counsel table during this trial—that the man you heard from this witness stand for the better part of three days—has the capacity for evil, because there is no other word to describe what happened out there at Morses Pond on October 31, 1999? That he has the ca-pacity for evil that would permit him to brutally and savagely take the life of his wife of thirty-one years and take the life of the mother of the three children he loves and who love him and also love their mother?

"Has the Commonwealth done that?"

Murphy told the jury that this case was not just about a man and a woman, a husband and wife, but about a family as well.

"Before you reach any decision in this case, you have to ask yourself, are you morally certain—are you persuaded beyond a reasonable doubt—two weeks after Kirsten Greineder told her parents about her upcoming wedding—that Dirk Greineder would walk to Morses Pond with his wife, take a hammer and take a knife, and attack her and murder her in the most savage way imaginable?" he said, pacing back and forth in front of the jury box.

Murphy next turned to the decision of police to focus on his client almost from the minute they found May Greineder's bludgeoned body lying in the path at Morses Pond, even though police knew there had been two unsolved homicides in recreation areas in Norfolk County in the preceding twelve months

"This is a case about a family. It's also a case about an investigation; an investigation that began in the early-morning hours of October 31, 1999, and—the evidence shows, as I said it would in my opening—focused from the get-go, from the start, exclusively on Dirk Greineder. After five weeks of testimony, after hearing from seventy witnesses and seeing four hundred seventy-three exhibits, have you heard a word, a word, of any serious efforts by police to investigate the possibility that someone else even might be responsible for this?"

Murphy played up the fact that there were two other unsolved murders in the area in the year before May Greineder was killed. He told the jury that police never conducted an objective search to find out the truth about who really killed May Greineder.

Murphy informed the jury that the prosecution had not met its burden of proof in this case and it was not the jury's job to do the work for the state.

"You can't do the police work for the prosecution. You can't fill in the holes. You can't fill in the gaps. You can't even connect the dots. Your job is to evaluate the proof that you've been given from this witness stand," Murphy said, banging his hand on the stand for emphasis. "And

the proof isn't there. The holes, the gaps, the spaces between these gaps. It's not your job to fill in those gaps
and you can't do it with guesswork and conjecture and
speculation. And I suggest to you if we go through this
case, evidence item by evidence item by evidence item,
what you'll see is the Commonwealth hasn't given you
real proof beyond a reasonable doubt. They haven't
given you evidence without holes, without gaps. What
they've given you are facts that are to be connected together in a way that leads to the conclusion that the man
sitting at counsel table is guilty of the savage and brutal
murder of his wife requires you—[and it] requires you
to speculate and use guesswork and use conjecture."

Murphy reminded the jury that even though the
Commonwealth didn't specifically offer a motive in this
case—it didn't have to in order to secure a conviction—
the prosecution tried to impugn Greineder's character
by focusing on his secret life of prostitutes and pornography, implying that he killed his wife in order to keep
people from finding out about those activities. But Murphy told the jurors that visiting online sex sites and
cavorting with prostitutes did not make Greineder a
murderer. He said that if Greineder were planning to
murder his wife, he certainly wouldn't have left a trail of
his online sexual activities the week before she was
killed.

Murphy informed the jury that there really was no
motive, financial or otherwise, for Greineder to kill
his wife. And he said there was no evidence that May
discovered evidence of her husband's sexual proclivities in the early-morning hours of October 31, 1999.

"There's no reason to believe that anything that
happened out there at the pond on October thirty-
first had anything to do with prostitutes or Internet
pornography," Murphy said.

Murphy once again reminded the jury that the prosecution had no real, hard evidence showing Greineder killed his wife. All they had was circumstantial evidence—evidence that asked jurors to piece what really happened the morning May Greineder was murdered.

Murphy continued to chip away at what he considered the prosecution's so-called evidence. He told the jurors that police didn't prove Dirk Greineder put the work glove in the storm drain when he went across the circle and down the paved path.

"What did Mr. Kear say? Mr. Kear said he had a view of the entire front and left side of Dr. Greineder's body as Dr. Greineder was moving across the circle, behind the island with Zephyr on a leash in his right hand. Saw no hammer. Saw no knife. Saw no work glove. What about the backpack? Two small stains of blood. No evidence of blood on the inside of that backpack. No evidence of blood on the contents of that backpack—those balls, the leash, gloves. Were the hammer and the knife and glove inside the backpack when he ran across the paved pathway with Zephyr looking for the runner, looking for movement? If they were, don't you think there'd be some blood on the inside of the backpack? Don't you think there'd be some blood on the other items in the backpack?" Murphy asked the jury. "And what about the left-handed glove? Where's that? Where's that?"

Murphy said police just assumed it was Greineder who put the left-hand work glove in the storm drain because it was near his car, just as they assumed he brought the foil loaf pan, plastic bags, latex gloves, and lighter fluid to the pond. Murphy pointed out that there was no real proof that Greineder bought a hammer at Diehl's, like the one used to kill his wife, nor was there real proof that he even bought the nails that were purchased right before the hammer.

"Those items at the crime scene—Mr. Grundy says they're part of an elaborate plan. Well, it's been five weeks now. What was that plan? Lighter fluid—was that going to be used to remove stains? Was it going to be used to start a fire? Maybe we'll hear from Mr. Grundy in his closing, but one thing is for sure, whatever he says is not based on any evidence. It's based on guesswork. It's based on conjecture," Murphy said.

Murphy again hammered away at police for not conducting a thorough investigation and letting potentially important evidence go undetected.

"Proof that Dirk Greineder had no blood on his hands. Well, wouldn't it have been nice if police had conducted an orthotoluidine test? Wouldn't we know for sure? In the absence of an orthotoluidine test, can you say that Dirk Greineder had no blood on his hands?" Murphy asked the jury.

"What about the photos? The photos were seen over and over in this case," Murphy told the jury as he displayed the photo of Greineder's clean hands on the screen at the front of the room. "In a case like this, when this much is at stake, whether you're going to brand someone a murderer of their own [children's] mother, don't you want a scientific test?"

Murphy then focused on Greineder's yellow-and-white windbreaker.

"Where's the rest of the pattern?" Murphy asked the jury, pointing to a bloodstain on the end of the sleeve of Dirk Greineder's windbreaker. "Well, if you look at the jacket," he said, grabbing the windbreaker from the podium, "if you look at the left sleeve of that jacket, below that line, you see a stain," he said, pointing to the screen. "That's not the end of the line, members of the jury. And the message being sent by that photograph that the line stops because there were gloves there is not borne out when you look at this jacket," Murphy explained as he unfolded the rolled-up cuff of Greineder's jacket to show the jury the rest of the stain.

"Remember what Mr. Englert said when I showed it to him? 'Well, I don't know when that stain got there.' He doesn't know when any of these stains got there, members of the jury. Not even Rod Englert found a bloodstain in a corresponding part of the left-hand glove found at the scene," Murphy said as he flung Greineder's bloodstained jacket in a box on a courtroom bench. "Did the blood come off Dr. Greineder's hands because he was sweaty or he wiped his hands on the jacket?"

Murphy next tried to portray Rod Englert as a hired gun for the prosecution—one without very much experience in the area of blood spatter.

"Do you think he was a scientist, members of the jury? Police officer for thirty-eight years. Nothing wrong with that. Paid consultant, National College of DAs. Nothing wrong with that. He came in here, no education, [no] biology, chemistry, physics. Was he here as an objective forensic scientist, or was he here, as he said, to assist the investigation?" Murphy asked.

Murphy told the jury that the only person they should believe was Stuart James, author of a leading textbook on blood spatter interpretation.

"What did [James] tell you about the impact spatter Rod Englert saw, Lieutenant Martin saw? That there were a number of different causes for the same kind of stains. What did Rod Englert say? He didn't even know the velocity that medium velocity spatters traveled when he was testifying about all the impact spatter he saw," Murphy said. "Nothing that

Rod Englert said, nothing that Lieutenant Martin said, contradicts or should outweigh in your mind what Stuart James, real scientist, author, leading expert on the subject, told you."

Murphy now tackled the prosecution's DNA evidence, asking the jurors if they were satisfied with the work Cellmark did on the case and whether they could convict Greineder of murder based on the company's work.

"Are you satisfied when the expert (Robin Cotton) that the Commonwealth brings in, after more than fifty thousand in expenses, hasn't even looked at the raw electronic data? Are you satisfied when she's confronted with alleles (alternative genetic formations) and the data that are inconsistent with Dirk or May, she said she'd have to consider the possibility . . . but hadn't done it before she came? Didn't come back to rebut any of the questions we raised about the stranger DNA in the evidence samples. Are you satisfied with that?" Murphy asked.

Murphy told the jury that the DNA detailed in the case was at such trace levels that some of the items that were sent to the FBI came back blanks.

"No person would be identified as having contributed to that DNA," he said.

Murphy said that meant the jurors had to consider alternative mechanisms for the deposit of that DNA on this evidence—alternative mechanisms discussed by Professor Krane and Marc Taylor.

"Think about the experiment Marc Taylor told you he did—part of his work before he expressed an opinion that this transfer was possible," Murphy said. "Face to cloth, cloth to face, face to cloth. He told you that what happened here could happen and to rule it out requires conjecture and speculation. So, to choose between direct deposit in this case and another transfer mechanism is just a question of guesswork and conjecture."

Murphy continued his argument, focusing the jury's attention on the bloody towel and contradicting the prosecution's theory about when that towel ended up in the Greineders' Toyota.

"Now, Mr. Grundy mocked Dr. Greineder about the towel we've heard so much about, but mocking someone, that's no evidence," Murphy said. "What does the towel show—Dirk's DNA, May's DNA, spots of human blood. Mr. Grundy wants you to believe, somehow, by some means, that towel was created after the fact. Detective McDermott, Chief Cunningham, they told you they searched the car on November first. They looked on the driver's seat and didn't see any bloody white towel. Well, remember what happened when I asked Sergeant Foley whether anyone had even told him about a white towel with blood on it in the car. He said no."

Murphy again focused on the DNA found at the scene that didn't match Dirk or May.

"[There is] DNA inconsistent with Dirk, inconsistent with May, on all the significant evidence samples in this case," he said. "Whose DNA is it, members of the jury? If you don't know, you have a reasonable doubt. Don't you have a reasonable doubt? Can you label a man the killer of the mother of his own children when you've seen this chart?" Murphy asked, pointing to the chart detailing the alleles found on the evidence. "Can you?"

Finally Murphy asked the jury what evidence there was that Greineder formed a plan to kill his wife.

"The prosecution wants you to believe something happened early in the morning of October thirty-first when there was something discovered on the computer. Did he have these items lying around the house? Had he pulled them together in advance in the event his wife discovered what was going on? When he went to the pond that day wearing a windbreaker that looks like this, is that a good way to avoid detection?" Murphy asked, holding up Greineder's yellow-and-white windbreaker. "When he went to the pond, to a public place where people come and go all the time, is that a good way for a doctor with a Ph.D. in pharmacology to plan the murder of his wife? Leaving all those traces on People2People. Calling Miss Doolio the day before the murder. Is that a good plan? It's not a good plan, members of the jury."

Murphy told the jurors that they should use common sense when they were evaluating the prosecution's evidence. However, he said, they shouldn't use their common sense to fill in the spaces and gaps or to connect the dots in the prosecution's case.

"You can use it to think about judging people and what they're capable of and you can use it to decide whether it makes any sense at all for Dirk Greineder to put on this yellow jacket and go out to the pond that morning with a plan to kill his wife with a hammer, knife, work gloves, latex gloves, loaf pans, lighter fluid. Does it make any sense to you at all when you know someone else is out there in that pond with aluminum pans and fires? Can you convict a man; can you find him guilty beyond a reasonable doubt? Can you really conclude that an intelligent man, a doctor—Ph.D. in pharmacology—would choose this way to kill his wife? No evidence, no evidence he formed that kind of plan at all. Guesswork and speculation."

Murphy told them that when they were back in the jury room they had to ask themselves whether Grundy gave them real proof—proof beyond a reasonable doubt, that Dirk Greineder killed his wife that Halloween morning in 1999.

"My last chance, members of the jury, my last chance to talk to you, to try and persuade you. The case is going to be over, over for you, over for me when you reach your verdict. No chance for new decisions, to rethink, no chance. This is it, and I ask you to go back to those three questions I started with: Has the Commonwealth given you any evidence Dr. Greineder wanted his wife dead? Has the Commonwealth given you any evidence that anything happened before October 31, 1999, that made Dirk Greineder do this? Has the Commonwealth given you any evidence to conclude the man sitting with me at counsel table through this trial the man who stood up and took questions for three days—[is] so evil—because that is the only word, 'evil'—that he could take the life of the mother of the children he loves?

"Members of the jury, this is a case about family. Thank you."

And with those words, Marty Murphy concluded his defense of Dr. Dirk Greineder.

Throughout his closing argument, Murphy repeated three words over and over, "conjecture, speculation, and guesswork." Using these words, Murphy reinforced for the jury members that they couldn't decide such a serious case without real, hard evidence. In his closing argument, as he did throughout the trial, Murphy portrayed his client as an intelligent man, asking the jury why a doctor with a degree in pharmacology would choose such a gruesome, amateurish way to murder his wife.

After a five-minute recess, Grundy got up to deliver his closing remarks to the jury.

Chapter 24

After addressing the court, opposing counsel, and members of the jury, Richard Grundy explained at the start of his hour-long closing statement that juries were made of "folks just like yourselves" and not various experts because all the evidence in a trial is subjected to common sense and not dependent on DNA or other scientific evidence. And he told the jury the case was about one thing and one thing only.

"And no matter what flurries around this case—this case is about one thing and one thing only, May Greineder," Grundy said. "She wasn't exclusive to this defendant, and she wasn't exclusive even to her children. You've heard and seen from family members whose lives she touched and from whom she was taken. This is what this case is about—a life taken. This woman. What was going on in her life just prior to October 31, 1999? What was going on in her family?" Grundy asked, holding up May's picture in front of the jury box.

Grundy explained to the jurors that in order to reach a verdict they couldn't just look at one piece of evidence, disregard it, and move on to the next piece of evidence but rather needed to consider how one connected to the other.

Grundy thanked the jurors for their time and attention during the five weeks of trial and asked them to forgive him for sometimes being brash and not to let his demeanor influence the information provided by the witnesses.

"Take note of the information that was gotten from the stand. Take note of all those photographs and all the evidence you have before you go through each piece of it and relate it to the evidence. Everywhere the defendant went that day, the killer left pieces of evidence behind. Everywhere the defendant went at the pond, he left the defendant's DNA behind.

"Not only were those Ziploc bags from the home, but they had a print from those gloves on them. Is Mr. Murphy suggesting to you that the strange killer went into May's pockets, removed some Ziploc bags, and then chose to just throw them down there in the pathway after he'd put his glove print on them?" Grundy asked, his voice dripping with sarcasm. "I suggest to you that, in fact, you did hear concrete evidence that Diehl's buys these gloves from Norman Libretts. The closest place that they're sold, other than Diehl's, is in western Massachusetts, covering a tristate area. You saw that man, the salesman, look at each glove, tell you the distinguishing marks, how he could tell the gloves from the storm drain, the gloves from the defendant's doghouse, and the gloves that were bought from Diehl's, the known samples. And he distinguished each of those and he compared them. He could tell that they were all the same, as opposed to Mr. McGloin, who came in here."

Grundy then highlighted the defense's biggest blunder—Murphy called Joseph McGloin, a salesman, to say he sold the gloves in question at numerous stores in the area, only to find out when he questioned McGloin on the stand that the gloves found at the murder scene, in Greineder's doghouse, and at Diehl's were not the ones McGloin sold.

Grundy next moved on to the relationship between May and Dirk and what was happening in her life just before she was murdered. Grundy told the jury that in the weeks leading up to her death, May was pursuing a new career as a nurse practitioner. She was also trying to look better. She had a face-lift, lost some weight, and was dressing more stylishly. Grundy said that May wanted a more romantic relationship with her husband, even though he testified his wife had no interest in sex. Grundy reminded the jury that May was also suspicious of her husband's activities.

"We also know that the defendant was involved in a myriad of activities that don't need to be gone into in detail here now," Grundy said. "The information is before you, but characterized by him as a side activity. It included prostitutes whom he told he was getting divorced; that he was separated; that his wife was old and soft; that he was seeking out Elizabeth, whom he had a long-term standing relationship with; that he was seeking out alternative sexual styles; that he had at the ready naked pictures of himself to send out to try and bring about further meetings; that he's sending out his cell phone number to these people. It's real, ladies and gentlemen, and this is not a small departure in a relationship. This is not a blip on the screen in a marriage."

The prosecutor then turned to Greineder's possible motive for killing his wife and reminded the jury that May, most likely, knew about her husband's proclivity for prostitutes and pornography. He advised them to use common sense to connect the evidence, rather than focus on a motive, because the Commonwealth didn't need to provide a motive to prove Greineder was guilty of murdering his wife.

Grundy mockingly began to pick apart Greineder's testimony, telling the jury the defendant invented various scenarios, like the simultaneous nosebleeds and back rubs, in order to explain away police evidence. Grundy told the jury that the best evidence was the evidence that was simplest to understand, saying it just didn't make sense for Greineder to leave his injured wife in the sand pit to walk back alone to the rock in the circle area.

"Wouldn't it have made sense just to come through that path, leave her at the rock, and go on his walk, rather than leave his injured wife in the sand pit alone?" Grundy asked.

Grundy said it also didn't make sense that Greineder didn't scream out for help after he found his wife lying in the dirt pathway. And he had an explanation for why Bill Kear didn't see the murder weapons in Greineder's hands when he crossed behind the circle and proceeded down the paved path to follow what he said was a shadow or jogger or movement.

At that point, Grundy bent down, picked up in his right hand the hammer used to bludgeon May Greineder, and holding the handle tight against his body, making it almost invisible, walked in front of the jury asking, "Is this difficult? Do you see this? Is it unreasonable that Bill Kear didn't see that? I suggest to you that, in fact, it's not at all. What's unreasonable, ladies and gentlemen, is that the defendant didn't raise a voice and yell during this whole time."

Showing the jury pictures of the horrific wound to May's neck and her bloody T-shirt, Grundy ridiculed the notion that Greineder's hands would be clean after touching his wife's carotid artery and trying to lift her several times.

"And Mr. Murphy now wants to say that the person who checked this person's neck, or the person who attempted to lift the person who was in this T-shirt on three occasions—who was specifically asked if he had washed his hands and said no—came away with these hands," Grundy said, showing the jury the photograph of Greineder's clean hands taken by Wellesley police.

"Is that guesswork? Is that speculation? Do you need an expert to come in?" he asked, turning Murphy's catchphrases against him.

"Let's hook that up, ladies and gentlemen. Back up, down the alley. No blood on the defendant's hands. Glove. Does that make common sense? Is there a connection to that?"

Grundy paused, not speaking, his arms folded across his chest, for a few awkward moments.

"I just counted off ten seconds. Did it seem like a while? Were you waiting for me? Bill Kear said the defendant was down that path thirty to forty seconds. Three to four times longer than that, minimally. Long enough to get the job done? Absolutely. Is there a reason for going down that path at all if you see absolutely nothing but your wife in that condition? I suggest to you that there's not."

Grundy again reminded the jury of Greineder's behavior after finding his wife brutally murdered.

"The defendant comes down with Paul Fitzpatrick, runs to his wife's body, and [Fitzpatrick] tells him, 'Be careful of the scene. Back away.' [Greineder] goes out to the circle. 'Is she dead? Am I going to be arrested?' Is that reasonable, ladies and gentlemen? Within twenty to thirty minutes after your wife is found is that what a reasonable person is going to be thinking? Are you going to be yelling and screaming, or are you going to be thinking about that? The defendant would have you believe that at that point he felt that he was a suspect. And, yet, for those twenty to thirty minutes, he never once says, 'I saw somebody go down that path.' He talks to Sergeant Nahass— never does he say, 'I saw somebody go down that path.'"

Grundy told the jury that Greineder only mentioned the shadow after he saw Officer Lamar Hughes taping off the paved pathway with yellow tape.

"It takes yellow tape to jog the defendant's memory about a shadow going down that path. And from there on, it's incorporated into the statements to Detective McDermott and Sergeant Foley," Grundy said.

Deriding the defense's theory of a conspiracy to frame Greineder for his wife's murder, Grundy asked, "Are these people all involved in this conspiracy that spans the police department, the prosecutors, the independent laboratories that were involved? Why does everyone want to put it on this defendant? Is it also nonsensical?"

Grundy now held up the various items found near May's body and talked about the lack of fingerprints on each of them—the loaf pans, the lighter fluid, the Ziploc bags that came from Greineder's home. He reminded the jury that Sergeant Rebeiro didn't find any unidentifiable footprints in the area around May's body.

"If there was another person there, he didn't leave a footprint. Is that possible? Yes. And you've heard that throughout this trial—possible, possible," Grundy said sarcastically. "Is it probable that this person dragged another body without leaving any footwear impressions? Is that probable? I suggest to you that it's not, ladies and gentlemen. I suggest to you that it's not, because we have that footwear. It's the defendant's heel mark right where he would have picked her up. With bloody arms under the jacket, he dragged her backward," he said, pointing to the picture of Greineder's sneaker projected on the screen.

"And finally, ladies and gentlemen, what's so important about Sergeant Rebeiro's work. The defendant's heel mark, an undisturbed furrow—drag mark—directly to May Greineder's body. Left heel, undisturbed. Picked up three times, ladies and gentlemen, dropped, had to reposition her body. Is that truthful testimony? When does a person lie, ladies and gentlemen? You lie when you're in trouble. You lie when the truth hurts you."

Grundy then mocked Greineder's testimony that his dog licked May's face.

"How many people did the defendant tell that the dog licked May Greineder's face?" he asked. "Look at her face in those photographs when you're deliberating this case. Look at the blood spatter on her face. He testified and said he loved her."

During this part of Richard Grundy's closing, Greineder sat next to his attorney at counsel table, showing no emotion. May's sister, Ilse, however, broke down and cried.

"That drag mark, ladies and gentlemen, is in the same area where the defendant tried to tell you he went down on his knees, when he testified. That, ladies and gentlemen, is powerful evidence—strong, powerful evidence—that the wearer of those shoes dragged May Greineder to right where that heel sits and that heel stayed there until the police were there," he said.

At this point, Grundy scoffed at the defendant's desire to leave Morses Pond shortly after he found his wife brutally beaten and stabbed to death to take care of his dogs.

"Now, we know, the defendant told us, that he wanted to get out of that scene. He had to take care of his dogs. He'd been there almost a whole hour. He wanted to get away from there. I certainly agree with that. I'm sure he did," Grundy said.

Throughout his closing argument, Grundy turned the catchphrases Murphy used in his closing against him.

"The chemist tested the defendant's [cell] phone [for blood] that he used to call police and there was not one drop of blood on it," Grundy said. "That's not conjecture. Paul Fitzgerald's cruiser. Checked that door that he was pushing on to get out. Orthotoluidine test. Nothing. That's not conjecture—that's real."

Grundy now focused on some of the odd statements Greineder made to police after his wife was murdered.

"The defendant gets to the police station and right away he calls Terry Segal. Nobody's threatened him, 'I've got your DNA,' but he's saying to Jill McDermott, 'My wife gave me a back rub, so you'll find my tissue under her fingernails.' That's what he's thinking. That's what this defendant is concerned about two hours after his wife is murdered."

Grundy began to talk about all the inconsistencies in Greineder's testimony.

"When he testifies, he can't remember if it's a back rub or a back scratch. There has got to be some consistencies in matters so important," he told the jury. "Can it be inconsistent as to where you touched your wife when you found her in that condition? Whether you checked her carotid artery? Whether you picked her up three times? Whether you've been talking to the police or talking to your own child—this defendant never once said he picked that woman up three times, because it didn't happen.

"Those simultaneous nosebleeds, the sharing of a towel in the garage. May Greineder has two packs of Kleenex. She's got one dirty Kleenex in her jacket. She's got two more in her pants. And not one of them has a bloodstain on it. How many married couples have had simultaneous nosebleeds?" Grundy asked.

"Is it just another lucky break for the killer in the woods with the gloves? Following the same path as the defendant, buying the same gloves. Dropping them off by [the defendant's] van. Dropping them off down the path [the defendant] goes into. Putting [the defendant's] DNA on them. . . . The killer did it all. The defendant is talking about fibers in his pants at that same time. He's talking about a second autopsy. He's talking about he found May's dilator, so he's got to have a second autopsy."

DNA now became the focus of Grundy's remarks. Grundy pointed out that although Greineder testified that after he found his wife he took the leash from around her waist, and although he said he was not wearing gloves, none of his DNA was present on the leash.

"Ladies and gentlemen, [you heard testimony] with respect to the transfer of DNA. Professor Krane told us he read nine articles [about transfer] . . . and none of these articles talked about anything beyond secondary transfer—that is, I leave my DNA here," Grundy said, touching the rail to the jury box, "and somebody comes along and picks it up. What the defendant is talking about with his bloody towel is minimally, minimally, from May's nose to the towel, from him to the towel, from the towel to May's face area, and from May's face area to the killer's glove . . . from the towel to May to the [killer's glove] . . . and [the killer's] not leaving his own behind."

Grundy then told the jurors that if Greineder picked his wife up three times and touched her neck like he claimed he did, her DNA should have been under his fingernails, but it wasn't. And he said the transfer theory offered by defense witnesses to explain how Dirk's DNA ended up on the killer's gloves and the knife used to slash May's throat was not based on any scientific fact.

Grundy then displayed a picture of Greineder's yellow windbreaker on the projection screen and told the jurors that if, after seeing the bloodstain patterns on the cuffs of the jacket, they believed the person wearing that jacket was wearing gloves, then they should consider that evidence during their deliberations. He also told them when they retired to deliberate, they should look at the patterns of dots on the jacket, on the plastic bag, on the hammer, and decide if they thought those dots were made by the murderer's gloves.

"And again it's your decision whether or not those exist," he said. "Whether or not they're important evidence."

Continuing, Grundy asked the jurors to consider the fact that Greineder had a pair of work gloves like those worn by the murderer in a doghouse in his backyard; that he bought nails at Diehl's right before someone bought a hammer like the one used to bludgeon his wife. He told the jurors not to pay too much attention to Colin Greineder's testimony that he was the one who bought those nails because Colin was obviously biased.

Finally Grundy told the jurors to pay special attention to the testimony of an important witness who never took the stand or swore to tell the truth—May Greineder. "She told you several things," Grundy said, holding up the picture of May's body lying in the path at Morses Pond. "She tells you in her positioning that she was never picked up, as the defendant now claims to explain the blood spatter; that she was never moved; that she was left at the end of that drag mark. She tells you that her clothes were cut in a manner to make it appear as a sexual assault, but that, in fact, she was not sexually assaulted in any ways or means. She tells you that she received a blow to the back of her head, examined by Dr. Kessler, that was nonfatal. She tells you she went down on that pathway with a mortal injury, was cut, and that she was then dragged away."

Grundy suggested that the defendant's greatest defense was that jurors didn't want to believe that an upstanding physician with good standing in his profession, loved by his children, could commit such a crime.

"As Mr. Murphy said, 'pure evil.' And if we could gauge pure evil, see pure evil, hear pure evil, it would make all of our jobs a lot easier," he told the jurors. "But I'd ask you to do something, ladies and gentlemen, I'd ask you to close your eyes and put in your mind who you think the killer is, what he should look like, how he should appear, how he should come across, and apply the exact same facts to that image that has been brought before you in this case. Let me suggest to you, ladies and gentlemen, that if that image in your head, with those facts applied, is guilty, then so is the defendant. And I suggest to you, ladies and gentlemen, this defendant, on October 31, 1999, killed his wife. It's the ultimate act of control. I would ask you to do one thing. Return a verdict that speaks that truth, a verdict of guilty."

And with that, Grundy ended his summation.

Chapter 25

After listening to five weeks of testimony from more than 70 witnesses and viewing 473 trial exhibits, the 7-man, 5-woman jury got the case about 2:00 P.M. on Tuesday, June 26, 2001. Two jurors had been selected at random to serve as alternates.

Before they retired to deliberate, Judge Chernoff told the jury, "You'll be taking another path and you'll be on that road alone."

The jurors were then taken to a small room, where they were to hold their deliberations. The first thing the jurors noticed when they entered was how jampacked it was with evidence from the weeks-long trial. The jurors soon realized that they were going to have to figure out a logical way to sift through the voluminous amounts of information presented at trial.

The jury foreman was Wellesley resident Stanford Smith, president of a software start-up company. Contrary to public opinion, the foreman was not selected by the jury. Instead, the two attorneys, one court officer, and the judge actually decided who would head up the panel. Each of these people kept a short list of jurors they felt would make a good foreman. Throughout the trial, they had observed which jurors were paying the most attention and taking good notes. At the end of the trial, the judge looked over these lists and then asked the court officer questions about how the jurors interacted with each other and which juror, he thought, could help people get through the process. They felt Smith fit the bill.

After kicking around some ideas and talking about the case in general, the men and women decided to set some ground rules, including that people would only speak when Smith called on them. Still, it got pretty noisy in the jury room, and at times people walking by thought the jurors were arguing. But they were merely sharing their opinions and recollections about the testimony and the case in general. Yes, they were loud, and sometimes out of control, but Smith presided over his fellow jurors with a firm hand and the utmost respect. Even so, he often wondered how twelve people from different walks of life, who didn't know each other, could agree on anything.

Smith likened a juror sitting through a trial to someone watching a movie, one character at a time. When the first character gets up and throws out his lines and acts out his part, the moviegoer isn't really sure why that character did what he did. But then he watches the second character act out his part and he starts to understand how their two parts fit together.

The problem was, at the end of five weeks, the jurors didn't really remember a lot of the pieces of the trial. So in order to put the jigsaw puzzle together, they decided to separate the evidence into different categories such as DNA, blood spatter, timing of certain events, and then they conducted a very organized review of that evidence, category by category. Before the jurors left one category and went on to another, each person was asked if he or she was ready to use that piece of evidence to form an opinion and make a decision about Greineder's guilt or innocence. If the answer was yes, then the jurors moved on to the next subject. But if jurors still had questions, the discussion would continue until everyone's questions were answered before they moved on to a new topic.

Throughout this process, jurors took anonymous votes to determine if they were ready to move on. On Thursday afternoon, they took two straw votes on guilt or innocence and seven jurors voted guilty, three said they were not sure, and one person voted not guilty. But the only vote that meant anything was the one they took on Friday, June 29.

One of the first things the jury did was create a timeline of the events surrounding May Greineder's murder. They used testimony from the various people who were at the pond that day—where they were and where they weren't; what they heard and what they didn't hear; and what they saw and what they didn't see. The jurors placed colored pushpins—one color pin represented one person—in an aerial photo of Morses Pond and soon got a very clear picture. It showed them that if the murderer was in the Morses Pond area and all the other people were also in the Morses Pond area, it was virtually impossible for the murderer to have escaped without being seen by someone.

"We developed this timeline and it began to look like if there was another person who committed this crime, somebody should have seen him—Dirk himself should have seen him. Coming back from the pond, [Dirk] should have been able to see this person run across the trail in front of him, because [the murderer] had to go to that storm drain to put the knife, the glove, and the hammer in it," said juror William Giesecke, a dentist who lived in Walpole, Massachusetts. "But Dirk didn't say that he saw anybody. He said he caught a glimpse. And nobody else saw anybody else—all they saw was each other and Dirk."

After reviewing the testimony of all the people at the pond the day May was murdered, the jurors also concluded that the murderer would most likely have been seen at the spot where May was murdered, the storm drain where the knife, hammer, and one glove were found, and the second storm drain where the other glove was found.

"And Greineder was seen leaving the area of the murder and going to the first storm drain and Greineder was seen near the other storm drain," said Smith.

Giesecke, Smith, and juror Sara Barbera, a product manager at Tyco HealthCare in Mansfield, Massachusetts, said the timeline had the biggest impact on the jury.

For thirty hours, the jurors, who were sequestered in a nearby hotel during deliberations, went through every significant portion of the trial from an evidence standpoint.

Although some jurors felt the DNA evidence was pretty strong, Giesecke didn't want to rely too heavily on the DNA because he felt the samples Cellmark used were very, very small.

"They couldn't get good samples and, at some point, they were using a sample of about six cells, which is not very big," he said. "And contamination can be a really big factor. I probably understood the DNA as well as, or better than, others on the jury, but I warned them that I didn't want them to use that as their sole reason because of the sample size. But I didn't think we needed the DNA anyway, because we had lots of other evidence. But the DNA does fit and

it makes you feel a little more comfortable overall. I
just didn't want people to put the sole emphasis on
the DNA and I thought some of them tended to do
that. My feeling was, I wanted to be absolutely con-
vinced he was guilty, because I have to live with this
the rest of my life."

Smith's take on the DNA evidence was that although there was DNA from some unknown person
on one of May's blue fleece gloves, it really didn't
mean much.

"Where the third person's DNA was, it looked like
it could have been picked up from her clothes,"
Smith said. "We all have DNA from people all over
our clothes. All you need is six cells to get DNA. But
in places like inside the gloves, where it mattered,
there was no other DNA but his. If the DNA had excluded Greineder, it would have been the first chunk
of reasonable doubt, but the DNA, although it didn't
necessarily convict him, it didn't exclude him at all."

Even though the prosecution placed a lot of weight
on the fact that Greineder didn't have any blood on
his hands, the jurors didn't place a lot of emphasis on
it. It was a factor, but not a big factor. Giesecke didn't
think there was any real proof that there wasn't any
blood on his hands because the police didn't test for
it. In fact, he kept saying the police would have made
the jurors' jobs a lot easier if they had.

"It was a dewy morning—[Greineder] was laying
down on the grass. He could have wiped his hands on
the grass," Giesecke said. "You had to listen carefully to
the police. I would never accuse them of perjury, but
everyone's recall functions for them the way they want
it to. There were times when the defense attorney de-
fused a lot of this stuff—he'd say to the police, 'You
said this about [a certain subject] and you took notes

that day and you read your notes before you came in,' and then he would produce their notes and the best of the police would be wrong about certain facts. They would have said one thing in court, but in their notes they didn't put it that way. They're not lying, but if one of the policemen says there's no blood on his hands, I'm not sure they noticed that until later. So can you put a lot of weight on that and what does it mean? Does it mean he was wearing gloves, because if he was wearing cloth gloves and they were blood-soaked, he still should have blood on his hands. And there were a lot of bloodstains on his jacket and pants that could have been from his hands. I'm not sure they tested absolutely everything."

At one point in their deliberations, the jurors asked the judge if they could have a ruler. They wanted it so they could measure a pattern of dots on Greineder's windbreaker and compare the measurement to the dots on the gloves that had been worn by the murderer.

"We were going to try and measure the distance between dots on the jacket and the distance between the pattern of rubber dots on the gloves to make sure they matched exactly, but we were turned down because the judge told us later it would have been a reversible error because the ruler wasn't entered into evidence," Smith said.

So Smith and Giesecke did the only thing they could do—they put the glove on the smear-type stain on the jacket and lined up the dots on the glove with the pattern of dots on the smear. For the jurors, it was pretty conclusive. Before they started their impromptu experiment, they had said that if they could somehow place the gloves on Greineder's hands—or even put the gloves in contact with his jacket—then that meant he must have been wearing the gloves. And if he was wearing the gloves, then that meant he was the murderer, because if the gloves touched the jacket and he never had contact with the murderer, then how did the pattern of the gloves get on his jacket?

"Through the stains, it surely looked like there was a really good chance he had contact with those gloves and the stain on his jacket," Giesecke said.

Giesecke also conducted another little experiment. He took one of the gloves and smeared a peeled banana with the finger of the glove. Initially the jurors didn't see anything.

"But ten minutes later, someone else picked up the banana and said 'Holy shit,' because there was a streak similar to the mark on the jacket," Giesecke said. "And that was one of those moments—'Hey, that does look like that'—that helped us piece that evidence together."

The blood spatter evidence also played a part in the jurors' decision. The jurors thought the experts who testified about the spatter evidence were very convincing. They felt that if Greineder wasn't near his wife when she was bludgeoned and stabbed to death, then he shouldn't have had blood spatter on his shoes and on his jacket.

Greineder's testimony was also an issue for most of the jurors.

Although thirty-one-year-old Barbera, who was eight and a half months pregnant, believed him to be a credible witness, other jurors just did not believe him.

Smith felt the doctor did very poorly on the witness stand. Greineder's life was on the line, but he just didn't give a convincing performance. The consensus among the jurors was he was not believable—his mannerisms made a poor impression and it didn't strike the majority of the jurors that he was sincere. They didn't think he demonstrated the level of pain a person would feel if they lost a loved one.

And they were struck by the fact that he changed his story on the stand when he was being cross-examined by Grundy.

The jurors had continually heard from the other witnesses that Greineder said he got blood on his clothes when he picked his wife up to check her and then put her back down.

"But while he was being cross-examined about where the blood was on him, he said to the prosecutor that he had picked her up multiple times—the prosecutor basically stopped and said, 'Multiple times,' and he said, 'Yes.' I looked over at the defense attorney and saw him shaking his head. Greineder was clearly flustered; he didn't know what to do. You can presume, since I believed he was guilty at the end of this thing, that he made up the story about what he had done anyway and he couldn't keep it straight in his head and he messed up. And the prosecutor was just all over him," Smith said.

Giesecke noted that during a sidebar when the attorneys were talking with the judge, Dirk, still standing in the witness stand, picked up a pitcher, poured a glass of water, and drank it without trembling.

"He was solid as a rock," Giesecke said. "To me, that was a scary moment. I said, 'What kind of a man is this that he can do that?' I mean, he is so good at compartmentalizing things that he can separate everything, and at that moment he appeared to be calm, cool, and collected. I would have been a wreck—most normal people would have been a wreck—especially if I was innocent. These are little things that don't weigh heavily, but you note them and they do weigh on your decision as long as the rest of the stuff fits."

Smith noticed that most of the time Greineder didn't look at the jury when he was testifying, even though every single witness had been coached by both lawyers and reminded by the judge that the questions would be asked by lawyers, but the answers should be directed to the jury.

"Dirk did not look at us; I watched his attorney pointing to us and giving him hand signs to look at the jury, but he couldn't do it," Smith said.

The jurors discussed Greineder's interest in pornography and prostitutes and why someone who appeared to have a normal family life would go so deep into that deviant world. However, they decided as far as Greineder's guilt or innocence was concerned, it really didn't matter. They felt they didn't need to understand it; they didn't have to believe it; they didn't have to agree with it. So, from a legal standpoint, they just threw it out.

"If you're the prosecutor, it's motivation—or it goes to motive," Smith said. "So, okay, there might be a motive there, but there might not be. And do we even care? It doesn't really have a material impact on our decision, so I think we all considered it, but then we said, 'Let's move on.'"

As for the other murders in Walpole and Westwood, the jury didn't buy the defense's implication that the same person who murdered Irene Kennedy and Richard Reyenger also murdered May Greineder.

"Even if you told me there was another person in the park that day that had murdered people in the past, I would say if that person killed May, then he would have been seen in one of the areas where Dirk was seen," Smith said.

For some of the jurors, the DNA evidence might have been stronger than the blood spatter, or the timeline might have been stronger than the physical evidence at the site, but nothing excluded Greineder. And when they looked at all the evidence, everything pointed to him. The jurors did everything they could to try and find him not guilty, but they felt that the only way someone else could have killed May was if Greineder had had an identical twin brother, who was invisible most of the time, but right next to him all the time.

"He almost got away with it," Smith said.

Smith believed that if Greineder had murdered his wife according to plan; if he knocked his wife out cold with the first blow of the hammer and not panicked; and if he was then able to clean up the scene and destroy the evidence with the materials he had brought to Morses Pond—the plastic bags, the lighter fluid, the foil loaf pans—he wouldn't have been convicted because he was a well-respected doctor.

After nearly thirty hours of deliberations, the jury reached a guilty verdict on Friday, June 29, 2001.

When they announced their verdict in the hushed courtroom, Smith and other members of the jury looked right at Greineder, who let out a big sigh and slumped his shoulders. His three children, who had been holding hands, broke down.

There were hugs and tears all around for the prosecutor, the investigators, and May's sister and niece. But for the Greineder children, there was nothing but heartache and disbelief. They were led out of the courtroom by the back door and didn't return for his sentencing.

To say Marty Murphy was devastated was an understatement. He sat alone at the defense table, in total disbelief, continuously tapping the top of the table with his hands.

Before Greineder was sentenced to life in prison without parole—Massachusetts does not have the death penalty—May's sister, Ilse Stark, made the following victim impact statement:

"Your Honor, I have not prepared anything. Ladies and gentlemen, I'm speaking from the heart, so please forgive me if I'm not eloquent, but listen with your heart rather than your ears. I think we have already been sentenced. A sentence has been imposed upon myself, my daughter, our family, my nieces, nephew, and grandchildren, and so forth. And we've been sentenced to life without my sister, who, as a human being, had her foibles and her baggage; we all do. But as a human being, also, is an extremely special person who had a sense of humor, a wit, and such a profound sense of right and wrong and helped you to see it without being judgmental about it. And my grandmother used to say [that] when a person dies, a library burns. With the loss of my sister, the Smithsonian is gone. I thank you all for everything. God bless you."

Epilogue

Dirk Greineder is currently serving his life sentence in the Souza-Baranowski Correctional Center in Shirley, Massachusetts. As of this writing, he is asking the state's supreme judicial court for a new trial, because he contends Judge Paul Chernoff violated his rights by allowing the jury to hear evidence about his secret life of prostitutes and pornography. Greineder is also challenging blood spatter, DNA, and other forensic evidence used to convict him. If a new trial is not granted, Greineder will appeal his conviction to the state's appeals court.

On Wednesday, November 14, 2001, the Massachusetts Board of Registration in Medicine revoked the license of Dr. Dirk K. Greineder, who had been licensed to practice medicine in the state since 1976. Also in November 2001, Greineder voluntarily agreed to give up control of his wife's assets. A month earlier, May's sister, Ilse, had petitioned the Norfolk Probate and Family Court to remove Greineder as the executor of his wife's estate. Because of a loophole in Massachusetts law, which has since been closed, Greineder would have been able to manage his wife's estate, even though he had been convicted of her murder.

Former state senator Cheryl Jacques was the lead

sponsor of a bill signed into law that now prevents a person charged with homicide from inheriting property, money, or assets from his or her victim's estate pending the outcome of a criminal trial. The law also prevents a murder victim's estate from being controlled by the person who has been found guilty in that person's death. The legislation was prompted by Greineder's case.

ABOUT THE AUTHOR

Linda Rosencrance is Senior Editor and reporter at *Computerworld,* an information technology publication. She has thirteen years experience as a reporter, writing for both the *Boston Globe* and the *Boston Herald,* as well as many community papers in the Boston metropolitan area. Her articles include numerous investigative pieces and coverage of the Boston political scene. Ms. Rosencrance has also written an anthology examining various crimes on college campuses. She lives in the Boston area.